PERSONAL LIBERTY AND PUBLIC GOOD

The Introduction of John Stuart Mill to Japan and China

Blame for the putative failure of liberalism in late-nineteenth-century Japan and China has often been placed on an insufficient grasp of modernity among East Asian leaders or on their cultural commitments to traditional values. In *Personal Liberty and Public Good*, Douglas Howland refutes this view, turning to an examination of the introduction in Japan and China of the seminal work on liberalism in that era: John Stuart Mill's *On Liberty*.

Howland offers critical analyses of the translations of the book into Japanese and Chinese, which at times reveal astonishing emendations. As with their political leaders, Mill's Japanese and Chinese translators feared individual liberty could undermine the public good and standards for public behaviour, and so introduced their own moral values – Christian and Confucian, respectively – into *On Liberty*, filtering its original meaning. Howland reflects on this mistrust of individual liberty and the reception of Mill's work both in Asia and in England itself, where his liberal vision was greeted with considerable apprehension.

A welcome addition to the corpus of writing on the work of John Stuart Mill, *Personal Liberty and Public Good* will be of great interest to scholars in the areas of political history and theory, translation, and East Asian studies.

DOUGLAS HOWLAND is a professor in the Department of History at the University of Wisconsin–Milwaukee.

DOUGLAS HOWLAND

Personal Liberty and Public Good

The Introduction of John Stuart Mill to Japan and China

UNIVERSITY OF TORONTO PRESS
Toronto Buffalo London

© University of Toronto Press 2005
Toronto Buffalo London
utorontopress.com

Reprinted in paperback 2020

ISBN 978-0-8020-9005-8 (cloth)
ISBN 978-1-4875-2615-3 (paper)

Library and Archives Canada Cataloguing in Publication

Title: Personal liberty and public good : the introduction of John Stuart Mill to
  Japan and China / Douglas Howland.
Names: Howland, Douglas, 1955– author.
Description: Paperback reprint. Originally published 2005. | Includes bibli-
  ographical references and index.
Identifiers: Canadiana 20200209981 | ISBN 9781487526153 (paper)
Subjects: LCSH: Mill, John Stuart, 1806–1873. On liberty. | LCSH: Mill, John
  Stuart, 1806–1873 – Influence. | LCSH: Liberty. | LCSH: Common good. |
  LCSH: Political science – Japan – History – 19th century. | LCSH: Political
  science – China – History – 19th century.
Classification: LCC JC585 .H78 2020 | DDC 323.44–dc23

University of Toronto Press acknowledges the financial assistance to its
publishing program of the Canada Council for the Arts and the Ontario Arts
Council, an agency of the Government of Ontario.

Canada Council   Conseil des Arts
for the Arts   du Canada

Funded by the   Financé par le
Government   gouvernement
of Canada   du Canada

ONTARIO ARTS COUNCIL
CONSEIL DES ARTS DE L'ONTARIO
an Ontario government agency
un organisme du gouvernement de l'Ontario

*To my parents
and to Kathleen*

Contents

Acknowledgments

A fellowship at the Institute of Advanced Study (Princeton, New Jersey) provided quiet concentration to develop much of this book. I remain grateful to Benjamin Elman and the faculty of the School for Historical Studies for their interest and encouragement. I would also express my appreciation to a number of scholars and friends who have critiqued parts of this project in earlier guises: Tomiko Yoda, Luise White, David Tucker, Stefan Tanaka, Margaret Storey, Kenneth Pyle, Elizabeth Lillehoj, Dorothy Ko, James Hevia, R. Kent Guy, David Gilmartin, Kevin Doak, and Wah K. Cheng. In addition, it is a special pleasure to thank Peter Zarrow, Richard Reitan, and Michael Dintenfass, who did me the great favour of reading through the penultimate draft, and the David D. Buck Professorship of Chinese History Fund at the UWM Foundation, for financial assistance. And finally, special appreciation to Rob, for making so much possible.

A Note on Conventions

The romanized pronunciations in this book are typically Chinese and Japanese terms. When the context is not clear, or when I have occasion to give both Chinese and Japanese pronunciations of a term, I use the according notation: C: *ziyou* / J: *jiyū*.

And in keeping with the Japanese and Chinese convention of giving precedence to translators of works over their 'original' authors, I cite Nakamura Keiu rather than J.S. Mill as the main entry for *Jiyū no ri*, Yan Fu rather than J.S. Mill as the main entry for *Qun ji quan jie lun*, and so on.

PERSONAL LIBERTY AND PUBLIC GOOD

Introduction

On Liberty did much to disseminate modernity as a global project. Translated into Japanese and Chinese in the last third of the nineteenth century, John Stuart Mill's 'modest work' endorsed two key aspects of the ideology of modernity. One was the epic dimension of progress asserted confidently throughout the nineteenth century, the other that building block of enlightened civil society, individual liberty. Mill envisaged a social order whose dedication to protecting individual liberty promised the advancement of humankind. A society of rational, responsible, and independent adults would allow one another the freedom to pursue their higher interests and would support a regime of public discussion that furthered humankind's search for truth. Mill's vision endowed the individual with meta-historical purpose and valued the genius above all. Freed from the claims of traditional authority and received custom, the superior individual's spontaneity and creativity would lead humankind to better, more rational ways of living.

This promise inspired both curiosity and muted enthusiasm among many of the educated elite in Japan and China, where Mill's liberal vision was perceived with some ambivalence – starting with his translators. In this book, I compare those local receptions of Mill's theory, for they share a significant point of criticism. The translations of *Liberty* expressed a deep suspicion that Mill's theory threatened to engender conflict between personal liberty and public expectations for moral behaviour. Mill's translators in Japan and China, respectively Nakamura Keiu and Yan Fu, were apprehensive that Mill's endorsement of individual liberty made no provisions for public good. They worried that his presentation of liberty in terms of the so-called harm principle might undermine the public good, because his preference for the individual seemed to negate public morality. That is, Mill hoped that society would cease to interfere with individual behaviour, with the sole exception of protecting itself from harm. But how, then, was society going to maintain standards of personal conduct so that a diversity of individuals could interact cooperatively toward collective ends – with a minimum of violent disagreement or irrational waste?[1]

Moreover, these suspicions of Mill's theory in Japan and China are strikingly similar to those raised in England by Mill's critics of *Liberty*. From his contemporaries to scholars working today, English reactions to Mill's presentation of individual liberty and the progress of humankind paralleled reactions in Japan and China; this book treats that set of reactions to Mill as an international phenomenon. Contrary to most scholarship on Mill, liberalism, and political thought in East Asia – much of which relies on the hoary contrast between a 'rational West' and a 'moral East,' the former committed to modernity and the latter to tradition – this book demonstrates that his translators and critics in Japan and China were much more like critics such as Thomas Hill Green in England. Readers everywhere raised concerns over Mill's representation of the individual, his seeming indifference to morality and the public good, and his minimization of equality. They all found his theory of self-interest inadequate, his theory of liberty too selfishly narrow, and they preferred a constructive approach to liberty – as a positive political force that enabled us to make something of ourselves for the public good. Thus, this book is an exercise in comparative history, and I treat liberal theory as a global concern. In fact, given the degree of neoliberal activism in much of the former colonial and socialist worlds, Mill's liberalism represents a persistingly widespread and contemporary set of issues.

From the vantage of *On Liberty* and its translations, it is clear that perceptions of conflict between liberty and morality proceeded in part from Mill's presentation of the individual in an atomistic manner – as though the individual existed in isolation and could be treated as the fundamental constituent of society. Mill's critics in the late nineteenth century – in England, Japan, and China – found this an implausible abstraction. Individuals are born into society; they are thus constituted by society. They enter the world with a given set of customs, values, and cultural habits; it is thus more appropriate to think of individuals as social beings embedded within these predetermined institutions and values. In the 1870s, T.H. Green in England, as well as Nakamura Keiu in Japan, would foreground the social being of the individual in order to identify personal interests with those of the community and thereby produce a structural basis for public good. In the 1890s, Yan Fu in China would reinterpret Mill's individual in the terms of classical Confucian ideals, imposing on each a personal commitment to collective practices of moral self-development that would integrate self and society for mutual good.

But perceptions of conflict between liberty and morality also proceeded from the ambivalence with which Mill treats morality in *Liberty*. In his essay, he disapproved of middle-class moralizing – the Christian piety and uninformed judgements of busybodies. In accord with his assertion that society should not interfere with an individual except to protect others from harm, Mill also implied that an individual should be free from the interference of irrational moral claims that had no bearing on purely personal actions. He was particularly critical of Christian doctrines of morality for their negative and passive focus on abstinence from putative evils; he felt that this focus distracted from the genuine value of moral training. Mill did not appreciate the way in which the petty attitudes and interests of the middle classes informed the ascendant morality of his day, which he found to be marked by a sanctimonious sense of middle-class superiority. (An unstated sentiment that likely informed this position was his own objection to the idle gossip directed at his platonic friendship with a married woman, Harriet Taylor.) In sum, *On Liberty* attempted to clear the ground for a 'political morality' or rules of conduct based on the liberties.[2]

But at the same time, implicit in Mill's argument was the confident assumption of a moral code shared by himself and his readers. This is the ethos that several scholars have identified as Victorian, best represented by its commitment to duty and hard work, its antipathy to selfishness, and its recommendation of virtue – particularly altruism. In recent decades, Stefan Collini, George Watson, and others have described Victorian morality as remarkably rational, in that every situation was believed to have one right moral answer, which every agent could come to understand. This knowledge was derived not from faith in God but from self-discipline and the cultivation of character. And character was the mark of a gentleman, for character determined the will, which in turn attested to discipline and virtue. A text such as Samuel Smiles's *Self-Help* (1859), which was extremely popular in Japan (and, with *On Liberty*, also translated by Nakamura Keiu in the 1870s), argued that perseverance, hard work, thrift, and a reasonable measure of ambition led to character and thence to wealth. One rightly sought virtue, which would be rewarded, and not gain, for greed was a mark of the vice of selfishness. As Watson notes, liberty from this perspective is not the right to do as you please but the opportunity to do as you ought.[3]

This second position, however – the Victorian ethos assumed by Mill – was neither explicit in *Liberty* nor necessarily obvious to his Japanese and Chinese audience. They saw most clearly Mill's denigration of thoughtless moralizing, and accordingly, his occasional references to the censure of public morality were a secondary and uncertain effort, because *On Liberty* gave greater prominence to Mill's argument that society should not interfere with the personal liberty of the individual. As Mill indicates, we may encounter inferior individuals in our daily affairs, persons whose opinion or behaviour is so obnoxious as to warrant our personal reprobation or even the censure of public morality – not the dogmatic moralizing sort but the serious morality that defines character. But collectively, we have no right to interfere with that objectionable behaviour unless it causes actual harm to others. Under these conditions, liberty seemed hardly the opportunity to do as one ought but more the self-indulgence to do as one will. Thus, the seeming certainty of conflict between free but undeserving individuals and standards of public morality most concerned Mill's readers in Japan and China, and his translators would introduce explicit endorsements of moral standards in order to supplement Mill's argument.

Apart from this ambivalence surrounding Mill's own references to morality, a related problem for his translators was that of conceptualizing morality. Of course, the work of translating *On Liberty* involved coordinating concepts and categories of behaviour specific to different cultural contexts, and a great deal of effort was involved in producing meaningful terminology. Japanese and Chinese in the nineteenth century were familiar with a term key to Confucian learning, 'human' or 'personal virtue' (C: *rende* / J: *jintoku*), and this word *virtue* corresponds in many respects to the classical Greek notion of virtue, familiar to Mill and his contemporaries in Europe, which, to put it simply, represents the personal effort of self-development to make oneself all that a good human being can be.[4] But new to East Asia were the European notions of morality and ethics, and the most influential work of distinguishing those ideas was that of the Japanese moral philosopher Inoue Tetsujirō, who translated *ethics* as *rinri* (C: *lunli*), or 'the principle informing human relations,' and defined it as the philosophical and universal basis of morality. Morality, in turn, he translated as *dōtoku* (C: *daode*), or 'the way of human virtue,' and defined it as the historical and particular set of standards for behaviour found in a given human community – a 'way' is, after all, an actual path or model for behaviour. As several scholars have noted, these Japanese translation words drew on classical Chinese ethical terminology and were eventually borrowed back into the Chinese language, with the result that they are now standard terminology in both Chinese and Japanese.[5] As I have argued elsewhere, the work of translating Mill was made more difficult by the fact that the translation words for *liberty* and *freedom* in Chinese and Japanese suggested doing what one wants, regardless of others – an explicit connotation of selfishness.[6] So Mill's translators attempted to contain liberty within what they deemed to be more reasonable understandings of the individual's social relations and more reasonable demands on the moral expectations of an individual's actions.

In spite of this shared terminology, both the translations of Mill and the reactions to him had markedly different emphases in Japan and China. In a striking departure from Mill's attitudes and preferences, Nakamura Keiu introduced into his translation a notion of Christian love and duty to others as a means of circumscribing the selfish behaviour of free individuals – a move that Mill would surely have repudiated. In their eventual rejection of both Mill's liberalism and Nakamura's Christianity, Japanese leaders turned deliberately to the creation of a national morality in order to emphasize a set of moral standards for the subjects of the new imperial government. In time, Inoue Tetsujirō and other leaders would define this morality as a properly Japanese form based on Japan's unique body politic and its traditions. They advocated precisely what Mill condemned as a 'despotism of custom' – to him, the misguided effort to improve morals by forcing all to conform to a set standard. Yan Fu, by contrast, stressed a positive interpretation of liberty akin to T.H. Green's conception of individual self-realization as a full human being; this Yan presented in the familiar Confucian terms of virtue: the personal attainment of moral autonomy, represented as the perfection of the four fundamental virtues that defined the character of a good person – sincerity, humaneness, propriety, and rightness. Like Mill, Yan advocated the development of conscience as the way to improve morality; he was interested in the personal virtue that validated a man for public service, in a manner similar to classical traditions in Europe – and such an approach informed the plans of his contemporaries, from more conservative reformers to anarchist and nationalist revolutionaries.

Both Chinese and Japanese, in other words, worked to accommodate their apprehension that Mill's theory of liberty was certain to undermine either virtue or morality. To put the point more strongly, his translators implicitly challenged his argument that liberty for the educated elite would further the progress of civilization. Rather, Nakamura and Yan asserted that without some requirements for personal morality or virtue to serve to limit liberty, liberty would lead not to civilization but to selfish chaos. If liberalism had been grounded in John Locke's belief that the individual has an insatiable desire for acquisition, deemed both natural and rational, Chinese and Japanese generally believed that it was precisely such selfishness that must be curbed, lest it produce immoral human relations, social degeneracy, and political chaos.[7] Hence, many of Mill's critics argued that it would be better to treat individual liberty as contingent on the social whole and community values, lest liberty undermine its value by encouraging selfish egotism. As Japanese leaders in the 1880s would argue, on the basis of the German concept of *Rechtsstaat* or the 'legal state,' it was state law that created individual rights and liberties, and only within the state could individual liberty be defended. Or, as Sun Yatsen, the Chinese national revolutionary leader, would argue in the 1900s, liberalism produced 'loose sand' – a degree of social disorganization that invited the predatory incursions of imperialist powers into China. In the interests of social and national solidarity, individuals must recognize that they are beholden to society in a significant degree.

This book, then, is not only concerned with the translations of Mill as problems of textual transmission and interpretation. Rather, I am especially interested in *On Liberty* and its translations as political thought – that is, as texts offering new conceptual structures that propose to transform existing sociopolitical structures. Insofar as Mill's theory of liberty suggests a plan of political organization and claims to constitute a contribution to human progress, this book undertakes to situate his theory in the practical imagination of politically engaged readers in England, Japan, and China who were sensitive to ideas about personal liberty and virtue as well as the public good. I look outside of *On Liberty* in order to examine how some of Mill's readers evaluated the pertinence of his theory for their immediate and future purposes. Largely because Nakamura and Yan had visited England in the 1860s and '70s, when Mill was at the height of his public esteem, they perceived *On Liberty* as a milestone deserving of translation; aside from their concerns about morality and virtue, the book represented both a clear alternative to long-standing political habits in China and Japan and a useful vehicle for bringing liberal thought within new public spheres. Mill and the translations of *Liberty* became quickly associated with a 'liberal' position. In Japan, where Mill was translated at the start of the Meiji Restoration, this position informed the movement for a national assembly (1874–84), a movement opposed to the ruling oligarchy but that succeeded in wresting from the oligarchy only a minimum of liberal demands for rights and participation in political decisions; eventually, as I describe in chapter 5, liberalism would be undercut by the creation of a national morality. In China, by contrast, where Yan translated Mill at the zenith of Qing dynastic failures, the liberal position associated with Mill appeared inattentive to the national crisis; its emphasis on the individual was inadequate for what all acknowledged as an impending struggle against the imperial court – whether motivated by reform or revolution.

It was this political world outside of Mill's text that provided a second important source for a moral critique of his liberal theory. If Mill's translators took issue with his advocacy of liberty at the expense of morality, his critics took issue with the type of society that, for better or worse, came to be associated with his ideas. After his death in 1873, Mill became linked to the libertarian ideology of 'individualism' that developed around Herbert Spencer's 1884 polemic, *The Man versus the State* (articulated in recent decades by Isaiah Berlin, Milton Freidman, Friedrich Hayek, and others); this is the argument that the individuals of civil society are best left to their own self-government, marked by a laissez-faire attitude opposed to centralization and state initiative – especially state supervision of the economy.[8] But this was not an accurate or an appropriate assessment of Mill's position.[9] He had advocated the value of 'individuality' – the social good that was to result from leaving each person free to pursue his own experiments in living and so develop his own character – but as we see in chapter 5, Mill was also open to invoking the principle of utility in order to interfere with individuals in the interest of some benefit for all.[10] As both a member of Parliament (1866–8) and public moralist during the last fifteen years of his life, he used his public position to advocate reforms such as land taxation and public education in order to ameliorate problems of inequality.[11] He was not a simple advocate of libertarian individualism.

If anything, Mill's political theory provided mixed messages for readers in China and Japan. To be sure, *On Liberty* offers only a partial discussion of his reflections on government; in it, he describes the political form of liberal society simply as self-government. Elsewhere, he endorsed the constitutional republic, but in *Liberty* he was more concerned with a pair of fundamental conditions that would limit the composition and extent of self-government. In the first place, he stressed the tutelary role of the educated and rational elite over their social inferiors; only as the common people were educated according to elite standards would they become eligible to participate. In effect, the liberal theory of self-government implied the rule of some over others, and in Japan and China, this was a principle of elite rule familiar from centuries of authoritarian and bureaucratic practice. In the second place, Mill advocated a restricted role for government, what we might call the minimal or libertarian state. He argued that the protection of individual liberty trumped all other social claims, except for society's right of self-protection. This aspect of liberal theory seemed to fly in the face of not only the requirement of elite tutelage of the masses but also political habits in Japan and China, where the state of course managed the people.

Largely because he endorsed a minimal state, Mill became associated with individualism, and critics of libertarian liberalism and the society that it had produced found fault with him as a source for those ideas. By the 1880s, it was apparent to many observers in England, Japan, and China that the combination of liberal society and libertarian state idealized in Great Britain was responsible for a significant measure of oppression both at home and overseas. *On Liberty* reflected the individualistic preferences of the class of private entrepreneurs, the bourgeoisie, who had used their elite wealth and power not to prepare the masses for participation, either in England or in India, but to maintain the masses in servitude and dire poverty. The liberalism represented by Mill was criticized as a bourgeois theory corrupt in its inception; his endorsement of individual liberty was leading humankind not to greater knowledge and improved ways of living but to selfish riches and decadent habits for the ruling few. The British ruling class was arguably so committed to inequality – especially economic inequality through its policies of low taxation, rights of inheritance, and the tradition of entailed estates – and this inequality grew so apparent in the nineteenth century with the fact of poverty (whether or not it was causally related to economic inequality) that moralists such as T.H. Green were inspired to political action on behalf of reform (see chapter 2).[12] If, early in the century, some had seen the industrial order encouraged by liberalism as akin to the fulfilment of God's promise to man, others at the end of the century argued that the liberal order had been usurped by capitalist dictatorship. In China, both conservative reformers and anarchist revolutionaries rejected Mill's preference of liberty before equality. Because societies in Europe and the United States had demonstrated that liberty for the few produced impoverished dependence for the many, it was clear that equality must precede liberty, for only equal citizens could attain an equal measure of genuine freedom.

Certainly, *On Liberty* encouraged a persisting tension between liberty and equality. In his essay, Mill pronounced liberty the superior value, to which equality and justice were secondary. As he understood the nature of individuals, only those that were independent could become equal. Hence, his argument contains what I describe as a tension between a theoretical individuality and a practical inequality. All persons are, in theory, endowed with liberty and capable of self-government, but Mill makes clear that social practice necessitates the authority of some over the others. If the purpose of elite tutelage was to prepare the masses for rational adulthood and thereby the freedom of self-government, one can only assume that the masses would subsequently negotiate with their fellows in order to secure a comparable measure of equality and justice. By contrast, Nakamura Keiu's Japanese translation attempted to dissolve this tension by reducing society and the state to an allegorical village, in which all members of the community are simultaneously free individuals and self-governing members of the polity – an interesting if ideal solution that parallels some of T.H. Green's and his student Bernard Bosanquet's efforts to correct Mill.

This tension between liberty and equality was felt as well in the international arena by Japanese and Chinese leaders, as they meditated on the fates of India, Africa, and Southeast Asia. On the one hand, the new universalism promised by the international liberal order pointed toward the progress and civilization represented by the powerful empire of Great Britain; it would assist with removing traditional authorities and their parochial claims to corrupt universals: the Tokugawa shogunate (1603–1867) and the Qing imperial order (1644–1911) were doomed. But on the other hand, Japan and China were in the midst of revolutionary struggles to replace those traditional rulers and state structures, and their efforts were complicated by Western imperialists, led by Great Britain, whose demands for territorial and economic concessions gave the lie to their liberal pretensions.

The problem facing the ruling elites of Japan and China in the nineteenth century, in light of the demise of traditional regimes, was not only the creation of a new sociopolitical system to maintain the Chinese or Japanese state in the new international order and under the desirable conditions of constitutional government and industrial capitalism. As this book undertakes to explain, the problem also entailed the creation of a new sociomoral system to guide the behaviour of the people as society was reorganized to meet those new requirements of the new state. The obvious wealth and power of the West, and its claims to a new universal order, made clear to Japanese and Chinese elites that they would need to import some or all of the West – its ideas, science, institutions, even a religion such as Christianity. But to what end? The sigificant diversity of approaches to political change – represented by republicans, imperialists, constitutional monarchists, anarchists, socialists, and more – undercut what had been initially a common attitude that the Tokugawa and Qing regimes were utterly corrupt. The rapid success of the Japanese oligarchy during the Meiji Restoration, even as it suppressed liberal institutions, created conditions that became a model for Chinese activists in the 1890s as China was plunged into a genuinely revolutionary situation.

Mill's utilitarian argument in *Liberty* – that people were useful as individuals – proposed myriad separate paths to development, all of which would eventually add up to a comprehensive social transformation. The risk with such a proposal, from the point of view of state builders, was that moral liberation from the past marked the beginning of autonomy for an individual who might prove useful to the new nation. But where were any guarantees? Unfortunately for those committed to building the state, the liberated conscience of an autonomous individual did not legitimize any particular political action. As Irwin Scheiner has argued for the case of Japan, when the state finally intervened in the lives of individuals, personal conscience invited a retreat from social action and eventually led to alienation; as I argue, the turn to a national morality in the 1890s would displace traditional notions of virtue and moral autonomy in favour of duty to emperor and state as a moral requirement of citizenship.[13] The changes in conceptual structures proposed by a text such as Mill's *On Liberty* promised to subvert social structures, but the men who led the Meiji Restoration were especially committed to maintaining workable forms of subjugation and hierarchization. The common people, not welcome in either civil society or representative politics, would nonetheless need to be included within the new Japanese state; their inclusion made a necessity of creating a class of imperial subjects whose sociopolitical and moral role was marked by obligations and duties to the state. In China, by comparison, the imperial system had conditioned expectations for the coordination of Confucian ethical traditions, stable social order, and good government; the demise of that system left expectations for a new social and political order ungrounded in any specific ethical tradition. Of seeming necessity, many advocates of change turned immediately to the problem of public virtue as a basis for new stability and good government.

In sum, Mill's atomistic individual seemed to promote selfish egotism; his promotion of elite tutelage seemed to justify a society marked by vast inequalities. Some critics of *Liberty* concluded that these undesired consequences, selfishness and inequality, followed from the free individual's negation of public morality. Rather than see this sociopolitical arrangement as progressive, they supplemented Mill's argument with alternative priorities. Both Nakamura and Yan gave greater emphasis to the progress and moral cohesion of the social group, which, accordingly, made a necessity of restraining the individual and circumscribing individual liberty. Mill's defence of individual liberty was a defence of the liberty of select individuals; and he was motivated to protect the autonomy of the elite from the mediocrity of the masses. Nakamura and his Japanese fellows wanted to protect the social whole and social order from the chaos generated by the potential foolishness of free agents. Both English and Japanese would advocate the education system as the avenue to ready the masses for rational thought and political participation. Yan Fu, by contrast, objected to Mill's negative presentation of liberty – freedom from external interference – and would have each individual more actively undertake good behaviour and use his liberty constructively for the benefit of all.

Hence this book begins by asking, What circumstances surround the Japanese and Chinese translations of Mill's *On Liberty*? What were its conditions of possibility? That is, what did the societies of England, Japan, and China share that enabled the relocation of Mill's ideas to new social contexts? And can we explain the similar, negative responses to his vision of individual liberty on the part of moralists in all three societies? Mill's Japanese and Chinese translators had studied in England in the 1860s and 1870s respectively, where they encountered his reputation and the authority of *On Liberty*, which they determined to introduce to their own peoples. As I explain in chapter 1, there were social similarities linking England, China, and Japan that facilitated the introduction of Mill, but his message underwent changes in the transition. Chapter 2 continues with a discussion of Mill's argument and his critics in England, particularly T.H. Green and his students Bernard Bosanquet and David Ritchie. Chapter 3 analyzes Nakamura Keiu's translation of *Liberty* as *Jiyū no ri*, chapter 4 analyzes Yan Fu's translation as *Qun ji quan jie lun*, and chapter 5 treats the several attempts to recover some collective virtue or morality in England, Japan, and China: Mill's hope for a 'regime of virtue'; Japan's creation of a national morality; and the wish among Chinese reformers and revolutionaries for a reconstruction of the people under a regime of moral education.

For the benefit of readers in Asian studies, let me add that the interpretive framework of this book bears little relation to the two main bodies of scholarship on the transfer of liberalism and democracy to East Asia. The first of these, modernization theory, dominated much scholarship between the 1950s and 1970s; it has been so often critiqued that we need not repeat that here.[14] Suffice it to say that the intellectual history informed by modernization theory was constructed around binary pairs of terms – West versus East, modern versus traditional, liberal versus Confucian, value versus history, reason versus emotion, and so on – and generally undertook to explain the ways in which Asian intellectuals mediated the two opposites. Figures such as Liang Qichao or Nishimura Shigeki (discussed in chapter 5) were deemed insufficiently liberal and thus insufficiently modern; and their interest in public morality became especially a sign of their commitment to tradition and history rather than to reason and modernity – or, more germane to my argument here, to authoritarianism rather than to liberalism.

The second, more recent, body of work, which began in the 1980s, has focused instead on democracy and democratization, largely within the discipline of political science. This work dispenses with liberal theories like Mill's and instead foregrounds a minimal set of liberal elements – usually freedom of assembly, freedom of the press, and free elections – as key utilities in the service of democratization, the overall goal of which is to create governments more responsive to citizens and accordingly more legitimate governments in China and Japan. Typically, these works subject local versions of democracy to a 'pluralist' standard of democracy, which defines democracy 'in terms of procedures instead of substance.'[15] While political scientists of Japan usually treat Japan's problems with democratization as commensurate with those of the United States or Europe, political scientists of China have turned to a form of 'nativism' that mimics the binaries of modernization theory. That is, scholars often reify the 'distinctiveness of Chinese culture' as a historically constituted commitment to traditional values different from and opposed to those of the West; accordingly, these China watchers search either for signs of convergence between China and the West (that is, changes to Chinese tradition) or for the persistence of traditional values that forever mark China's difference from the West.[16]

This is all quite removed from Mill's more libertarian liberalism – which at times is misrepresented in this nativist work.[17] Instead of a political theory like Mill's liberalism, this scholarship on China's democratization dwells on 'political liberalization' as a precondition for democratization and focuses on four general problems: ideology (the commitment of Chinese leaders and intellectuals to authoritarianism, dictatorship, and nationalism); the Chinese Communist Party (and its lack of commitment to democracy); political economy (the growth of pluralism and globalization at the expense of a planned economy); and the expansion of political procedures such as elections and liberal utilities such as civil society, which inform the question of political legitimacy.[18] Mill's liberalism has been stripped of its comprehensive set of liberties, while his sole concession to the problem of political legitimacy has been retained: general elections whose purpose is to allow the dominated classes a periodic check on the momentum of their masters.

Both modernization theory and the more recent work on democratization find fault with the alleged failures of China and Japan to produce liberal societies characterized by multi-party democracy and industrial capitalism. Put another way, both assume that industrial capitalism and the domination of society by the entrepreneurial class and its corporate agents is both normative and good. In both bodies of work, concern for collective morality and the public good is seen as misguided – a sign of a premodern and illiberal consciousness that needs to Westernize and to commit itself to reason. That bourgeois democracies produce class divisions – the dependence of a working class on an entrepreneurial class, or the impoverishment of a rural class in the interests of an urban class – is largely irrelevant.

This book, by contrast, is not so much concerned with how Chinese and Japanese intellectuals mediated Western and Eastern political philosophy in the interest of developing modern states and capitalist economies in China and Japan. Nor is this book interested in judging the legitimacy of governments in China and Japan. Rather, the interpretive framework here accords with the intellectual history that has followed the linguistic turn into cultural history so as to grant Chinese and Japanese subjects the capacity to represent their world views as autonomous thinkers – persons not bound categorically by one or another cultural identity but constituted by the hybridity of culture and language that characterizes their international and intercultural lives. But unlike many such works of intellectual history, to which readers will find extensive references herein, and which treat large complexes of ideas such as evolutionism, Darwinism, liberalism, and so on, this book looks at the specificity of Mill's theory of liberty and in particular the tension it provoked between personal liberty and public virtue.

I argue that this was an international concern, for we find it among Mill's critics in England, Japan, and China. This book does not pursue an 'either-or' strategy of opposing the West and China or Japan, but a 'both-and' strategy: all were agreed that Mill neglected the importance of public virtue. If anything, this book discloses the utopian desire for social harmony (to be fostered by projects of education or 'harmonization') common to a wide range of intellectuals in the nineteenth century. Based on the evidence of social divisions and working-class misery in England and its colonies, for which libertarian attitudes and laissez-faire political values were held responsible, English and East Asian critics of Mill idealized a more 'constructive' liberalism that would better integrate personal liberties and public moralities. Again, I would emphasize that Mill's translators in China and Japan well understood Mill's *On Liberty* and chose to modify his argument – in very much the same way that some of his English critics had done. If Mill's elevation of individual liberties undermined public morality and threatened the unity of the nation, T.H. Green, Nakamura Keiu, and Yan Fu were agreed that some provision had to be made for the public good.

CHAPTER ONE

On Liberty and Its Historical Conditions of Possibility

On Liberty was translated into Japanese and Chinese in the last decades of the nineteenth century, and, with these texts, ideas and arguments central to the liberal theory of John Stuart Mill were transmitted to East Asia. This chapter examines the circumstances surrounding Nakamura Keiu's Japanese translation of *Liberty, Jiyū no ri* (The principle of liberty), published in 1871, and Yan Fu's Chinese translation of 1898, *Qun ji quan jie lun* (On the boundaries of the authority between the group and the self), published in 1903. But I must emphasize that this chapter marks a departure from problems of translation and historiography in order to examine what I call 'the conditions of possibility' surrounding *On Liberty*. That is, what did the societies of England, Japan, and China share that made possible the transfer of Mill's ideas from one social context to another? What elements in the historical conditions of Japan and China facilitated the respective translations of Mill and helped to familiarize his liberal theory for respective groups of readers? I argue that translation theory alone is insufficient for understanding the transmission of Mill's ideas to East Asia, and would draw our attention to the historical conditions of possibility informing *On Liberty* and its translations.

I use the term *translation* as an initial gesture to conventional discussions about the transfer of texts and ideas. Theorists of translation have long understood their topic in the same way that translators practice their craft: as a process of mediation between two distinct languages defined by two distinct linguistic groups. This assumption has given rise to an extensive literature on translation, ranging from linguistic analyses that compare lexical, grammatical, or stylistic aspects of translations and their original texts, to biographical discussions of the intentions of authors and translators.[1] Typically, the questions raised by this comparative approach foreground the fact of disparities between versions of texts: Is the translation (or translator) literal or paraphrastic? Accurate or interpretive? Aren't some genres, like poetry, simply untranslatable?

Many previous historical studies of translation have rested content with conclusions such as these – that so-and-so mistranslated such-and-such an idea or text. Benjamin Schwartz, for example, in his standard work of modern Chinese intellectual history, *In Search of Wealth and Power*, examines Yan Fu's turn-of-the-century translations of modern landmarks by Thomas Huxley, Herbert Spencer, J.S. Mill, and others; Schwartz periodically emphasizes the differences between Yan's translations and the originals, to accuse Yan of mistranslation or to point out where Yan diverged from the sense of the original or embellished points not in the original.[2] Likewise, in the March 1999 issue of the *Journal of American History*, which comprises a series of essays on the international circulation of the Declaration of Independence, several contributors make informative points about one or another translation of the Declaration, but a number of authors settle with conclusions that attempt to differentiate original, core, or timeless aspects of the Declaration from its translated, inaccurate, or timebound aspects.[3]

The shortcoming of such an approach to translation as historical event is the problem of semantic transparency – the notion that meaning is fixed over time and among disparate cultures and languages. Studies of the movement of ideas, texts, and institutions from one cultural setting to another assume the reality of semantic transparency when they do not problematize the language of concepts; some intellectual and political historians have been satisfied to discuss texts written by European authors and to assume that language is not bound by its historical context – that what a text meant to a nineteenth-century reader, in whatever language, is what it means to anyone reading it today.[4] So, for example, to equate what Huxley or Spencer meant by a theory of evolution with what Yan Fu proposed as a 'theory of evolution' (*tianyan lun*) is to treat evolution as a term whose meaning is stable from one time and place to another. As Schwartz concludes, 'It does not seem to me that the difference in cultural tone is more significant than the identity of the idea.'[5] Rather than compare the translations of texts and ideas in this manner, with reference to a notion of 'cultural tone,' an alternative approach would examine the role of translated ideas and texts in debates over evolution and progress – as Lydia H. Liu and James R. Pusey have done.[6] Another alternative, as I attempt in this book, would examine the ways in which translations engage and deliberately modify the arguments of their originals, in order to comment on those originals. My goal here is to move beyond a narrow, text-bound consideration of the Japanese and Chinese translations in order to look at that interlingual work as both interpretation of *On Liberty* and commentary on Mill – in short, as elements of an intercultural discussion on individual liberty and public virtue.

Translation in Theory

Long before textual analysis called into question assumptions regarding the unitary nature or singular identity of 'the text,' linguists had criticized the notion of translation as a mediation between different languages on two important accounts. First, Roman Jakobson pointed out forty years ago that 'translation' occurs daily among people ostensibly sharing 'the same language.' The most fundamental form of translation, he maintained, is the simple *rewording* (or 'intralingual translation') that constitutes the process of expanding one's vocabulary in one's own language. Translation between different languages is thus an extension of this metalinguistic procedure.[7] Jakobson developed his observation with two important comments regarding linguistic structure. On the one hand, given that a distinction optional in one language may be compulsory in another, he insisted that translation is rarely word for word; it is directed instead at the level of messages. So, for example, in order to translate the English statement 'I hired a worker,' a Russian needs supplementary information – whether the action was completed or not (because completive versus noncompletive aspect is obligatory with Russian verbs) and whether the worker was a man or a woman (because gender is obligatory with nouns). On the other hand, insofar as language occurs across the range of social interactions, Jakobson urged us to carefully consider the human experience within which these messages are necessarily embedded: 'In its cognitive function, language is minimally dependent on the grammatical pattern because the definition of our experience stands in complementary relation to metalinguistic operations – the cognitive level of language not only admits but directly requires recoding interpretation, i.e., translation.'[8] We would do better, in other words, to move beyond the arguably narrow cognitive concerns of contemporary linguistics and to consider translation in the larger context of the more common-place activity of transcoding. After all, as Henry Schogt has observed, the act of translation focuses on a target audience at the level of perfor-mance, or *parole*, and is hence largely incompatible with the concerns of linguistics, which claims to examine the paradigmatic structure of language.[9]

Accordingly, more specific acts of textual transcoding (Jakobson's 'translation proper') should be related to their social settings. The com-mon practice that we call textual translation, for example, has long been a pedagogic discipline central to elite education in both Europe and East Asia.[10] Far from being a simple and isolated transaction between texts and translators, textual translation has largely remained a social practice specifically intended to demonstrate linguistic compe-tence of a sort I might term, in light of what follows below, 'lexico-graphic.' That is, acts of textual translation on the part of an educated elite, like the compiling of interlingual dictionaries, are characterized by the desire for fixity in meaning, so as to provide an accurate or definitive version of an original; with all terms of the source language text rendered into the target language text, the translation achieves a mark of authority. Unfortunately, this comparative and lexicographic understanding of translation too often invites the conclusions men-tioned above – that so-and-so mistranslated this section, erroneously paraphrased that section, and so on.

In addition to Jakobson's criticism of simple notions of translation – and thus, as a second major critique of translation – theorists of lan-guage as a social practice have called into question the description of 'a language' as a unitary phenomenon. They criticize the academic posi-tivism of contemporary linguistics, because it first employs criteria external to language (like racial characteristics or national demarca-tions) and privileges an official form of language use over others in order to designate a standard, and then proceeds to examine the gram-matical and cognitive limits of language use according to the princi-ples of logical positivism. Instead, these theorists urge us to consider language activity as the production of signifying utterances within one or another discourse.[11] That is, we should understand language as a practice of human sociality in which we evoke or propose relationships among the things in our worlds; we should examine language not as a 'thing' but as a mediation among social positions.[12] With this perspec-tive of language-as-practice, it is claimed, we will avoid reducing social experience to simple acts of communication that require decipherment within a linguistic code, and will instead be able to analyse experience as the contextualization and contestation of ideological meaning or symbolic power.[13] Translation, in other words, need no longer be seen as a necessarily compromised mediation between two languages but as a creative act of generating meaning and constructing discourse in an interlingual context.

In this regard, scholars of historical linguistics present evidence that significantly challenges our desire to delimit one or another unitary language. The phenomenon of loanwords, words that are borrowed from 'one language' by another, demonstrates the existence of interlingual lexical material that crosses the boundaries of 'different' languages so defined.[14] (Admittedly, the phenomenon can only be described in the terms it seeks to undermine.) The interlingual discourse on liberty, prompted by Mill's text, includes much such material – such as *riberuchi* in Japanese and *liboerte* in Chinese. So rather than speak of an original and its translation, we would do better to dwell on the interlingual aspect of texts and ideas. To return to the points made by Jakobson, making sense of an 'original' text requires that a reader translate it into 'one's own language'; and to engage in transcoding a text necessarily enlists the terms of both original and translation – whether we think of these as two versions of 'one language' or as versions of two such 'languages.'

Some readers may object, however, that the conventional view of translation has been an adequate model in the past and continues to be so today, particularly in light of recent advances made in machine translation. Committed to the work of producing better – even automatic – translations, that branch of translation studies quite practically proposes theories of translation that can be empirically tested and judged on their adequacy. Such a project is thus closely affiliated with the positivism implicit in the linguistic demarcation of separate and independent languages.[15] But the objection overlooks a significant difference of scholarly goals. Obviously, the effort to produce machine translations is not concerned with translation as a historiographical problem and hence should not distract us here; rather, the objection speaks to the risks of interdisciplinary research. Noam Chomsky once offered a persuasive defence of 'idealization' as a condition of linguistics as a science – that is, as a rational method that aims to discover explanatory principles. But he also argued that interdisciplinary examinations of language, such as sociolinguistics, do not really contribute to our understanding of linguistics, which depends on the idealization of a language and its community of speakers.[16] Hence, I might refine the point made earlier: the problem is not how linguistics constructs and pursues its study of language but the way in which those who study translation draw on linguistics to conduct their research. I make no claim here to be contributing to the study of linguistics; my effort to better understand the practice and consequences of translation in specific historical and social settings is meant to expand on earlier studies of translation, and this necessitates a break with the models offered by linguistics.

Translation Words and Lexical Fields

Nonetheless, the two theoretical precautions outlined above (the nature of 'translation' and the putative unity of 'a language') go largely unheeded in ongoing efforts to understand the vast work of translation undertaken in East Asia. Because of the great differences distinguishing Euro-American societies from Chinese and Japanese societies in the nineteenth century, and the extensive processes of Westernization that ensued as East Asians developed their interests in the West, scholars of these intellectual, cultural, and linguistic histories have relied extensively on the concept of 'translation word' (C: *wailaici* / J: *hon'yakugo*) to analyse and describe the passage of meaning 'from West to East.' Such an approach to this transfer of meaning, I believe, has at best a limited value, because of two significant complications that have not yet been fully taken into account.

In the first place, given the nature of the linguistic sign as both material and meaning (in Saussure's analysis), the phenomenon of translation at the level of the word can occur with respect to either phonetic value (sound) or conceptual meaning.[17] The former are commonly called *loanwords* (or *phonetic loans*) and the latter *translation words* (or *translation loans*); both are important types of translations in East Asia, where the Chinese character can convey meaning independently of its pronunciation. For example, in translating the English word *liberty*, we might see in Japanese *katakana* syllabary the loanword リベルチ (*riberuchi*), or the Chinese use of Chinese characters for the loanword 里勃而特 (*liboerte*). Both languages, by contrast, currently use the same translation word in Chinese characters 自由, although pronunciations differ (C: *ziyou* / J: *jiyū*). While loanwords are very common in Japanese, they are rather uncommon in Chinese today, except for proper names like *Bolatu* for Plato, and so on.[18]

The difficulty in examining translation in this manner – at the level of the word – is that we are rarely certain of the exact denotatum of the translated word.[19] How can we be sure that the word *X*, from a source language like English, is being translated into the target language Chinese or Japanese as *Y*? In the case of a loanword ('sound transfer'), once one has learned to make the conventional phonetic shifts, the denotatum in the source language is somewhat clear. One learns to recognize *riberuchi* as a loanword for 'liberty,' and to attribute to *riberuchi* the meaning of the English word *liberty*. (And this procedure assumes familiarity with the English word *liberty*.) But the denotatum of a translation word is not so readily identified. In analysing language as a system, Saussure astutely pointed out that '[t]he content of a word is determined in a final analysis not by what it contains but by what exists outside it.'[20] That is, the synchronic dimension of language, where we distinguish synonyms from each other, frustrates our best efforts to specify any single word, say, in Chinese, that is serving as a translation word for a given word in English. In *On Liberty*, Mill makes frequent mention of *society, association, community*, and similarly related terms; given the relative interchangeability of these terms, we would have to contemplate an analogous range of Chinese translation words for the English set. So a single Chinese word might correspond to a single English word, or it might fit in a range of English synonyms, and a set of Chinese synonyms may or may not correspond smoothly with the analogous English set. To pursue translation at the site of the word (lexeme) must lead to treating concepts, reflected in sets of terms, as a 'lexical field' and thus investigating the interlingual relations between such lexical fields.[21]

It can be argued, nonetheless, that apart from loanwords we have an excellent tool available for the investigation of specific translation words: the dictionary. Indeed, as the Japanese school of National Philology (*Kokugogaku*) has demonstrated, a historical sequence of dictionaries allows the scholar to determine the standardization of translation words and the development of their morphology; in addition, the study of dictionaries invites conclusions regarding the sources for a translator's craft. So, for example, in one of the monumental works of National Philology related to my work here, Morioka Kenji evaluates the relative influence of the primary dictionaries available to translators in the 1860s and 1870s and concludes that Nakamura Keiu, in his inventive translation of *On Liberty*, was somewhat influenced by the most important Chinese-language dictionary available by 1870,

Wilhelm Lobscheid's *Chinese and English Dictionary.*[22] Be that as it may, the dictionary remains a problematic historical source, because it is a primarily synchronic representation of language and can only tangentially assist in examining the development of translation methods, lexical fields, and the new discourses associated with Western learning.[23] Certainly the case of Nishi Amane, a contemporary of Nakamura Keiu, demonstrates that the majority of his translation words failed historically; they were not reused and consequently do not appear in the dictionaries of the period. From the point of view of the dictionary, we are left with the marginally interesting conclusion that Nishi relied little on dictionaries and apparently had little influence on contemporary lexicographers.[24] A better approach, I believe, would be to examine translation words as they appear in translated texts – as utterances in discourses and thus as elements of the semantic fields constituted by these texts – in order to better analyse translation processes.[25]

In addition to this interference of the word's semiotic structure and the semantic field of the linguistic sign in the attempt to specify translation words, there is a second, pragmatic, problem that complicates our best efforts to examine translation at this level of the word. Given the relative incongruence of languages on the point of semantic equivalence and the constitutive nature of neologisms in the new discourse on liberty, to equate terms from source and target languages is not a sufficient procedure because it ignores what can only have been, for the majority of readers, a new and unfamiliar, even obscure, context.[26] That is to say, if little is equivalent at the higher level of context or discourse, it makes little sense to equate a lower level of mere uncontextualized terms.

Consider the following contrast, central to the challenge for anyone wanting to translate *On Liberty.* It was possible to speak of 'man' generally or 'humankind' in nineteenth-century China or Japan, because comparable terms could be borrowed from the language of Chinese moral and political philosophy: *ren* for 'man' or *zi* for 'self' in Chinese, and *hito* for 'man' or *ji* (*onore*) for 'self' in Japanese. At the same time, the would-be translator was assisted by a relatively straightforward abstraction: as a particular instance of the concept himself, the reader, as 'man,' was in a position to abstract from personal experience to the general concept. The same was not true of that difficult objectification 'society.' In addition to having to displace the sensibility among Chinese and Japanese that the family and village were the group units most natural to humankind, a great deal of linguistic and cognitive invention was required to objectify society as a thing unto itself. One might equate society with people, population, or citizenry, or invoke the individual as a bridge between society and nation; but in any case, effort was required to objectify this abstract concept, particularly because – as Saitō Tsuyoshi has pointed out – the Spencerian notion of social struggle as a given condition for humankind was simultaneously providing yet another unfamiliar context for this new concept, society.[27]

So in addition to moving from equating specific terms to examining the lexical field surrounding new concepts and neologisms, we would do well to understand textual discourse as a pragmatic activity intended to have an effect on the historical world of action. This is especially critical because the translation word neologisms are remarkably tentative in formative texts like the early translations of *On Liberty*. Rather than a fixed and hence repeated translation word for a term like *society*, one finds a series of terms that work collectively to construct a version of Mill's meaning. Translation, for Nakamura Keiu and Yan Fu, was not a lexicographic project but a discursive activity, intended not to fix but to generate meaning: their translations are not authoritative but are aimed at beginning the process of generating new textual authorities to guide the new projects of Westernization in China and Japan.

My point of departure, then, is to acknowledge that the Japanese and Chinese translations of Mill's *On Liberty* were deliberate contributions to nineteenth-century socio-political movements. In the midst of the European and American invasions of China and Japan, intended to integrate those two lands within the world capitalist market, Mill's translators created new versions of *On Liberty* in order to introduce to their respective readers the English-language terms of this new, liberal understanding of appropriate social and political forms, including liberty, morality, the individual, society, and the state. To be sure, both Nakamura and Yan decided to translate Mill rather than describe and critique him, so the question remains as to how their translations are related to Mill's original; the accuracy or inaccuracy of the translation is still implicit. But in this book, our focus is on the historical context surrounding these works of translation.

The Historical Conditions of Possibility

My discussion thus far has assumed that languages – and texts in particular – are infinitely amenable to intercultural transcoding. But such an assumption flies in the face of historical fact, for, as I acknowledged above, the translation of texts has long been a largely formal and pedagogic discipline of elite education. This is certainly true of the situation in nineteenth-century Japan and China. So if we think of translation as intercultural exchange and the creation of milestones of hybrid culture, the work of translation must have some material basis in social practices that permit such cultural transfer.

This is because, in the first place, translations do not appear in the absence of some social context. For example, one doesn't readily find nineteenth-century translations of *On Liberty* into southern African or native American languages, yet works of Mill, Spencer, and other British philosophers were translated into the Polish language in the nineteenth century and read avidly by Polish liberals reportedly concerned about the fate of their struggling nation.[28] This is not to say that southern Africans or native Americans were uninterested in Mill or incapable of translating *On Liberty* into an idiom of their own; indeed, the opposite may have been the case, but I have seen no published evidence. In the second place, translations can serve motives different from the intentions of either their originals or their translators. We cannot assume, for instance, that those interested in Mill were necessarily anti-authoritarian liberals committed to staking claims to their rights in the face of monarchical privilege. The aristocrat who translated *On Liberty* into Serbian, Prince Peter Karadjordjevi'c, remained an advocate of political reform even when he later reigned as king of Serbia between 1904 and 1914.[29] The Japanese and Chinese translators, as we shall see in subsequent chapters, were also committed to political reform, but they brought to Mill a somewhat collectivist perspective, with their keen wishes to maintain public standards of morality.

We should also consider the context of a translation's reception among its readership. Given that the Japanese translation of *On Liberty* was reportedly read by the entire generation of Japanese leaders who came of age in the 1870s, it seems appropriate to ask what historical conditions facilitated this intellectual work of translation? What factors in the historical conditions of Japan in 1871 familiarized *On Liberty* to Nakamura and his readers? Or again, what factors in the historical conditions of China in 1903 familiarized *On Liberty* to Yan and his readers?[30] Rather than focus exclusively on one or another translator's interest, ability, or motives, I would also examine the material ground of historical conditions, which, in this case, gravitates toward social institutions like the family and monarchy. If we examine the translations of *On Liberty* as contributions to the ideological project of individual liberty, the question of historical conditions comes to include the methodological problem of identifying those contingent assumptions that Mill, Nakamura, and Yan shared – that is, the conditions of possibility that permitted the transfer of ideas among English, Chinese, and Japanese.[31]

In other words, one problem that motivates this book is the historical condition of transcultural understanding. How was it possible that a Japanese intellectual like Nakamura could undertake to translate one of the most popular philosophical works of Victorian England? And what of liberal theory did Nakamura convey to the many Japanese readers of *Jiyū no ri* in the 1870s? This is not to ask how one or another reader responded to Mill in translation – for there was a range of elite intellectuals with various Buddhist, Confucian, or Western studies perspectives – but to inquire about the cultural assumptions surrounding the reception of Mill in translation. So, for example, as I discuss shortly, Nakamura's translation of Mill spoke to an issue at the heart of the Meiji Restoration: whether political participation was to be determined by merit or by heredity. If we consider Nakamura's text as an act of intercultural transcoding and a contribution to Japan's changing political discourse during a revolutionary period, what elements in the historical conditions of nineteenth-century Japan informed Nakamura's translation and helped his readers make sense of such a version of liberalism? The same questions apply to Yan Fu and the reception of *Qun ji quan jie lun* in China. By 'historical conditions,' I draw our attention to three specific assumptions, both explicit and implicit, that would inform a reader's understanding of *Jiyū no ri* or *Qun ji quan jie lun*: (1) the concepts of individuality and subjecthood; (2) the elite value of literary education; and (3) the class nature of civilized societies, which educated elites assist in ruling. I submit that these three assumptions provided a material basis for familiarity with Mill's argument in China and Japan.

Individuality and Subjecthood

Like Mill and his reading public in England, Nakamura and his Japanese contemporaries, and Yan and his Chinese contemporaries, were firmly grounded within a long literary tradition that, in addition to the benefits of elite culture, afforded each the self-conscious position of 'individual.' While it is not my intention here to survey the linguistic literature that accounts for the grounding of the category of individual (or 'first person'), it is clear that an understanding of oneself as an individual was a feature of English, Chinese, and Japanese literate culture in the nineteenth century, insofar as each made available (1) the pronominal position of *I* as an agent in discourse, (2) the reflexive notion of a self, which can be both generalized to others and particularized to oneself, and (3) the abstract notion of 'individuality.'[32] In translating Mill, Nakamura constructed a concept of individuality as a complex formed by an interior ego or self (*jiko* and *onore*) and an exterior, abstracted individual – that is, the individual as one of the people or humankind (*jinminkoko, ikko no hito*, and *kojin*), amenable to the new abstraction 'individuality' (*dokuji ikko*).[33] By comparison, Yan enlisted an identical Chinese character word for self, *ji*, but differentiated that personal self from the more abstract or impersonal self (*zi*) of an expression such as self-government (*zizhi*). Like Nakamura, Yan's terms for the objectified individual indicate the individual as one of the group (*yiren* and *yiji*), and from a poetic term of self-reference, *xiaoji*, he generated an awkward and defunct neologism for individuality, *xiaoji zhuyi* (see chapter 4).[34]

These two positions – the interior self and the exterior person – are mediated through the exercise of individual freedoms and rights, primary of which, to Mill, are belief or opinion, judgement, taste, occupation, and friendly assembly. That is, the individual is concretized in connection with a range of related concepts, including (1) those things that an individual may have or hold, such as opinions, duties, and character; and (2) activities in which an individual may engage, such as discussing, debating, considering, comparing, judging, and so on. Within the structures of grammar and syntax, exemplified by a phrase such as 'from my point of view,' Mill's rhetoric creates space for the authorial voice to give an analysis or an opinion as an individual. Hence, through mediating terms such as *freedom* and *right*, which come into play on the occasion of such free expression of opinion or assembly, the interior self and abstracted individual are ideally resolved for each person as a member of society, because all adult and functioning members of society ideally share these freedoms as individuals. That is, the linguistic material available in both Chinese and Japanese expressions for *I, me, oneself*, and *that individual person* served to translate those conceptual structures that proposed the new social relations implicit in Mill's theory of individual liberty.[35]

The converse of this category of individual, a second position that Nakamura, Yan, and their contemporaries shared with Mill, was subjecthood, that state (to Mill) of unreasonable dependence of people upon their masters. Nakamura and his readers came of age as subjects of the shogun, family elders, and bureaucratic superiors; if they chafed under the authority of the shogun and incapable superiors, as many historians argue, we can appreciate Nakamura's criticism of unreasonable dependence and his aspiration for the new independence of the people. With the removal of the Tokugawa shogun from power in 1867, many samurai-officials embraced their new roles as subjects of the emperor, a position that enabled them to participate actively with the emperor in the administration of a Westernizing Japan. This complex of identifications – as free individuals, advocates for self-government, subjects of royal masters, and targets of social or governmental interference – was available to both English readers of *On Liberty* and Japanese readers of *Jiyū no ri* and certainly grounded the reception of liberal theory in Japan. For someone like Nakamura, interested in private schools, the education of women, tolerance for Christianity, and other civilized social policies, the meaningfulness of Mill's liberal theory arose from this set of multiple identifications: in the position of free individual, one exercises one's freedom of opinion, discussion and so on, and thereby resists the subjecthood imposed by ruler, government, or society.

Likewise, Yan Fu and his readers came of age as subjects of family elders, bureaucratic superiors, and the imperial Qing dynasty. They chafed under the authority of an imperial institution dominated by the Empress Dowager and her reactionary allies, who seemed committed to little more than maintaining the status quo and silencing the growing calls for reform. But the presence of the treaty ports, urban spaces exempt from Chinese rule and under the authority of European powers, exposed some Chinese nationals to Western bourgeois culture and facilitated the growth of structures of civil society, such as Chambers of Commerce and newspapers. Some of these new structures took root in the provinces, where imperial and central authority had waned after the Taiping Rebellion at mid-century and forces for reform began to gather in the 1890s. In a number of cases, the provincial elite – with interests in the movement to recover railroad and mining rights from foreign concessions – began to construct local and provincial assemblies, newspapers, clubs, scholarly associations, and Westernizing schools – all of which corresponded to the public world imagined in Mill's *On Liberty*, where free discussion led to enlightened principles of self-rule.[36]

But the positions of individual and subject alone are insufficient for either an understanding of Mill's liberal theory or the creation of a liberal society. Missing is the cateogry of the citizen, which is closely bound to a concept of society and an understanding of representative government. As Saitō Tsuyoshi has pointed out for the case of Japan, although Meiji intellectuals like Nakamura saw themselves as individuals constituting a new society, the major problem they faced was procedural: they might have come to understand the theory that society and citizenry are equivalent and that this society of citizens and the nation-state are linked through the individual, but they failed to overcome the perception of family and village as natural institutions – with their assumptions of paternal hierarchy. Accordingly, they failed to establish the new institutions needed to reconstruct society as a body of individual citizens.[37] Irwin Scheiner, in his discussion of psychological dimensions of social protest in the Meiji period, points to the corresponding limitations imposed on the development of a socially critical position: without a concept of society, an individual cannot develop the personal conscience and identity of a citizen that differentiate one from the subject of an authoritarian state. Scheiner quotes Motoda Sakunoshin, president of Rikkyō University, who lamented in 1909 that without 'society,' there are only nation and family, and an individual's private concerns are thus divorced from the public realm and political life.[38] As I argue in chapter 3, the political consciousness of citizen seems to become available only when the conception of representative institutions creates a differentiation and mediation between society and government.

Elite Education and the Ruling Class

If both Nakamura and Yan imagined society as an authoritative group whose nature is less like a general association of free men and more like the institution of government, residing at the opposite extreme of this goal of a civil society of self-governing citizens is the individual constituent of the social. One of Mill's purposes in *On Liberty* is to reiterate the utilitarian value of the individual. People are valuable as individuals, in and of themselves, because their diversity is beneficial to all society as a prolific source of speculation and innovation. Liberty is therefore to be cherished because it is generally useful to the social whole. As Thomas L. Haskell observed in a brilliant essay relating Mill's utilitarianism and Max Weber's 'spirit of capitalism,' central to both theories is the ideology of opportunity – the conviction that individuals take advantage of the present in the interests of a better future, whether as future-oriented entrepreneurs or, more to the point in Mill, as more enlightened and hence more autonomous agents.[39]

Key to the future betterment of each individual is education, which is central to two further shared assumptions about the nature of society. First, Mill, Nakamura, and Yan understood that the paramount determinant of status in society should be education, which appropriately defines both a social elite and the progress of an enlightened society. In *Liberty*, Mill states that education cultivates the social virtues and leads to the maturity of an individual's faculties, both of which are prerequisite to rational, adult status and hence political participation. Mill suggests that education, if not provided to all children by their parents, should be guaranteed by the state. If education were extended to society as a whole, social conditions would certainly improve, since the pool of qualified talent seeking private and public employment would be larger. Given the competitive nature of free institutions, the best talent would rise to leadership positions, no longer fettered by mere ascriptions of birth.[40] This very sentiment had long justified the system of civil service examinations in China – although debate frequently rekindled around the practicality of the material tested – and was increasingly expressed by samurai intellectuals in the late Tokugawa period and by formative Meiji pronouncements such as Nakamura's translations of Samuel Smiles's *Self Help* and Mill's *On Liberty*. With the support of education, individuals could freely cultivate their special and diverse talents, and all society would benefit. Education was key to the dynamic principle of progress. To Nakamura, Yan, and so many of their contemporaries, progress is operable in historical time and accompanies the advance of civilization, that new and man-made order active in the world from the eighteenth century, marked by 'modern' technology like the railroad, steamship, and telegraph, and the rational modification of moribund custom.

Second, Mill, Nakamura, and Yan assumed that human sociality is marked by class divisions and that education rightly affords a man entry to the educated elite and ruling class. In Mill's England, the educated elite was largely identified with the ranks of the traditional aristocracy and the middle class – professional men who found occupation in the church, law, medicine, education, and government service and who, like Mill, read the press and paid taxes, and to whom the right to vote had first been extended with political reform in 1832.[41] In China, the educated elite – many of whom came from landowning and landlord backgrounds – rose to positions in the ruling bureaucracy based on successful performance on the civil service examinations; the aristocracy, however, continued to benefit from the privileges of nepotism, and fiscal emergency excused the occasional sale of examination degrees to merchants and others with available cash. In Japan, the educated elite were for the most part the samurai ruling class who dominated the academies and government offices of the Tokugawa period; as in China, their ranks were supplemented by talented merchants or those willing to purchase samurai privileges. Where the educated elites of England, China, and Japan overlapped was among the ranks of governmental and entrepreneurial bureaucracies, a social position observable in the lives of Nakamura, Yan, and Mill. All three took advantage of opportunities provided by education to secure positions within their respective bureaucratic classes – Mill in the East India Company while he pursued his avocation as political economist and philosopher, and Nakamura in the Tokugawa and Meiji governments as he pursued his career as educator, translator, and journalist. Yan, too, served in several official and advisory capacities, most notably as director and then chancellor of the Beiyang Naval Academy in Tianjin between 1881 and 1900. All three men, in other words, gave personal expression to the appeal in *On Liberty* to education as the mark of human progress and foundation of an enlightened ruling elite.

But even though Mill, Nakamura, and Yan assume the existence of an educated and bureaucratic ruling class, the social groundings of this class differed in nineteenth-century England, Japan, and China.[42] By the 1860s, England's bureaucratic class can be identified with what both Hegel and Marx call the 'middle' class – the educated class that serves first as a mediation between the state and (bourgeois) civil society, and second as a link between the state and the 'corporations' that structure civil society.[43] If the aristocracy prevailed in the House of Lords, the Commons was the platform from which the bourgeoisie worked to expand its power during the nineteenth century. According to Arno Mayer, the aristocracy tended to dominate the army, the foreign office, and the diplomatic corps, with their ascriptive claim to authority. By contrast, the bourgeoisie and their allies in the professions of law, education, and journalism – even though its members more often than not mimicked the education and manners of the aristocracy – represented an alternative authority based on specialized and practical knowledge, and served most often in the ministries of war, finance, agriculture, and justice.[44]

Nakamura's sympathy with Mill's endorsement of an educated ruling class underscores a significant element of the Meiji Restoration of 1867, which promoted the goal of replacing a hereditary ruling class, the samurai, with a ruling class defined by the alternative criteria of merit and ability. Most members of the Tokugawa and early Meiji bureaucratic officialdom, like Nakamura, were drawn from the samurai, a legal creation that grew out of the landed warriors of the medieval age and a ruling class to whom the Tokugawa shogunate had granted the privileges of hereditary status, a right to hold public office, a right to bear arms, and a cultural and moral superiority upheld through educational preferment.[45] Their intellectual, administrative, and military labour was bound to the interests of the state, particularly its economic goals: to manage the peasant class and to extract from its labour a portion of agricultural produce with which to maintain the samurai class.

But a significant effect of Tokugawa rule was the rationalization of the samurai class, which begged the issue, as in China, of heredity versus merit. The shogunate enforced the systematic segmentation of each status group into self-regulating sectors characterized by increasingly impersonal relations, so that the samurai band, peasant village, and townsman ward came to be structured less in terms of personal ties and loyalties than in a hierarchy of bureaucratic position.[46] Once the shogunate had contained the samurai's independence, by placing individuals in regional castle towns and in positions of loyalty and service to superiors in hierarchical structures, it demilitarized the samurai's warrior function, by proposing alternative programs of education that emphasized moral ideologies reinforcing the samurai's superior status. Through two centuries of Tokugawa peace, bureaucratic relations and the samurai's administrative function came to dominate their ruling-class function, a process that encouraged both a less arbitrary and a more coercive enforcement of authority. Tokugawa bureaucratic service was defined in Chinese Confucian terms, both as an administrative aid to the sovereign in exercising authority and as a moral authority offering behavioural examples to the lower classes of the people. Consequently, the moral authority that came with hereditary status and personal relations – that sense shared with Mill that an educated class has tutelary privileges over the uneducated – was in tension with these processes of political rationalization that encouraged the rewarding of talent and ability.[47]

The Meiji Restoration proved to be the moment at which samurai leaders – allied with key imperial court nobles and merchant banking interests – conferred on themselves that right of civil society to represent itself as an autonomous polity, and placed themselves in the closed circle of society, government, and the power to rule that we find in Nakamura's translation of Mill. It is the structural overlap of bureaucracy with the samurai class, I believe, that accounts for Nakamura's conceptualization of society as government (see chapter 3). Their mediating function in the transition from Tokugawa to Meiji was precisely the initial step of abstraction that must occur in the structural linkage from society to government, for it was members of the samurai class and aspirants to bureaucratic service who overthrew the shogunate in order to reconstitute themselves as the leading society of an imperial restoration. They mediated the old society and the new, the old class of subjects and the newly autonomous government; they spoke as members of government and men of the people, secure in their positions on account of education and samurai status. They possessed what Mill's theory required: a keen sense of responsibility for their own society and an equally keen sense of duty as civil servants to do what administration required.[48] So, for example, in the 1875 debate over freedom of the press in Japan, it was not that the new leaders failed to appreciate Mill's argument but that they chose to decline the freedom in the interest of solidarity with the government and public order in the streets.[49]

But it is important to remember that neither Mill's nor Nakamura's text endorsed rule by the elite alone. Suffrage should be extended to women and the lower orders, if only to allow them a veto on the policies of their educated superiors. Even though Mill and Nakamura viewed society from the perspective of an educated elite, they foresaw that as greater numbers of people took their place among the educated, so too would greater numbers of people qualify for participation.[50]

The Meiji Restoration thus intersected with a perennial problem in Confucianism raised but left unresolved by the ancient Chinese philosopher Mencius: was leadership to be based in hereditary status or in merit, the rewarding of talent? Under the Tokugawa system, most positions of leadership and responsibility were in practice filled on a hereditary basis and justified in the terms of loyalty that had been so pointedly eroded during the rule of the Tokugawa shogunate. The lower samurai who made up the majority of bureaucratic clerks and lowly functionaries, and who felt unjustly cut off from positions of power and respect, increasingly voiced the rationalizing opinion that official appointments and positions should be based on merit rather than hereditary factors. At the twilight of the Tokugawa age, these lower samurai became the group most willing to risk the present in the interests of fundamental political change.[51] Alienated from the Tokugawa state and motivated by notions of reform, some younger samurai – Nakamura, for example – began to interpret the question of political legitimacy in terms of representative institutions and replaced relationships of loyalty with an identification with independence – the very position of Mill's educated elite and middle class.[52] Nakamura's translation of Mill, then, reinforced the position of those who valued talent over status – as a criterion for bureaucratic service and political participation – and contributed greatly to the early Meiji political culture of freedom and independence. But Nakamura's silence on representative institutions left the problem of imagining democratic and republican forms of government to subsequent scholars and political activists. As a consequence of this delay, the political development of civil society in Meiji Japan paralleled other contemporary 'failed democracies' in Europe.[53]

By contrast, conditions in China at the time of Yan's translation of *On Liberty* – 1898 to 1900 – were becoming revolutionary. China had for centuries been governed by an absolute monarchy aided by a bureaucracy, and both claimed their authority to rule on the basis of moral superiority. But the reigning monarch traced his moral superiority to his dynastic founder, by way of filiation, while the civil bureaucrats allegedly demonstrated their virtue by passing the civil service examination, the content of which was linked to the ancient classics of Confucianism and subsequent commentaries. The problem in the nineteenth century was a dismaying lack of opportunities for educated men who had spent their youths preparing for the examinations.[54] A dramatic six-fold rise in population in the seventeenth and eighteenth centuries saw the numbers of people within each district more than triple, but the number of districts and local magistrates stayed constant; hence, society grew at the expense of government administration. Rather than become government officials, educated men had to look for work as tutors, local historians, writers, fortune-tellers, traditional medical doctors – like Yan's father – and so on. The social dislocation was demoralizing, the rise of opium addiction in the course of the nineteenth century appalling.[55]

China's foreign and domestic troubles at mid-century precipitated the undoing of imperial government. In 1839, Great Britain provoked the first of the Opium Wars in south China; in 1851, the Taiping rebels began a fourteen-year rampage that devastated much of China south of the Yangzi River. From 1856 the second series of Opium Wars ravaged Beijing, and calls for administrative reform and study of Western science and armaments were thereafter officially supported by the foreign affairs clique at the imperial court. But three decades of Chinese efforts to buy and copy Western ships and guns were proven utterly inadequate during the Sino-Japanese War in 1894, when small and late-comer Japan routed the great empire of China; the subsequent effort of the Guangxu Emperor to reform the imperial government and bureaucracy and a host of institutions was crushed by his aunt, the Empress Dowager, and her allies in 1898. One dire consequence of this event was that nationalist dissidents, especially Sun Yatsen and the United Alliance (Tongmenghui), began to blame China's ills on both the imperial institution and the Manchu Qing dynasty, characterizing that dynasty as a foreign, non-Chinese rulership that could not have the well-being of the Chinese people at heart. Yan translated Mill in the midst of xenophobic reaction and calls for national revolution. In fact, the Boxer Rebellion of 1900 curtailed Yan's plan to publish his translation of Mill that year; he resigned the chancellorship of the Beiyang Naval Academy and left Tianjin. Not until 1903 did he recover his Mill manuscript and publish it.

Although socio-political and institutional reform had largely failed in the latter half of the nineteenth century in China, small beginnings were well under way by the turn of the century. Imperial schools such as the Tongwen Guan, the school and translation bureau of the Jiang-nan Arsenal, and Yan's Beiyang Naval Academy were instructing Chinese in Western science and mathematics. Revived efforts to build a modern army and navy encouraged the importation of many Japanese, German, and other advisers to reform Chinese military practices. Chinese living in and around the treaty ports were exposed to Western business and culture. And increasing numbers of students ventured to Japan, the United States, and Europe to secure Western educations – especially after 1905, when the examination system was abolished and traditional educations became pointlessly detached from civil service. But if radicals began to advocate the elimination of the Qing dynasty and the abolition of the imperial state altogether, Yan remained committed to reform and shunned revolution during the last two decades of his life. For him, political legitimacy remained grounded in the imperial institution and its claims to moral superiority. Hence, Yan's translation of Mill must be understood as an effort at reform, to introduce Western methods and subjects of education, while maintaining the moral cohesiveness that could be brought to bear in unifying China.

Given the undercurrent of reform present in the political agendas of Mill and his readers in England, Japan, and China, we can conclude this much about the possiblities for some intercultural translation of the project of individual liberty in the nineteenth century. What Mill proposed was an indeterminate praxis based on expertise and individual liberties and values; this project was indeterminate because it was deliberately experimental: expertise was always open to debate and revision, and individuals were encouraged to speculate and innovate. And Mill would have his praxis replace the traditional authority of England's moral code defined by savoir faire and rooted in familiar patterns of heredity and hierarchy. From the point of view of aspirants to reform, if not self-government, Mill proposed the replacement of that allegedly moribund savoir faire with specialized knowledge and practicality, talent and ability. In China and Japan, this meant the capacity to construct new institutions that augmented the wealth and power of the state so as to better enable it to fend off the West – particularly Britain, whose growing world domination seemed to be traceable to those very institutions.

But implicit in this theory of individual liberty was a predominant risk that did not go unnoticed by Nakamura Keiu and Yan Fu. What in Mill's theory would safeguard the long-standing requirement for moral leadership? At least two aspects of the rationalization implicit in the liberal project threatened to undermine what seemed so necessary in Japan and China. First, the liberal project of education seemed intent on disengaging morality from its purposes and goals. When education is intended for the differential development of each individual's particular talents, moral instruction is subordinated to the experimentation promoted generally by education. Moreover, as Max Weber noted at the turn of the century, the development of national educational institutions demonstrates a tendency to bureaucratize institutions of higher learning, in that they supply the demand for specialized expertise through regular curricula and specialized certificates. Tokyo Imperial University, for example, after its reorganization in 1886, became the main source of supply for officials to staff the Japanese bureaucracy. Rather than reproducing the moral ethos for a ruling class, what the Japanese government subsequently arranged for its new imperial subjects was a somewhat primitive ideology of loyalty and commitment of service to the emperor and his government. Although this speaks to the failure of the liberal project in Meiji Japan, however one tried to imagine the successful liberal project of education in late-nineteenth-century Japan, the masses of speculating individuals did not add up to a cohesive society or nation. A moral code was absent, and with it the moral function of the educated elite and ruling class.

Second, because the long-term benefits that accrue to society from the utilitarian value of individual liberty are slow to appear and not necessarily obvious when they do, the outcomes of Mill's theory of individual liberty betray a tension between the system of values and the rationalization of values. As Weber noted, a principle such as 'equality before the law' tends to encourage an abstract regularity of the execution of authority and the principled rejection of doing business from case to case. Principles of rule in the form of rational values tend to encourage bureaucratic rule by experts. Precisely because of the specialized expertise and status of civil servants, people may turn against those civil servants responsible for maintaining such equality in the interests of popular rule, a principle that expresses the ideal system of values.[56] Or again, Thomas C. Smith has noted that, with the elimination of legal status in the course of the Meiji Restoration, all Japanese were freed on matters of residence, name, dress, and occupation, and granted greater access to education. One important result of this concession to the rationalization of talent and ability was that outward signs of status were no longer reliable; accordingly, status became understood as the outcome of success or failure in competition, as competition was asserted as a systematic value.[57] In other words, individual development of talent and experimentation with morality seemed to offer no public standards for behaviour. And if the rationalization of values perpetually renegotiated what was to be valued, the competition native among individual efforts to excel could scarcely encourage a unifying moral ethos – *pace* the utilitarian proposition that competition serves as the mechanism by which self-interested individuals work for collective goals.[58] Weber had argued that rationalization was not ideal but inevitable; accordingly, as I demonstrate in this book, critics of Mill's libertarian approach to individual liberty – in England, Japan, and China – had much more in common than is usually acknowledged. The situation at the end of the nineteenth century was not one of a rational or modern West committed to 'fact' versus a traditional and moral East committed to 'value'; rather, educated persons in all three societies were apprehensive for the stability of the common good.

To reiterate: Mill and his translators, Nakamura Keiu and Yan Fu, shared a set of cultural assumptions that facilitated the transmission of *On Liberty* to Japan and China – the positions of individual and subject, and both the value of elite education and its connection to practices of tutelage among the ruling class and its bureaucracy. But *On Liberty* generated dissonance with another assumption dominant in Japan and China, the expectation that elite education encompassed the cultivation of virtue. For the educated elite were also a moral elite, one of whose roles was to foster the moral ethos that unified their respective societies.

CHAPTER TWO

Mill and His English Critics

Published in 1859, John Stuart Mill's *On Liberty* concerns the legitimate power that society can exercise over an individual, and Mill states clearly that the 'self-protection' of society is the only valid reason for interfering with an individual's liberty of action.[1] Mill impressed this point on his readers with a reference to the 'tyranny of the majority' suffered during the French Revolution, and suggested that a similar 'despotism of custom' among the ascendant middle class in England threatened to squeeze progressive individuals into the confines of popular conformity.[2] As J.C. Rees pointed out fifty years ago, whether or not a reader accepts Mill's argument depends on whether one agrees with his perception that individuality was declining under the growing domination of social conformity and public opinion. Apparently, Mill's peers among the educated elite did not share his alarm at the time; and he himself would later admit in his *Autobiography* that he had perhaps overstated the case. Nonetheless, contemporaries report that he was widely read by a sympathetic audience of both lay readers and the younger generation of students.[3]

Self and Others

The problem with Mill's main argument, according to many contemporary critics, was that it depended on a dubious distinction between 'self-regarding actions' and those affecting others.[4] According to Mill, 'the fact of living in society renders it indispensable that each should be bound to observe a certain line of conduct towards the rest. This conduct consists, first, in not injuring the interests of one another ... and secondly, in each person's bearing his share ... of the labours and sacrifices incurred for defending the society or its members from injury and molestation.'[5] Mill acknowledged that citizens rightly pay for police and military protection, and must be willing to serve in their armed forces – these he termed our 'social duties' – but Mill's interest in *On Liberty* concentrated primarily on the first point of conduct: not injuring the interests of one another. Mill insisted that '[t]he acts of an individual may be hurtful to others, or wanting in due consideration for their welfare, without going the length of violating any of their constituted rights ... As soon as any part of a person's conduct affects prejudicially the interests of others, society has jurisdiction over it, and the question whether the general welfare will or will not be promoted by interfering with it, becomes open to discussion. But there is no room for entertaining any such question when a person's conduct affects the interest of no persons besides himself ...'[6] In more forceful language, Mill declared that 'the individual is not accountable to society for his actions, in so far as these concern the interests of no person but himself.'[7] The exceptions to this principle were children, minors, and the 'backward races' of barbarians, because of the 'immaturity of their faculties.'[8]

A great many critics simply denied the validity of Mill's distinction, declaring that there were no actions that concerned only oneself. As they saw it, he misunderstood the relation between the individual and society – that is, he overlooked the social nature of humankind. Society is not simply an aggregate of independent individuals but an organic unity itself. Robert Bell, for example, writing in the *Westminster Review*, asserted that within the divine order of natural law, we are created as individuals for whom liberty is a 'necessary external condition of law'; but in complementary fashion, society too has a real and natural existence as a higher unit in the scheme of evolution, and hence we are required to obey our fellows in society.[9] Other contemporaries emphasized the embeddedness of individuals in society. R.H. Hutton faulted Mill for ignoring the fact that social organisms precede and surround the individual; since the 'natural organic action' of an aggregate of Mill's intellectual elite would not, on its own, constitute a free society, Mill should approach the problem of liberty by thinking not that society is composed of individuals but that individuals are members of society.[10] And Herbert Cowell found Mill's implicit social theory indefensible; liberty is not the freedom of each to do as he likes or the simple negation of another's power but 'an assertion of authority, of the right to compel the observance of other people's duties to ourselves.' Cowell compared Mill's effort to say no to one's own community to the absurd effort to claim one's own cubic air for oneself.[11] Simply put, Mill's notion of harm or injury could not be construed as a set of effects limited either to oneself or to others in society.

In fact, critics charged, none of Mill's examples demonstrated an action whose effects are entirely confined to the agent alone.[12] Even where he points to obvious excesses of individual liberty, like drunkenness or gambling, he readily admits that more often than not these acts prove harmful to others and cease being cases of liberty, becoming instead cases of morality or criminal law.[13] Consider the perhaps simplest case, that of expressing obnoxious opinions. Mill allows that in the case of someone who is lacking in taste, or foolish, or contemptible, we are under no obligation to seek his society; we can avoid him, even urge others to shun him. But opinions that challenge the prevailing views on matters central to the alleged interests of society are seldom perceived as harmless – and Mill's recurring example is religious opinion contrary to Christianity. Rather, governments will invoke their duty to uphold certain beliefs, and leaders will inflict vituperation on those who express such obnoxious opinions as the atheist.[14] But as a writer for the *British Quarterly Review* noted, there is little recourse against such an unwise exertion of society's power. If one appealed to Mill's criterion of self-protection from harm to justifiably limit society's coercion against the atheist, the principle invoked would be so vague as to be without value: the atheist, even shunned by all, remains free to 'discuss' by himself, which is meaningless. In the face of others' moral convictions, all that he is likely to be able to do is to persevere with moral courage. To ask the majority to be more willing to hear out the minority is largely useless, as the two meet on quite unequal footings.[15] Assuming that the atheist has strong and sincere convictions, how much less compelling – as Yan Fu would subsequently conclude in China – would be Mill's defence of disingenuous opinion that takes the form of asinine parody or destructive sarcasm.

The most systematic of Mill's critics, Fitzjames Stephen, took the argument even further. Not only was Mill illogical when he attempted to determine which spheres of social action merited the consideration of government involvement and which did not, but the entire effort was ill advised. To Stephen, government was precisely that body in an appropriate position to encourage socially desirable ends among its citizens.[16] What was needed was not *less* interference by society into the affairs of individuals, but *more* – a point that resonated soundly with Japanese critics of Mill's position in the 1880s.[17]

The Individual as Ground of Liberty

After making his distinction between self-regarding actions and those affecting others, Mill's argument proceeded by insisting that our first priority is to safeguard the individual and his freedom of expression – in thought and discussion – for this fundamental freedom determines the progress of society. Like many of his supporters – as well as critics, including Stephen – Mill assumed that humankind is rational by nature and inquisitive of the world. But Mill gave particular weight to this natural inquisitiveness. Insofar as individuals grow by interpreting their respective experiences and discussing their subsequent convictions, they advance the collective search for truth; and it is this competitive and dynamic advancement of truth that defines the progress of human knowledge and human society. Mill pronounced it 'the *duty* of governments, and of individuals, to form the truest opinions they can; to form them carefully, and never impose them upon others unless they are quite sure of being right.'[18] The present danger to individuals is that they are under pressure to conform and to cease their self-development – that search for truth in interpreting experience.

Two aspects of this argument have troubled readers since the 1860s. First, Mill betrays what some see as a romantic preference for the genius, that special individual who, in exercising his free choice often in the face of custom and convention, has developed far beyond his peers. Where his contemporary Thomas Carlyle concluded that human history becomes a history of great men, Mill stressed that since human progress depends on the genius, it is the originality and eccentricities of such a highly developed individual that are in danger of succumbing to a tyranny of public opinion.[19] Hence, critics argue, he would have society organize itself so as to safeguard the interests of that rational and educated elite, whose own narrowly defined individuality – in terms of education and the 'cultivation of the higher sentiments' – risks subverting the principle of equality in a democratic society.[20] Although Mill may advocate universal education as a guarantee of some 'standard of rational conduct,'[21] critics have seen this as unrealistic, if not disingenuous. Providing such a level of public education is beyond the competence of society, and at the same time, most people are simply incapable of questioning the grounds of their convictions and are quite willing to respect convention. So why should society formally treat each person as an original thinker and expect him to analyze his experience in order to support his convictions?[22] To this way of thinking,

Mill's position on liberty is necessarily and inexcusably elitist, and seems to be more a commitment to elite education than to democratic institutions.[23]

Indeed, a pervasive issue in this book is the lingering tension between Mill's theoretical individual, who constitutes the ground and purpose of liberty, and his understanding that social practice necessarily involves tulelary responsibilities of the enlightened over the irrational: parents over children, adults over minors, and colonial rulers over natives. If, in the phase of his life marked by his important essay 'Coleridge' (1840), he was willing to honour the received institutions of all cultures for their positive role in developing the emotive life and national character of each man, he later returned to abstract and rational standards like that promoted in his youthful utilitarianism for the reform of man and society.[24] In *Considerations on Representative Government* (1861), a major work that followed *On Liberty*, he held, for example, that the principle of legality served as a standard to which a barbarian country could be held as it developed into a nation. (This was, in fact, the basis for the unequal treaties that Britain forced on China and Japan in the 1840s and 1850s.) In other words, not all human cultures are equal and valuable; some, in fact, are better, and the elite of these more civilized nations might, in time and with great care, extend their progressive learning to their inferiors.[25]

Far from being a simple endorsement of the individual per se, *On Liberty* reflects this enduring tension between a theoretical individuality and a practical inequality. Not all individuals are equal and valuable; and Mill's solution in *On Liberty*, to treat individuals in a progressive continuum and to honour the genius above all, is but one 'liberal' approach to mediating individuality and nineteenth-century assumptions about human social progress. Some critics continue to be disturbed by this formulation because it does not advocate equality and democracy; indeed, Mill admitted his fear that democracy promises a form of government by the masses, the character of which will be as exclusive and mediocre as rule by aristocracy, but which, worse, will create a tyranny of the majority – a degree of vulgarity against which society must be on its guard.[26] Although he advocates a 'free constitution,' he is silent on the details; in *Considerations on Representative Government*, he clearly prefers a republican model led by some wise and gifted minority and dedicated to improving the virtue and intelligence of the people.[27] But suffrage must be extended to the people – particularly women and the working classes – so that they may exercise a popular veto on the decisions of the more enlightened few; otherwise, the way is opened for an authoritarian state ruled by experts who use education to their own ends in forming the minds of their charges.

Apart from Mill's preference for the genius, a second objection to this understanding of individual freedom has been his presentation of liberty as a prerequisite to the search for truth. Critics charge that in subordinating liberty to the perpetual task of producing true knowledge, Mill interjected an unwarranted, abstract, and metaphysical distortion of an otherwise political principle.[28] Fitzjames Stephen insisted that truth is more often the imposition of the will of a minority on a majority forced to tolerate the minority opinion; truth, he concluded, has less to do with freedom of discussion than with power.[29] William Thomas and others, by comparison, questioned the ability of Mill's thinking individual to contribute to nineteenth-century knowledge. The alliance of scientific positivism and empiricism constructs a body of knowledge as a fully formed science and thereby tends to restrict the openmindedness and freedom of discussion imagined by Mill. Apart from the groundbreaking experiment that offers new empirical evidence, there is little likelihood that any individual's convictions would substantially affect the truth of a scientific body of knowledge.[30] To these critics, Mill would do better to emphasize the political nature of liberty.

Negative and Positive Interpretations of Liberty

It was especially Mill's insufficient discussion of the political and social context of individual liberty that invited the most comprehensive repudiations of his fundamental position. Like many nineteenth-century and libertarian views of liberty, that of Mill's construes the freedom of a single individual in a negative fashion: each is free from the interference of others.[31] This grounding of negative liberty in the individual was targeted by several alternative arguments in favour of positive liberty, which we might construe most simply as the freedom to make something of oneself. Among the more metaphysical versions, a reviewer for the *Southern Review* maintained that freedom was a moral state, man's highest achievement, in which an individual demonstrated a perfect development of the three aspects of the soul – the intellect, which conquers ignorance and error; the heart, which conquers evil passions; and the will, which conquers vicious habits. Civil freedom of the kind Mill outlined was a minor and subordinate version and rightly subject to the promotion of this higher moral free-dom.[32] Other commentors quite explicitly equated this moral freedom with the spiritual freedom promised by Christianity and redirected attention to the doctrine of obedience to God as a liberation from spiritual bondage, which would encourage human affections and our yearning for our fellow men.[33] As we will see, such an argument informed Nakamura Keiu's wish to subordinate liberty in Japan to Christian love and duty.

A second approach to a more positive interpretation of individual liberty was to link it to the social configurations of humankind. R.H. Hutton, as we noted above, maintained that Mill would do better to recognize individuals as essentially members of society. So in contrast to Mill's emphasis of individual freedom, it would be more appropriate to understand liberty as 'social liberty,' or 'liberty for the free play of social character.' Hutton sought to validate the moral bonds that structured the social organism, and he meant to encourage individual participation in the social development of morality. To that end, he insisted that the 'principles which go to the very root of social life,' such as national character, fraternity, and solidarity, are prior to and hence take precedence over the liberty of individuals. Otherwise, Mill risked the danger of 'severing the roots of social purity and unity.'[34] But it was precisely this affirmation of the social grounds of liberty that Mill had criticized in condemning 'social rights' – the putative rights of democratic legislatures to invade the liberty of individuals under the mistaken belief that their communities have 'a vested interest in each other's moral, intellectual, and even physical perfection.'[35] Mill did not trust either the middle-class majority or the untutored working masses with the power to legislate matters of morality, character, or solidarity.

What we don't find among Mill's contemporary critics is the classical notion of positive liberty that figures in the writings of political philosophers like Machiavelli, Hobbes, Locke, or Constant. This is the idea, suggested in *On Liberty* but not developed by Mill, that liberty is the self-realization of the individual enacted politically through some system of self-government. In such a theory of positive liberty, political participation guarantees the legitimacy of the laws; and accordingly, liberty conveys the right to be subjected only to laws – and not the arbitrary force of mobs or monarchs. For example, the Roman republican theory of citizenship, according to Quentin Skinner, was founded on two principles: only as members of a community do we retain our individual freedom; and only those who share cardinal civic virtues are assured liberty. As opposed to modern notions of liberty, such as the pursuit of private pleasures within the world of commerce or some notion of human progress, classical liberty was a collective civic project. To paraphrase Cicero, the free citizen is slave to the public interest.[36]

By contrast, a deliberate critique of the libertarian notion of negative liberty appeared with the German concept of *Rechtsstaat* ('legal state' or 'state of law'), which some interpret as a variant of positive liberty. This took as its point of departure not the theory of civil society that informed the position of Locke and Mill, in which civil society constructs the minimal state to administer its needs for protection, but a theory of the sovereignty of the state constitution and its laws. In Japan and China, the *Rechtsstaat* would provide an influential critique of Mill's concept of liberty, as its advocates asserted that the state establishes liberty as a positive notion of individual conduct under the influence of national attitudes. Such statist ideas are not absent among Mill's contemporaries. Fitzjames Stephen, for example, insisted that liberty is based on a national power to protect individuals; insofar as our government guarantees our liberty, we are obliged to exercise our freedom and to behave in certain socially sanctioned ways. This socially sanctioned behaviour is the basis of moral systems, the coerciveness of which Stephen justified as necessary and appropriate – a point emphasized by Japanese leaders in the 1880s and 1890s.[37] Eventually, statist critics of Mill's liberalism would insist that the concept of negative liberty implies that justification for intervention rests with the state, which it supplies through positive law. Liberty and rights thus become obverse sides of the coin of law, snugly in the pocket of the state.[38]

Mill's strong endorsement of negative liberty has generated much discussion of both the differences between positive and negative liberty as well as their compatibility. In denigrating the notion of positive liberty as not really a serious concept, for example, Isaiah Berlin argued – perhaps disingenuously – that positive liberty involves a shift in analysis, from the sphere of action in which the individual is best left unhindered to the issue of who is to do the interfering.[39] By contrast, Wilhelm von Humboldt ranked the two in *The Sphere and Duties of Government* (also known as *The Limits of State Action*), such that the negative liberty of freedom from restraint is a precondition for the pursuit of positive freedom.[40] However one might pursue differences between negative and positive liberty or the reality of individual versus social groundings for liberty, the matter is often beside the point, as W.L. Weinstein argued nearly forty years ago. All advocates of liberty, in whatever way it is construed, assume that it is good for its own sake – an end in itself; the point of debate is instead the purpose to which liberty is intended, or the justification for being free.[41] Where a libertarian or utilitarian advocate of negative liberty might believe that each individual is best left unhindered to do the best he can, with the confidence that society will eventually benefit from his accomplishments, a republican advocate of positive liberty, convinced of the great need for social cohesion, might make mandatory our civic duties to participate in local government as the best expression of our liberty.

The issue is not so much the nature of liberty but the purposes to which it is put. Hence, of the many attempts in recent decades to define liberty with philosophical accuracy – whose sophistication is beyond the purposes of this chapter – H.J. McCloskey is most pertinent in arguing that negative liberty and the understanding of positive liberty as self-realization are both subsidiary interests to other social goods.[42] One of Weinstein's points in his important essay was to show that arguments about liberty are most often arguments about the phenomena and values that encircle the concept of being free – and these social goods are entirely appropriate objects of social and political debate. It may be, for example, that we would want to reduce the liberty of some in order to give more citizens more stability and a more decent life.[43] As I demonstrate in this book, East Asian reactions to Mill's liberalism would repeatedly take up these questions of how to reconcile liberty with the related concerns of morality, equality, and the common good.

Society and Morality as Ground of Liberty

The most systematic of liberal attempts in late-nineteenth-century England to reposition liberty within a social context came from the group of social reformers and ethical philosophers often identified as the British Idealists – the group of men associated with Thomas Hill Green, who taught at Oxford University in the 1870s and 1880s. Green and his students, particularly Bernard Bosanquet and David George Ritchie, argued that the development of society depends on changes in moral attitudes among citizens, so that moral development informs the state's work of both fostering a collective sense of community and citizenship and promoting the common good. In advocating political and social reform, they sometimes turned to the intervention of state legislation, which would impose new obligations on individuals and thus new limitations on individual freedom.[44] Although it was their interest in the German idealism of particularly Kant and Hegel that encouraged their positive re-evaluation of the moral value of the state, it is important to stress that Green and his followers saw themselves as furthering the cause of liberalism – Green described his own position as 'constructive liberalism.'[45] They maintained the focus on the individual as the fundamental component of society and the site of self-improvement, but they chose to elaborate on the social context of the individual and his important moral role within the state. After all, Mill had advocated a self-perfection based on individuality in *On Liberty*, but his subsequent essay 'Utilitarianism' (1861) pointed toward the individual as a social being, and Mill acknowledged that one aspect of personal development was the gradual strengthening of the 'social feelings of mankind.'[46] Like their contemporaries in East Asia, Green and his followers drew out aspects of liberal theory present but never centrally developed in Mill's oeuvre.

T.H. Green's accomplishment was to argue that the social recognition of liberty endorsed both the centrality of the public good and the equal liberty of all individuals. The individual had no such natural freedom but acquired liberty as a member of society and as a citizen of a state that had sufficient means to defend that recognized measure of liberty. Individuals each possessed an equal measure of liberty, as the freedom of external interference and as the freedom to participate in self-government. In philosophically grounding a concept of liberty that encompassed both its negative and positive nuances, Green opened liberalism to a consideration of equality and to society's use of the state as an advocate of the common good.

Green's expansion of liberalism paralleled Mill's expansion of utilitarianism in two key respects. Mill had reacted with dismay to the mechanistic utilitarianism of his father and Jeremy Bentham, who found no place in their theory for human emotion, altruistic motives, and the like, so Mill felt compelled to rethink utilitarianism with a conception of the individual as constituted by an entire range of needs, capacities, and talents. Similarly, Green found the libertarian theory of Spencer and Mill profoundly disconnected from the social realities of poverty and inequality, and he revised liberalism in order to encourage the self-determining individual to become more responsive to his fellows in society. In addition to this awareness of a gap between social theory and reality, both Mill and Green introduced significant measures of idealism into their revised theories. Under the influence of von Humboldt, Mill supplemented negative liberty with the goals of personal self-development – especially the cultivation of the 'higher pleasures' – and the advancement of humankind. (We address these issues in chapter 5.) Green accentuated this idealist goal for man, by grounding his theory in the moral philosophy of especially Kant and by conceptualizing self-development as moral action directed toward the idea of the good life. Green maintained that a man seeks to realize a conception of himself as a freely willing, self-conscious subject. Where Mill only awkwardly imagined a society of free individuals tending toward a 'regime of virtue,' Green explicitly made a moral society the goal of his endorsement of liberty.[47]

Green's point of departure was a critique of the naturalism that informed both utilitarianism and the atomistic individualism of thinkers such as Spencer and Mill, for neither set of ideas made it possible to constructively discuss moral action. Utilitarianism and its validation of desires offered no moral criteria by which to evaluate the various pleasures available to humankind – one was as 'good' as another. By comparison, the libertarian insistence on individualism assumed a set of largely middle-class values implicit in behaviour – rationality, dignity, character, and so on – without explicitly endorsing them or arguing for their necessity. As Green understood it, the self-conscious subject whose moral experience depended on moral freedom could only be a subject capable of self-evaluation. And self-evaluation, in turn, meant that an individual depended on the received knowledge of others insofar as he conceived of himself as an end to be realized – as an individual in a social context.[48]

Because Green's starting point was to identify the subject of freedom, two significant corollaries followed. In the first place, liberty was inconceivable apart from Green's commitment to a moral goal for it. In his several definitions of freedom, Green consistently tempered the negative 'freedom from restraint or compulsion' with the social limitations advocated by Kant in his principle of freedom as 'self-determination': we are free from the interference of others because we are individually obliged to determine ourselves according to the moral law. Green insisted that the concept of freedom necessarily includes such a moral end that gives value to freedom as a means. In a manner entirely compatible with John Locke's statement that law is a necessary condition of freedom, Green concluded that 'to submit [to the restraint of society] is the first step in true freedom, because [it is] the first step towards the full exercise of the faculties with which man is endowed.'[49] In the service of self-consciousness and self-control, liberty made one more capable of choosing rationally and morally.

In the second place, liberty was inconceivable apart from its social determination. If self-evaluation implied a collective moral knowledge of individuals – a knowledge of needs, appropriate satisfactions, and values – it also provided a common interest and goals common to the members of the collectivity. Green described these common interests and goals as 'the common good.' The common good – that social ground of individuals – was a condition of pluralism, characterized by society's commitment to the ability of all members to participate on equal terms. Green explained that society and individuals mutually recognized their shared liberties, rights, and obligations, and accordingly, freedom necessitated a commitment to the liberation of the powers of all men equally. That is, the social basis of liberty implied that society's constituent individuals must recognize the equal freedom of all. Thus Green bound individual liberty to the equality of individuals in society, for individual liberty depended on an equality of respect for all to realize themselves as moral constituents of society.[50]

Green's commitment to equality is a startling contrast to the example of the Chinese anarchists who, at the end of the century, embraced equality but rejected liberalism because of its complicity with bourgeois oppression of the working classes (see chapter 5). Green's theory of the social determination of individual liberty clearly shared that motivation to change the status quo in order to obtain the equality of individuals in society. Unlike the anarchists, Green was not a revolutionary but a revisionist; he was committed, like Mill, to the theory of civil society, industrial capitalism and its market economy, and the expansion of political participation. Hence, Green's turn to the state as an instrument with which to expand the equal liberty of all depended on a carefully nuanced argument, for he ultimately wanted to justify the state as the environment for both self-realization and the enforcement of an individual's obligations to his fellows.

The political thrust of Green's understanding of the self-determining individual and his socially grounded liberty followed primarily from two premises. One was the common good represented by common interests. As mentioned above, common interests were Green's expression for discussing that mutual recognition of our liberties, rights, and duties. At the same time, common interests formed the substance of law, which bound a political society to collective obedience once the law was established through a collective process of debating and negotiating our common interests. Green's identification of common interests and law made a necessity of political participation, for he argued that citizens assume a 'higher feeling of political duty' only when they take part in the work of the state – either directly or through their representatives. Only when citizens participate in the maintenance of law are they able to transfer to the whole society that particular interest they would otherwise have in maintaining their own personal liberties or rights.[51] Thus, the creation and maintenance of law was pre-eminently a moral activity (the work of self-restraint and self-realization), and marked for Green the fact that a civil society had developed into a formal state. In moving beyond personal, family, or local interests, the state depended on the moral agency of its citizens. Green's concept of the common good served to legally bind citizens into moral relationships that determined our liberties, rights, and duties. There was nothing at all natural about the arrangement.[52]

Thus the second of his key premises was the fact of historical change. Green acknowledged that social conditions change, social conflicts arise, and elements of social good, once overlooked, may be newly taken into account. Moreover, persons once deemed unworthy of political participation may be newly reckoned capable of participating in the common good. His point was that no arrangements are permanent, that no configuration of liberties, rights, and duties was eternal.[53] And Green used this argument both to explain the successful enactment of reform in the past and to urge continued reforms in the present. The reform laws that had liberalized trade, ameliorated working conditions in the factories, and established compulsory elementary education had been a set of first steps in the attempt to 'liberate the powers of all men equally.' Green contemplated further interference with liberty of contract, and asked if society might choose, in the public interest, to further regulate labour or land – the inheritance and settlement of estates – by virtue of labour being a key commodity and land being a key raw material.[54]

Green understood that libertarian individualism had become obstructive to the well-being of society and that the conflicts it had engendered invited a collective rededication to the common good for the purposes of removing the obstacles to society's well-being. He dedicated much of his adult life to three such causes: education reform, the expansion of political participation, and temperance – all of which, he believed, would serve to diminish the moral degradation of the working classes and create better conditions for all citizens to pursue self-determination. Far from describing such proposed changes as a tyrannous majority invading the personal liberty of the few, as Mill might have done, Green saw reform as a process of collective self-restraint. Faced with new social conditions and common interests, a society can democratically choose to redefine and limit collective rights and liberties.[55]

But Green was nonetheless committed to the kind of society that Mill had envisaged. Like Mill, Green advocated the use of the state not to promote or to enforce moral goodness but to create better conditions for the flourishing of individuals. Like Mill, Green accepted the gradual expansion of political participation as the lower classes cultivated themselves through self-reliant charitable associations. But to a degree more than Mill, Green was acutely aware of the dangers to society posed by civil inequalities. Green noted a wide range of fractious issues that threatened to divide society, including the treatment of immigrants, colonial populations, and religious minorities; and he was dismayed that the privileged classes invited the hostility of the suffering classes.[56] His theoretical pronouncements were committed to forestalling violence; his analysis of political economy thus emphasized the need to include the workers within the system of capitalist wealth, as full participants in the common good. In an eccentric fashion, Green blamed the poverty of the working classes not on industrialists but on their background in the feudal age – their 'habits of serfdom.' Excluded from the landed wealth of the privileged aristocracy, the working classes had once farmed in their capacity as serfs and tenants, a marginal status antecedent to their new role as unskilled workers. Thus, the problem for the working classes was not the capitalist market economy but the fact that the market economy was not open to all for self-development. In fact, Green maintained that capitalist wealth is good in that it is constantly redistributed to workers in the form of wages. Although he sometimes doubted that the working classes could manage to amass property within the current economic structure, he placed his hopes for the economic improvement of workers in the increased opportunities for access to the capitalist market that might follow from reforms.[57]

The Individual and the State

By the end of the century, some in England had come to believe that Green's moral conception of the state and its citizenry had successfully overcome Mill's distinction between self-regarding and other-regard-ing actions.[58] Be that as it may, the practical problem yet remained much as Mill had raised it in *On Liberty*. He had emphasized the nega-tive injunction that the state cannot act except out of self-preservation, but positive practice remained undetermined: how exactly was the state to be used to ameliorate the lives of individuals and to promote the common good?

Green's students Bernard Bosanquet and David Ritchie attempted to provide some direction. In addition to their many practical commit-ments to social reform, they reconsidered the problem of state action in terms of what they described as the contradiction of self-government in the libertarian position of Mill and Spencer. Bosanquet asked, How can the self exercise social authority over itself? Or again, How can the self be both agent and patient in the social coercion exercised by some over others?[59] To Bosanquet and Ritchie, this was particularly a prob-lem when liberty was understood as the absence of restraint, when law was seen as a curtailment of the human nature represented by the orig-inality and eccentricity of solitary individuals, and when authorities such as Mill and Spencer argued that moral judgements of actions properly excluded the 'inner' intentions of agents.[60] Bosanquet and Ritchie found Spencer's 1884 polemic, *The Man versus the State*, the extreme of this amoral and apolitical mode of argument. Bosanquet criticized Spencer's conclusion that self-sustaining action was categori-cally non-social and that social aggregation was a purely negative development; and Ritchie deplored Spencer's dismissal of the notion of common welfare and any possibility of improvements in govern-ment action, which, he judged, rendered Spencer's sociological theory incapable of 'any coherent theory of politics.' In Spencer's view, the state was but one of several voluntary associations, and always a minority within the larger body of society. Hence, their alternative was to consider the goals of the state – that is, the nature of coercive author-ity and what it could do to promote the good. It was, in Bosanquet's words, an effort to reconcile the self and government.[61]

Bosanquet and Ritchie accepted much of Green's analysis of the moral individual in society, and they chose instead to examine social institutions, notions of community, and the nature of the state – a dif-ference from Green that sometimes results in their being considered something other than liberal.[62] Like Green, they were committed to the individual and the moral development of character, self-reliance, and self-realization. But where Green's idealism grew especially out of a

Kantian understanding of the self and its realization in terms of the moral law and collective goals for human communities, Bosanquet's idealism grew out of a Hegelian interest in institutions. In developing his theory of the state in opposition to naturalism, positivism, and empiricism, Bosanquet turned to law as an obvious ground for what he called 'ideal facts' – formal acts of mind that receive social recognition. Jurisprudence demonstrated that these ideal facts are social phenomena posited in a manner quite contrary to notions of natural growth. That is, where Green based social recognition of liberty and rights on society's capacity to acknowledge a common good and so begin to construct a state, Bosanquet located social recognition in the formal establishment of permanent state institutions like law, which formalized the common good.[63] His and Ritchie's interest lay in a point further along in the developmental process. They were, in other words, often reticent on matters of morality and discussed instead the efforts of society to formalize the common good through state institutions.

The concept for which Bosanquet is best known – and to the discussion of which Ritchie contributed an influential dose of scepticism – is that of the general will. Borrowed from Rousseau's *Social Contract*, the general will is in theory that which replaces the social contract in providing political unity to a people and a democratic will to the state. If Ritchie at one point judged the notion of general will unrealistic, because it failed to account for the fact that an organic whole is more than the sum of its parts, he remained nonetheless interested in Bosanquet's work on the concept, because he saw general will as a possible alternative to the concept of sovereignty, which represented an excessively authoritarian power to command. Ritchie was especially concerned that in a sovereign state, the will of the majority would safeguard minority rights.[64] For his part, Bosanquet pursued an analysis of general will because he saw it as a point of mediation between citizens and the common good, a means of political unity by establishing linkages between individuals, communities, and the state.[65]

In developing his theory of the general will, Bosanquet pursued an important critique of Rousseau. According to Bosanquet, Rousseau had differentiated the 'will of all' from the 'general will'; where the will of all represented a mere aggregate, a sum of particulars, or 'allness,' the general will represented a true common interest, an organic unity, or true universality. As Bosanquet explained the problem, the will of all could very well represent the condition in which individuals, each motivated by private interest, coincided as to their individual wills – as in an election, for example. By contrast, the general will was a truly integrated community interest arrived at through reflective discussion. Rousseau's error in *The Social Contract* was to accept the will of all as a substitute for the general will – a fatal error, according to Bosanquet. Only the general will could unite all citizens for a true common good, and Bosanquet stressed the important functions of criticism and interpretation that must enter into legislative debate and the formation of the general will.

Unfortunately, he turned to the difference between a crowd and an army in developing his explanation of how a general will is embodied in a state. If a crowd is a mere association of persons connected by virtue of some incident qualities or interests, an army is an organization of persons bound by operative ideas that are expressed in structures of training and obedience and in patterns of leaders and followers – a systematic group. Bosanquet's choice of analogies was inept – liberals didn't appreciate the comparison of a healthy state to a well-managed army – but even more unfortunate was the mentalism that Bosanquet engaged in when reducing organizations like the state to their operative ideas. He maintained that organizations are more than their physical manifestations – that a school, for example, is much more than a mere building, since it encompasses teachers, students, pedagogies, skills, and expectations. This is true enough, but Bosanquet leaves his reader with the understanding that organizations such as society or the state are best understood in terms of the apperceptive systems by which we recognize them and their operative ideas, a conclusion that departs noticeably from the actual work of criticism, discussion, and the integration of private interests.[66] It is surprising, then, that Bosanquet, in *The Philosophical Theory of the State*, suddenly shifts from the general will to his unanticipated assertion that the end of the state is the realization of the best life – a key point of idealism which he shared with Green and Ritchie but which had no logical necessity as the next step in his own argument. For who directs this project of realizing the best life?

Given their premise that the modern state is created for the good of the nation – that is, for the good of all citizens – Bosanquet and Ritchie agreed that its actions must generally undertake to promote freedom in a social and moral context, so as to realize the best life for the individual. The problem of what action to take, however, remains ambiguous in terms of the utilitarian principle that operates in Mill's *On Liberty*: depending on how one interprets the self-protection of society, one could very well justify interference with individual liberty. As noted earlier, Green described reform through state action as an act of collective self-restraint. In determining what exactly to do, Bosanquet proposed the rather minimalist principle that the state serves to 'hinder hindrances to the common good,' in effect aligning himself with those who advocated a minimalist state that intervened only to protect citizens. Ritchie, by contrast, asserted that there are no a priori principles to determine the sphere of state action.[67] Accordingly, where Bosanquet was quite cautious in offering charity in the interests of social reform, insisting through his work with groups such as the Charity Organization Society that self-reliance and the development of character must be primary goals of any charitable work, Ritchie stressed the careful identification of our principles of action in order to determine how we apply those principles. We must take care that the disadvantages produced by successful intervention do not outweigh the actual advantages secured.[68]

Ultimately, Bosanquet's philosophical theory of the state settled with Hegel on the rather conservative proposition that social reform would best proceed through the established institutions of civil society (what Hegel called 'corporations') – the families, trade unions, commercial associations, neighbourhood and civic groups, and so on that mediate private and public interests and that, in effect, do the primary work of socializing the private sphere.[69] Like Mill and Green, Bosanquet and Ritchie were both opposed to centralization in government, and judged local government in local districts as the best venue for social reform – this in spite of Ritchie's awareness that citizens were increasingly at the mercy of powerful private interests such as the water and electric companies, and that the formation of political parties was undermining citizen interest and involvement in government. They judged the state of local government deplorable at present but suggested little more than proceeding within the status quo. Bosanquet made a revealing comment in an early essay, noting the need for the *practical* organization of society as a means to encourage reflective discussion, but such a proposal did not figure in his fully developed theory of the state. When he directly posed the question, How does the state pursue the common good?, he had no specific answer other than to obliquely recommend the institutions of civil society as the appropriate venue.[70] Thus the way was left open for those who could provide an answer, as in Japan.

This somewhat conservative commitment to gradualist reform

found a convenient metaphysical principle in the concept of social evolution widespread at the end of the nineteenth century. Ritchie and
Bosanquet engaged theories of evolution in ways that confirmed their
idealist approaches to citizenship and the common good. Ritchie
rejected notions like Spencer's that society is an organism evolving in
a natural course through the action of individuals. He accepted struggle and competition as forces that encouraged individuals and societies to develop, but he credited consciousness with a capacity to
intervene in evolutionary processes. The human capacity for self-
awareness and critical attitudes toward individual and social positions
invited moral choices and purposes that displaced so-called natural
evolution and tempered competition over time. Natural development,
in other words, was supplemented to a significant degree by historical
experience and society's commitment to law and the common good.
Ritchie thus concluded that the unit of evolution was not the individual but society, as demonstrated by the important development of solidarity, and that society was less like an organism and more a human
construction. If anything, the state was the entity most like an organism, because it was most capable of regulating its tendencies; and
morality could accordingly be understood as an adequate determination of the health of the social organism.[71] Similarly, Bosanquet interpreted evolution not as an ethics of competition but as a process of
natural selection that encouraged the work of 'soul formation,' a social
and moral process that promoted self-sufficiency and the growth of
character in the interests of citizenship.[72]

As Sandra Den Otter has so aptly noted, and as their views of evolution indicate, the idealism of Green, Bosanquet, and Ritchie was suffused with a leitmotif of harmony. They certainly did not regard
society as free of conflict, but their orientation toward moral self-realization and the value of community tended to emphasize unity, solidarity, and harmony. Implicitly, in their work, development tends
toward harmony and moral freedom toward unity, and their emphasis
on community undercuts the political language of class as the common
good diminishes conflict.[73]

The inverse of this assumption of harmony was a profound ambivalence over equality, so much so that we might suspect Ritchie and
Bosanquet of undercutting the significance that Green had accorded
equality. Where Green discussed the equal participation of all in society, the equal freedom of all, and the equality of respect for all to attain
moral self-realization in society, Bosanquet had little to say about

equality. By contrast, Ritchie was distressed by what he called the 'dogma of equality' – the legacies of the French and American revolutionary proclamations of equality as a natural right of man – for he judged the assertion of natural equality a misleading and unhelpful concept. Obviously, talents and natural abilities were distributed in an unequal manner among humankind. Thus, on the one hand, following Green's work on the social recognition of liberty and rights, Ritchie restricted the meaning of equality to those aspects that were socially recognized in the state's law: equality before the law, and equality in political rights. But on the other hand, he was dismissive of unreflective and troublesome claims to equality – in regard to age and maturity, the civilized and the inferior races, and aspiring social reformers versus the slaves whose freedom they advocated or the working classes whose betterment they sought. These he deemed too often dependent on utilitarian considerations, so that equality served as 'a rough and ready device for escaping the difficulty of judging correctly and the discontent which arises from suspicion of unfair judgments.' Equality was for Ritchie too often a flashpoint of social discontent that drew attention to differences of status and marked the necessity of self-sustaining charity as advocated, for example, by Bosanquet's Charity Organization Society.[74]

Ritchie preferred to consider equality from its obverse: the problems of real social inequalities. These were the object of his social work and social reform, and he felt that such inequalities could be ameliorated by education, for example, which allowed for greater opportunities. Rather than pursue a positive endorsement of equality, he preferred to work on rectifying inequalities. For he seemed always to hesitate at the point of according some measure of equality to all individuals. At times he acquiesced in Green's prior analyses, reiterating, for instance, that equal liberty follows from the recognition of the common good, or that the law determines our equal liberty in rights.[75] But elsewhere he asserted a collective significance for equality, as 'an important precondition for harmonious, unconstrained social relationships' insofar as it ensured 'that artificial barriers were not placed in the way of sections of the community whose abilities would allow them to make worthwhile contributions to the welfare of society.'[76] He drew the line at attempts to establish the equality of social conditions for individuals. Equal wages for workers (which might upset the ability of one or another to support more rather than fewer children), or equal rights for husbands and wives, or equal political and economic rights for men and women were impossible at the time, for they would require an inappropriate measure of state interference with the family institution. At most, Ritchie averred in 'The Moral Function of the State,' the state's indirect moral function was to encourage legislators to consider the moral interests of the community in considering reform.[77]

What this points to is the enduring tension in liberalism between the earlier description of the state as a necessary but minimal instrument for maintaining order and the newer description of the state as a moral institution to encourage the self-realization of individuals within a society committed to a common good. It also points to the centrality of charismatic leadership and compelling logic in not only persuading a majority of those in power of the need for social reform and state action but also, and perhaps more fundamentally, in persuading a significant majority to reconceive individual liberty in terms of its idealist groundings in morality and society. Both Bosanquet and Ritchie insisted that we need to approach the individual not as a datum but as a problem, so that the aim of our politics is to find and release the individual.[78] But ultimately, liberalism in the latter half of the nineteenth century remained committed to the status quo; both its libertarian and reformist positions marked a largely conservative tendency that was best identified by its difference from the more radical proposals of socialism.

CHAPTER THREE

Nakamura Keiu and the Public Limits of Liberty

Nakamura Masanao (1832–91), who is better known by his pen name, Nakamura Keiu, was born into a family of samurai status in Edo (now Tokyo) and was a central figure in the intellectual transition from the Tokugawa shogunate (1603–1867) to the modern state created during the Meiji period (1868–1912). With early recognition of his intellectual promise, Nakamura won a scholarship to the shogun's academy, the Shōheikō, where he studied between 1848 and 1853. He was eventually appointed an official Confucian teacher there in 1862, at the unusually early age of twenty-nine. But Nakamura was also a student of Dutch learning and was one of those who led the way in studying English after the Perry Expedition of 1853. The shogunate sent him to study in England between 1866 and 1868, and on his return to Japan immediately after the Meiji Restoration, he joined the abdicated Tokugawa family in Shizuoka, where he taught until 1872. In Shizuoka, he translated into Japanese what are his best known works, Samuel Smiles's *Self-Help* (as *Saikoku risshi hen*) and J.S. Mill's *On Liberty* (as *Jiyū no ri*). Both were quite popular – *Jiyū no ri* was reportedly read by the entire generation of educated Japanese who came of age during the Restoration, and *Saikoku risshi hen* stayed in print until the 1920s; both helped to spread the Western ideas of individuality, self-reliance, and liberty. In 1873, Nakamura became a member of the Meirokusha, the first scholarly society of Westernizing educators in Japan; in 1874, he was baptised a Christian.

Nakamura is best remembered as an educator, and particularly for his commitment to the education of women. He opened a private school in 1873, the Dōjinsha, which specialized in moral and political education for both men and women and published a journal committed to the same, the *Dōjinsha bungaku zasshi*. He served as head of the Tokyo Women's Normal School between 1875 and 1880 and became professor of Chinese learning at Tokyo Imperial University from 1881. Honours were showered on him in the last decade of his life; he was elected to the Tokyo Academy in 1879, he became a member of the senate-like imperial advisory body, the Genrōin, in 1886, and a member of the House of Peers in 1890. At the same time, Nakamura lost his specifically Christian faith and became a Unitarian.[1]

The intense interest in *Jiyū no ri* among Nakamura's contemporaries had several motivations. One important reference was the foundational Charter Oath decreed by the Meiji emperor at the start of the Restoration. The Oath declared the set of principles that guided the samurai oligarchy responsible for the new government and included broad injunctions to 'establish deliberative assemblies,' to 'unite officials and commoners in administering the affairs of state,' and to 'seek knowledge throughout the world' in order to 'strengthen the foundations of imperial rule.' Nakamura informs us specifically that he intended his translation as a contribution to Japanese examinations of the political forms of Western countries. Insofar as the publication of *Jiyū no ri* coincided with the Meiji government's Iwakura Mission to the United States and Europe in 1871 – a delegation instructed to revise Japan's unequal treaties and to conduct general investigations of Western institutions – Nakamura anticipated that his translation would give his readers some understanding of Western political thought and would inspire discussion of these matters so crucial to the future of the imperial domain.[2]

In addition, Nakamura's translation spoke directly to the sense of urgency for change in Japan. In *On Liberty*, Mill warned against the 'despotism of custom' that fosters a deplorable uniformity, stagnation, and decline; for evidence, he added, one had only to look to Asian nations like China. This point roundly resonated with Japanese readers of Mill in the 1870s, who were intent on avoiding the appalling fate of China in the wake of the Opium War – a decline that left it unable to fend off the West.

Furthermore, Mill spoke to a key tension at the heart of the Japanese project of social and political reconstruction: the extent of popular participation in political processes. Although the Charter Oath encouraged the creation of a less exclusive government, the Meiji oligarchy's intention was arguably to extend political participation not to all the people but primarily to the ranks of the former samurai and the new bourgeois elite of entrepreneurs. A majority of scholars, who otherwise disagree about the social or class nature of the Restoration, interpret formative documents like the Charter Oath as a call for the participation of hitherto disenfranchised or lower-ranking samurai in policy decisions, expressly on the basis of a new principle: political participation should follow not from ascribed conditions like birth or status but according to the principle of ability or merit. However defined, ability would serve to identify those acceptable to the oligarchy for political participation.[3] Mill, too, advocated such a view of limited participation, which Nakamura's translation reproduces – even though *Jiyū no ri* has been often understood as inaugurating the tradition of popular rights that figured so centrally in Japanese political developments between 1874 and 1884.[4] If Nakamura's translation encouraged new principles of liberal thought, in that it argued for the promotion and protection of individual freedoms and rights, it simultaneously reinforced a long-standing restriction of political participation in Japan, on the same grounds that Mill himself described in *On Liberty*: education and the development of rational thought were prerequisite.

But more important, Nakamura's translation of Mill attempted to resolve a significant tension noted in chapter 2. *On Liberty* endorses, on the one hand, a theoretical individuality that assumes the individual is the basis of society, rather than the alternative position that society is natural and organic and that each individual is thus a component of society. On the other hand, *On Liberty* acknowledges a practical inequality, in that not all individuals are equally committed to intellectual advancement – hence Mill's turn to the genius as the agent of progress. In his translation, Nakamura worked to resolve this tension; first, he modified Mill's theoretical individuality by equating society and government in the ideal social unit of the village, so that the individual and his social and political being coincide. In this circumscribed social setting, each person can adequately fulfil an integrated existence as both autonomous individual and self-governing member of society. Second, Nakamura lessened Mill's practical inequality by suggesting another form of intellectual advancement: the search for religious truth, a task that demanded neither intellectual superiority nor public debate. Nakamura emphasized the liberty of the Christian to maintain his private faith, and he foregrounded the interior space of freedom of conscience as a space protected from government interference and public morality. The search for religious truth was especially a personal undertaking.

Although Nakamura's translation of *On Liberty* was a painstaking effort to render Mill's argument into Japanese, Nakamura's additions to Mill, particularly those regarding village society and Christianity, served to restrain Mill's theory and begin the work of placing public limits on liberty and individuality. One unintended consequence was to make Mill's theory better cohere with Japanese government needs at a time of massive social and political transformation.

Village Society and Government

Perhaps the most striking idiosyncrasy in *Jiyū no ri* is that Nakamura does not consistently differentiate between 'society' and 'government.' Nakamura's reproduction of Mill's text in Japanese is persistently simplified by the interchangeability of *seifu* ('government' or 'administration') and a host of translation terms for society, which cover a range of phenomena: active interactions of people, which we could call 'sociality' (*kōsai*); concrete groupings or associations, as in a club, company or a society (*kaisha, nakama*); conceptions akin to the public (*kōshū*) or the whole group (*sōtai*); and, quite simply, the people (*jinmin*), including the people of the domain or nation (*kokumin*), all the people (*shūmin*), or common people (*heimin*), and specific affiliations that the people can assume – parties, sects, churches, and so on. Nakamura also refers to the people's division into classes, including a Confucian conception of the 'four classes' (officials, farmers, artisans, merchants) and less formal notions of higher and lower, rich and poor, noble and mean, aristocrats and commoners. Most of these terms are equated with *seifu* at one point or another.[5]

To be fair, Mill himself in *On Liberty* does not consistently name the force that so threatens the freedom of the individual; although he most often writes 'society,' he occasionally uses 'mankind,' the 'public,' 'public opinion,' the 'government,' and the 'state.' But given Mill's analysis of the threat to individual liberty, it is clear that the middle class who constitute 'society' are the root of the problem facing the individual, for it is they who authorize the government – by means of representative institutions – to interfere with an individual's liberty. That Nakamura does not differentiate between society and government certainly follows in part from the lack of an abstract conceptualization for 'society' in Japanese thought during most of the nineteenth century. But his deliberate and persistent conflation of society and government demonstrates that he conceives the problem of the human exercise of authority over one's fellows as essentially the problem of governmental exercise of authority over its subjects. To paraphrase Hegel, Nakamura is like the eighteenth-century burgher who experiences the externality of the state as a subject of the prince, but who has not yet arrived at the political consciousness of a citizen, that site where universal and particular interests are synthesized. The burgher sees that the government subjects him, but he has not yet seen his own role as a citizen in a burghers' government, where his particular interests are synthesized with those of the whole.[6] For Nakamura, interference with individual freedom is necessarily governmental interference, and accordingly, the variation among his translation words for society in *Jiyū no ri* is symptomatic of his attempt to explicate Mill's charge that society interferes with individual freedom.[7]

A key passage might best clarify the set of issues here. One of Nakamura's important additions to Mill's original is an extended analogy intended to illustrate Mill's concept of civil liberty by means of a Japanese village setting. Having carefully translated Mill's first paragraph, which distinguishes between 'liberty of the will' and 'civil liberty' in order to indicate that *On Liberty* concerns only the latter, Nakamura interjects the following as a second paragraph:

> Although it can be readily understood from what follows that 'social group' [*nakama-renchū*] in this text refers to the power exercised over the individual, let me explain rather crudely by imagining the entire country as a single village. Imagine one hundred households in the village. The hundred families in these houses are composed of equal-ranking commoners, without any differences as to rich or poor. Thus they all live in peace, working diligently at their family occupations, following their various desires, engaging freely in all matters, and seeking their interests in right accord with natural principle. Once they were the dependents of another man, receiving his commands for no good reason – and worse, forced by him for no good reason to forgo the purposes of their own minds. But [now] these hundred households have gathered together to form a village, as if each were a master with legal authority or rights [*ken / kabu*] (that is, 'rights of liberty'). Maintaining that it is reasonable to plan freely for the benefit of each, they found it imperative to proceed by planning for the benefit of the whole village. Suppose a thief invaded from a neighbouring village. They would gather their strength in numbers and protect themselves against the thief. Given such a case, agreed the one hundred families, they would each contribute a little cash every year for a

collective village fund, establish a system of annual service, cooperate in groups of five or six households, and thereby manage village affairs. With the collective village fund, they could build bridges, dredge rivers, repair roads, furnish themselves with suitable weapons, or stockpile reserve rice for a bad year. This is the nature of taxation. Or again, if a man were murdered in the village, the social group would debate the matter; to pardon the murderer would be an act harmful to the entire village, so a penalty would be imposed. Such is the nature of a court of criminal law. Now, if the social group fulfilling the annual service maintained their official work of safeguarding the entire village, they would of course have the authority to adjudicate village affairs. However, when this authority became excessively strong, and if it became an obstacle to anyone's free action on some matter, then the social group – that is to say, the government – would deliberate and determine a limit to the power it could exercise over any individual, for the purpose of increasing the well-being of all the people, a matter of utmost concern.[8]

Nakamura proposes an analogy between the entire country and a single village. It is a potent analogy; like many would-be reformers of mid- and late-Tokugawa Japan, Nakamura imagines a natural village community and economy. In this both legal and spatial setting, the parts equal the whole. His particular village embodies both liberal and Confucian concepts: it is an egalitarian village in which there is no significant division between rich and poor, a peaceful society whose exemplary morality is 'in right accord with natural principle,' and a pure democracy in which all households (working in groups of five or six) collectively make village decisions. In the manner suggested by Rousseau's *Second Discourse*, this ideal political order is a small community in which political participation is a condition of living within the community. Although Nakamura retains the Confucian's pragmatic understanding of the purpose of the polity – it is intended to benefit the well-being of all the people – he overrules the social hierarchy that Confucians understood as an aspect of the natural order. The people have relinquished their dependence on the master, becoming independent and self-determining – according to natural principle.

Nakamura's negation of social hierarchy is specified in the first of two key translation words that carry the burden of creating the new distinctions at the heart of Mill's liberal theory. *Ken* encompasses our concepts of power, privilege, authority, and right; it originally meant a balance scale, the act of judgement, and in turn the power or authority to judge. However, because Nakamura specifically translates 'power' as *kensei* (a long-standing term meaning the power of authority), the more simple *ken* is best construed as authority and hence a legal right or privilege.[9] He indicates (with *furigana*, or pronunciation notations) that his first usage of *ken*, in 'a master with legal authority,' is to be read *kabu*, a licence or legal privilege; he then equates this 'privilege' in parentheses with the 'right [*ken*] of liberty.' The context supplied here for his discussion of rights is the Tokugawa background of legal claims to guild monopolies, land tax revenues, and the like, ultimately sanctioned by the authority of shogun or local daimyo.[10] In a process of substitution, the power and authority of the former master give way to the rights of the commoners' households and are thence transferred to that social group as the self-governing political community. Their self-determined purposes and interests displace the master's power to command others; debate and collective decision making among the unified whole replace the unilateral decisions of the authoritative master. To recall John Locke: in so consciously representing itself as a political association and assuming an official capacity to act as a body, the village or social group empowers itself to act as a government.

The difficulty for liberal theory lies in a second key translation word, *nakama-renchū*, which, in the logic of Mill's text, could be understood as 'society,' but which I have retranslated more narrowly as 'social group' to stress the concrete and face-to-face nature of Nakamura's exemplary village. In an initially perplexing series of moves, he refers *nakama-renchū* to both the power exercised over an individual, and the social group – or government – that exercises such power. In so conflating power, society, and government, Nakamura closes the theoretical circle of pure democracy. Government becomes the social group, where it was once the master, and society becomes government, in the political self-representation of the social group constituting the village. This political manifestation of the social group confers on itself the right to safeguard the entire village by providing for village affairs through taxation and the adjudication of criminal cases.[11]

A comparison with Alexis de Tocqueville is instructive: where Tocqueville describes the creation of 'general government' as the union of individuals to form a sovereign authority and hence a people who can choose representatives, Nakamura bypasses sovereignty and representation.[12] The social group simply usurps the power of the sovereign in the name of self-government – as took place in the Meiji Restoration with the overthrow of the shogun. Since society and political authority overlap in a homologous space, resistance to tyranny becomes a secondary concern. Nakamura comfortably imagines that liberal society is open, inclusive, and egalitarian, and that the social group as government will simply choose to limit its power, since all are bound by a common goal, their collective well-being. As an elucidation of civil liberty, Nakamura's confidence rests on the unspoken guarantee of a right to participate.

But he ignores a classic analysis of state and civil society merely implicit in *On Liberty*. Rejecting the formulation of Locke and Rousseau, who foregrounded the social contract as the occasion that differentiates civil society from the state of nature and thereby gives birth to the state, Mill seems to assume instead the analysis of the Scottish philosopher Adam Ferguson, developed further by Hegel in his *Philosophy of Right*, which foregrounds civil society as the mediation between humankind and the state. Although both approaches, social contract and civil society, were based on the experience of the English Revolution as a bourgeois political movement in which the self-appointed representatives of civil society rose against the tyranny of the monarch's unrestricted state, Ferguson and Hegel are uninterested in the question of the origin of political legitimacy in nature and reflect instead on structural points of mediation between humankind and government: institutions of civil authority like the police and civil service; the 'corporations' to which one chooses to belong and which organize particular interests or needs as universal and abstract rights; and the representative institutions of constitutional government.[13]

Nakamura is certainly aware of the mediating institutions of civil authority and 'corporations' to which Mill makes reference in *On Liberty* – he translates many examples of associations, companies, parties, churches, guilds, and bureaucratic offices – but he seems to lack a developed theory of constitutional law and a grasp of the representative processes that theoretically mediate political society and state and thereby legitimize such law. This is not to say that Nakamura fails to understand the concept of representative institutions; rather, the important distinctions that they mediate are simply in abeyance in his version of the text, and in that regard, it is unfortunate that Nakamura chose *On Liberty* to translate, for it is not Mill's purpose therein to justify his preference for representative government. (He would do so in *Considerations on Representative Government*; see chapter 5 below.) Nonetheless, at key points in *On Liberty*, Mill describes the development of 'constitutional checks' in ancient society as the means 'by which the consent of the community ... was made a necessary condition ... to the governing power.' In translation, Nakamura renders these constitutional checks as 'regulations and orders' (*ritsurei*) – necessarily authoritative acts of rule, that form a collective means by which people can limit the power of a ruler. Indeed, constitutional government is in part a usurpation of the privileges of monarchy, but the procedure of consent so critical to Mill's argument is absent in Nakamura.[14] Similarly, Mill's mention of 'popular institutions,' representative bodies elected by the people to create a government, is rendered by Nakamura as 'discussion government' (*gisei*), a general public forum rather than a specifically representative institution. Likewise, Nakamura translates 'democratic republic' as 'country under popular administration' (*minchi no kuni*) or 'people's government' (*minsei*), choices which again omit the role of citizenship that theoretically embodies the political expression of civil society.[15] Nakamura lacks first-hand experience and abstract understanding of civil society – which his analogy is in part meant to explicate. The people do not move to restrict the power of the master; they replace him in a rupture of historical continuity. In this regard, Nakamura's analogy recalls the reform proposals of the Tokugawa scholar Andō Shōeki (fl. 1744–63), who imagined eliminating outright the samurai class of overlords and allowing the self-sufficient agrarian village to pursue its own political requirements autonomously.[16]

One can only conclude that Nakamura's harmonious village is not an appropriate analogy for Mill's 'society,' which Mill repeatedly represents as a site of differentiation and debate. Although Nakamura's village does serve to illustrate the political principle raised with the Meiji Restoration – that administration of the affairs of the new state would be more inclusive, extending to members of all classes and embracing public discussion – the very concreteness of Nakamura's village has inherent conceptual limitations. By 'imagining the entire country as a single village,' Nakamura offers a discrete setting that runs counter to the abstraction necessary for conceptualizing representative institutions. The pure democracy of the village, which assumes the full participation of all residents, precludes both a need and an occasion for representation.[17] Without the concepts and vocabulary for the representative institutions that mediate society and government, Nakamura cannot think beyond a closed circle of society, government, and the power to rule. If each member of the village is a 'master with legal right,' which is simultaneously considered a 'right to liberty,'

Nakamura implies that the power to rule is the freedom to make laws that both coerce the ruled and restrict the rulers. He rests confident that such a law-making community will choose a self-imposed limit on its power, because the well-being of all is both the condition and the goal of political action.

This is a peculiar setting for Mill's discussion of individual liberty, ostensibly the focus of *On Liberty*. In the absence of constitutionalism and representative government, which are theoretically an individual's sole collective recourse to tyranny, the problem of the 'tyranny of the majority' can be understood as only a conflict over power between a majority and a minority that are not amenable to institutional forms of representation and that drift conceptually from people to social groups and to government. Nakamura's innovative solution, in paraphrasing Mill, is to 'harmonize' and to encourage cooperation between people and government.[18] The individual, in other words, struggles to maintain his independence in the face of the group, who have an absolutely legitimate claim to power and political authority. As Nakamura seems to conclude in the village analogy, should some individual find his or her free action obstructed, the guiding principle of political process is nonetheless the well-being of the whole. Although an excess of governmental power is registered as an obstacle to any member's freedom of action, the main criterion for governmental self-limitation is, after all, that goal of safeguarding the entire village. Nakamura has created an impossible context for individual liberty – a situation we will see again with his introduction of Christian love and his emphasis on moral conscience.

This is not to accuse him of broadly misunderstanding or mistranslating *On Liberty*. Rather, my purpose here is to disclose the limits of Nakamura's discussion of liberal theory in 1871: without an expression for 'society,' how much can he express? As a first and formative step into liberal theory, *Jiyū no ri* was limited by the capacity of Japanese language and political discourse to encode new abstractions. An abstraction like society is, after all, a difficult concept in any language; Mill's own usages of society demonstrate connotations that indicate multiple references like the masses, the middle class, or Mill's educated peers. Whether we understand Nakamura's multiple terms for society as metaphors for the English word, or Mill's society as a metaphor for these several terms, the fact remains that translation proceeds necessarily through metaphorical extension of meaning, by trial and error, quite like the fundamental habit of expanding vocabulary within one's own language.[19] Where Mill stressed the fact that society often presents an obstacle to individual freedom, Nakamura made sense of that tension by imagining the process by which the society represented in a self-sufficient village freely managed its affairs as a popular government. But as Motoda Sakunoshin noted at the turn of the century, there was no concept for society in Japan, only nation and family, so that an individual's private concerns were separated from both the public realm and political life.[20]

Some readers may wonder whether Nakamura's focus on the village is a response to the great interest among nineteenth-century Europeans in the village as the fundamental unit of society and government. Such interest arose in reaction to nationalist, democratic, and socialist movements and the issues they raised regarding land redistribution and nationalization. German and British scholars expended a great deal of effort debating, first, the relation between the ancient German mark and the Anglo-Saxon village, in order to identify an original Teutonic village community form; and second, the political economy of such a village community, either as a democratic, self-governing community of individual private-property holders, or as a largely collectivist group maintaining primarily common lands according to some democratic socialist plan, or subject to an authoritative master (as in the Roman villa or feudal model). Paramount in these debates were the implications of their differences for theories of social evolution and efforts to explain the origin and development of contractual relations, commercial economies, and progressive modernity.[21] Moreover, these debates were taken up by British colonial officials in India and Africa, where they introduced profound changes in local village governance, land distribution, and taxation, on the basis of these historical and anthropological judgements.[22] But to my knowledge, although Nakamura was in England at the time this scholarly debate began and could certainly have been exposed to it, I find no evidence in his writings that he attended to it at all. Rather, I believe that his interest in the village grew out of his Japanese background and the sense that the village, like the family, is a natural social unit.

Christianity and the Personal Liberty of Conscience

The reader familiar with Mill in English is surprised to discover that *Jiyū no ri* includes a number of additional references to religion and to Christian liberty and love. Alongside the epigraph by Wilhelm von

Humboldt in Mill's original – which speaks to 'the absolute and essential importance of human development in its richest diversity' – Nakamura added a second epigraph by Francis Bacon: 'A little philosophy inclineth man's heart to atheism; but depth in philosophy bringeth men's minds about to religion.'[23] Nakamura would have us understand that the man who commits himself most deeply to the search for truth will arrive at God's truth about the Messiah. His translation of Mill, in part, recommended Christianity in an effort to circumscribe Mill's presentation of liberty.

Nakamura's interest in Christianity was largely specific to contemporary conditions in Japan. To him and his generation, Christianity was above all an alien ideology that had served to define the Westerners as a group beginning in the sixteenth century and, after 1639, had been ruthlessly prohibited by the Tokugawa shogunate. Just as *Jiyū no ri* was published, the debate over Christianity in Japan advanced a significant step. When the new government in 1868 adopted a policy of Westernization, European and American missionaries (who had begun arriving after the Perry Expedition of 1853–4) renewed their desire to serve as educators in Japan but were officially prohibited from teaching Christianity; in many parts of Japan, their illegal efforts and their few converts among the Japanese were punished severely by local authorities.[24] Edward Warren Clark, Nakamura's friend and spiritual counsellor, was the first foreigner to be granted permission by the national government to teach the Bible and Christianity in 1871, and he and Nakamura were prominent in urging the Meiji government to lift its ban on Christianity.[25] In a memorial publicized in 1872, Nakamura suggested that the Meiji emperor endorse – even convert to – Christianity, since it was the basis of Western wealth and strength.[26] Nakamura, who was publicly baptised on Christmas day 1874, understood that in Japan Christianity was an obstacle to the kind of liberty that Mill advocated, but he implicitly recognized that Mill's own difficulties with Christianity were a useful forum within which to advocate the freedom of thought that would necessarily include a tolerance for faith in Christianity. If Japanese were to understand and accept Mill's libertarian position on the freedom of individual thought and expression, they would have to curtail the long-standing ban on Christian belief among Japanese individuals.[27]

As we know, Mill was not enthusiastic about Christianity. *On Liberty* makes repeated reference to the intolerance of the Christian majority among Britain's middle class; thus freedom of religion becomes one of several necessary correctives against the tyranny of the majority.[28] But at the same time, Mill does not reject Christianity outright. His commitment to a dialectic search for truth encompasses religious truth; if he singles out Calvinism expressly to criticize the dangers of its excessive teaching of obedience, or sabbatarian legislation as an infringment on individual liberty, he also cites the case of Jesus as an outstanding example of the superior individual whose message of truth was ruthlessly suppressed by hostile contemporaries, and the case of Luther as an example of how an initially persecuted doctrine can in time and for some become truth.[29]

All of this is intact in Nakamura's translation. But it is overlaid with a series of additions that so extends the possibilities in Mill as to begin to transform the argument of *On Liberty*. Nakamura sought to stress the freedom of religion as a fundamental principle of Westernized society, and Christianity as a central example of individual freedom. In comparison to his many translation words for 'society,' his remarkably consistent translation of 'liberty' and 'freedom' as *jiyū* reproduces what we find in Mill: liberty is presented as a balance of forces; it is the limit placed on a ruler's privilege and power as the people establish the alternative rule of law. Liberty is thus both principle and right, and can be specified as a set of plural liberties: of judgement of right and wrong; of taste and occupation; of friendly assembly; of thought, of speech or discussion; of publishing; of religion; of action. (As I discuss shortly, Nakamura also emphasized the principle of free trade.)

But at the same time, Christianity becomes the quintessential form of freedom for Nakamura and plays a central role in his elaboration of the theme of human and institutional limits. Christianity does not lend itself to a discussion of human equality; rather, Nakamura invokes civil law and Christian love to rein in the threat of selfish and egotistical behaviour connoted in Mill's theory of liberty and Japanese conceptions of liberty generally.[30] In a preface to Mill's chapter 'Of the Liberty of Thought and Discussion,' Nakamura again quotes Francis Bacon to point out the difference between God's limitless love for man and man's limited institutions; just as God loves all men without limits, so we too should love God and all men without limits. But human capacity is limited, and hence man's control over other men is rightfully limited, and the boundaries we rightly place on our individual freedom deserve diligent maintenance.[31] In his introduction to *Jiyū no ri*, E.W. Clark spoke of liberty in terms of Christian responsibility for self-development and self-enforced limits:

> Liberty in its highest sense must have limitations; though men are less apt
> to respect its bounds than to accept its freedom. In some, there is a certain
> restless spirit which brooks no restraint, either from civil code or from indi-
> vidual conscience, & which feigns itself free in proportion as it is indepen-
> dent of rightful rule. But such a conception of freedom, is as far as possible
> from the truth: it defeats its own aims by substituting servility to self, to
> submission to lawful requirements. No form of bondage is more pitiable,
> than that of a soul taking the liberty to enslave itself; & no truer freedom is
> ever to be enjoyed than that of thorough submission to righteous law. And
> just in proportion as the 'perfect law of liberty' rules in our members, just
> in that proportion do we rise to the standard of true freedom.[32]

True liberty is not licence or total independence, which enslaves the
soul, but liberty from sin in the interests of a self-development to the
glory of God.

Moreover, Nakamura expands on this Christian notion of love to
address the Japanese goal of civilization: love for others is a mark of
civilization. Hatred for others is primitive; hence, barbarians readily
hate and kill others. Love, by contrast, is a more developed notion, and
civilized peoples progress from self-love to love of others, in accor-
dance with the injunction to 'love others as you love yourself.' Nakamura imagined an international project of civilization based on the
love of one's fellows: 'With a heart loving others, nothing is limited;
with our feelings approximate and our force united, our undertakings
will succeed; the spirits will harmonize with man and our prosperity
will be full.' In a truly ideal scenario, a civilized Japan would become
one with a Christian and peaceable order of civilized states.[33]

Although Mill and Nakamura elsewhere question the rightness of
the range of laws established by the middling majority, submission to
the right rule of law and to the moral conscience is prominent to Nakamura's thinking. But his position is not to be mistaken for mere obedience of religious authorities. Mill, after all, had praised 'the great
writers to whom the world owes what religious liberty it possesses' for
having 'asserted freedom of conscience as an indefeasible right.'[34]
Nakamura supports Mill's insistence on a 'living belief.' Mill warns
about the dangers of hypocrisy: the Christian who gives homage to
certain standards in religion may very well give his real allegiance to
the worldly life. Hence Mill and Nakamura promote the need for free
discussion of religious truth in order to test belief. After all, Christian
morality, its laws and rituals, have changed considerably over the cen-

turies.[35] For Mill, the goal for those committed to religious truth is identical to our collective goal of political truth, both of which demand the maintenance of liberty of discussion.

The problem of moral authority, however, that Mill discloses in *On Liberty* persists in Nakamura's translation in a new form. Given the conviction with which individuals maintain religious faith, and given the propensity for that religious faith to inform public standards of morality, there is always a danger that a self-righteous 'moral majority' will establish laws that either prescribe its religious truths for others or proscribe the public debate over religious truth. The close relationship between religion and morality is problematic when matters of faith become authoritative grounds for judging the moral value of the actions of non-believers. Hence, Nakamura cannot escape from engaging the problem of authoritative standards for public morality. If anything, he complicates the problem by foregrounding the development of the individual's moral conscience as a primary solution.[36] On the one hand, as Mill had asserted, the principle of liberty insists on freedom of thought and discussion in order to debate the truths that inform the laws that we establish; on the other hand, Nakamura's new endorsement of personal obedience to that law and the personal development of Christian love and moral conscience creates a new tension. As Ogihara Takashi put the point, Nakamura's notion of truth is substantive and unitary, since the goal represents a common point to which we all aspire, but for Mill, truth is fragmentary, partial, and plural, a perpetually constructed object of debate and cooperation.[37] For Nakamura, then, the individual becomes the site for an internalized debate over the moral authority of law: in the event that one's social obligation to obey the law overrules one's liberty of belief, what are the consequences for freedom of discussion or freedom of religion? Individual liberty retreats from the public arena of debate to the private and interior space of thought and belief.

The tension that Nakamura feels between public morality and the possibility of alternative private morals could be resolved by splitting the two: publicly, one conforms to the public standards; privately, one holds one's own beliefs according to liberty of conscience. Where Mill is comfortable to challenge the authority of public standards – indeed, *On Liberty* can be read as a manifesto in favour of the individual's variance from public morality – Nakamura hesitates to fully endorse this position, as would any number of Japanese social critics during the Meiji period, from Christians to popular-rights advocates to socialists.

In developing his argument for liberty of thought and discussion, Mill is clear that this human activity ensues in a public and social setting. Thought is concretized in beliefs and opinions and is brought forth in speech, whereupon individuals contend over the validity of their beliefs. Where Mill occasionally makes references to 'mind' and its intellectual operations (the human faculties of perception, judgement, and so on), Nakamura invests in terms from Confucian teachings that point to the interiority of the individual, like the 'human heart-and-mind' and the 'soul' or 'spirit.' Both Mill and Nakamura, for example, describe an individual's engaging in the self-correction of error by weighing and comparing others' opinions with one's own; the goal of this activity is the establishment of truth. For Mill, this self-correction occurs in tandem with public debate; Nakamura adds, however, that the 'human heart-and-mind' turns to goodness and corrects mistakes: the personal practice of the self may work its effects in the public sphere, as public morality advances.[38] Nakamura emphasizes at the outset that liberty is key to self-development; in translating and expanding on Mill's epigraph from William von Humboldt's *The Sphere and Duties of Government*, he adds that liberty is something for 'all people to obtain and thereby develop their talents and natures.'[39]

Critical to both Mill's and Nakamura's explanation of the advance of truth is the interpretation of experience. Mill again treats this as a largely public activity with social consequences – one learns through observation and conversation to judge whether another's experience is pertinent to oneself, and then chooses a mode of action, all of which is an exercise in the education or development of the human faculties. By contrast, Nakamura emphasizes the internal orientation of such interpretation: 'To follow only custom and standards ... neither expresses nor develops the Heaven-granted [innate] talent and intelligence that defines the nature of man. Rather, the spirit's talent and intelligence – namely, sagacity and insight – affords man choice in judging affairs, evaluating good and evil, and aiming at morality and etiquette, and only this exercise of comparison and choice in worldly affairs gives expression to man's innate talent and ability.'[40] Internally perfected individuality is manifested outwardly for others to observe and to take note. Here and elsewhere, Nakamura's vocabulary for morality and metaphysical principles like truth and understanding is largely borrowed from Confucian teachings. This language stresses, in the first place, the public and social nature of morality itself, defined as 'the way of humanity' (C: *shidao* / J: *sedō*) or as the 'fundamental human relations' (C: *renlun* / J: *jinrin*) – a concept that denotes the natural hei-rarchies of age, gender, and status.[41] In the second place, Nakamura's Confucian terminology stresses the centrality of moral instruction to education and the role of the perfection-seeking conscience (C: *liang-xin* / J: *ryōshin*) in moral self-criticism and improvement. And indeed, we have contemporary accounts from a number of Nakamura's peers, reporting that their engagement with *Jiyū no ri* took the form of a fasci-nated, self-transforming reading.[42]

This is not to argue that because of his choice of translation terminol-ogy, Nakamura is necessarily bound to the Confucian project of self-rectification through personal reflection (as is the case of Yan Fu in China). Rather, Nakamura has discovered in Mill – if not introduced to *On Liberty* – an interiority that takes precedence in belief and self-improvement: the spirit's talent and ability, which is expressed in expe-rience and can be extended by religious instruction.[43] Hence, in addi-tion to valuing Christianity for its centrality to arguments about the liberties of thought, religion, and discussion, Nakamura found in Christianity an expression of individual liberty that highlighted an interiority answerable directly to God and potentially out of reach of society or government. This perspective is boldly announced by E.W. Clark in his introduction: 'The mission of the world's Messiah was one of deliverance. As foretold by the ancient prophet it was "to set at lib-erty." It was to unchain the captive, not from a temporal, but from a spiritual despotism. It was to open prison-doors, & to let light into dark places. It was to rescue us from the thralldom of sin & Satan, & to usher us into the "glorious liberty of the children of God!"'[44] Here, in its most Christian formulation, Nakamura would have us believe that liberty is most pertinent for religious salvation. God grants each of us liberty and a measure of talent and ability, and the responsibility of each of us is to develop that liberty, talent, and ability in order to liber-ate the spirit and thus to live as moral testimony for others.

The difficulty with Nakamura's position is that we are left ambiv-alently between the centrality of 'character' in Mill's original argument, and the importance of 'conscience' in Nakamura's interpretation. Both Mill and Nakamura present character as an essential sign of 'different experiments of living.' Both discuss character as a balance of impulses and self-control; both denigrate mindless imitation, adherence to old forms, and self-indulgence; and both praise love of virtue and stern self-control. In Nakamura's rendition, the fundamental nature of individu-ality is the free expression of character.[45] But in the face of Mill's absolute commitment to the freedom of any individual to behave as eccentrically as he would (within the limits of public safety), Nakamura balks and turns to the individual's moral conscience, introducing a prior principle of Christian love and harmony that deserves to be perfected through the individual's project of self-development.

The problem, left unresolved in Mill, remains this tension between public morality and individual conscience. As scholars such as Irwin Scheiner have demonstrated in their accounts of the development of Christianity and social protest in the Meiji period, the debate between character and conscience in Japan was dominated by the state. If religion (especially the newly constructed imperial state religion of Shintō) and morality are the basic influences on human character, one might remain always within national traditions or priorities. The danger of the individual's conscience as a source for moral authority is its relation to eternal truth, unmoored from any specific social system: the individual is inherently free from social norms and structures.[46] The Christian activist Ebina Danjō declared that once he had found a personal relationship with God and welded his faith and his inner self, he realized the authority of his conscience.[47] But Japanese critics of Christianity would ask, Is the good citizen a loyal one or a moral one? Are public moral values derived from the individual conscience or from the state – or some other public ethical sphere? The problem that a Christian posed to the Japanese state is evident in the career of Niijima Jō, who wrote of his transformation in the United States as a student during the 1860s; he discovered an internal, personal freedom that made him no longer a slave to the Japanese government. He had earlier gleaned from Francis Wayland the point that secular progress depends on the cultivation of conscience, and once he became a Christian he realized that self-reform is the key to social reform, since the individual is bound only to and by God.[48] Japanese tolerance of Christianity promised to subvert the group differences once constructed around Christian beliefs, which defined Christian Westerners as alien and thus invoked some alternative Japanese grouping. As I relate in chapter 5, Japanese unsympathetic to Mill or Nakamura, those nation builders desiring to construct some positive Japanese identity in an analogous fashion around a set of beliefs, found this subversive potential of Nakamura's Mill quite threatening and worked to confine Christian conscience to its internal liberty of faith by demanding a public manifestation of civic morality.[49] Nakamura's Christianity had far less influence than his presentation of liberty.

Free Trade

If Nakamura seems somewhat naive in emphasizing harmony as a goal toward which the members of a community should strive, by submitting their individual liberties to the group out of Christian love for each other or a sense of collective well-being, we are reminded by another of Nakamura's surprising additions to Mill that the tyranny of absolute authority was a most powerful point of reference as he considered new social and political institutions in the face of the Meiji Restoration. If he seemed much more willing than Mill to grant the community or majority the benefit of the doubt where individual liberties are concerned, this was perhaps because he was much more concerned with the absolutism personified by the Meiji oligarchy. Nakamura concludes Mill's first chapter with a series of paragraphs derived from Dugald Stewart's contribution to the *Encyclopaedia Britannica* on the subject of François de Fénelon (1651–1715), who, as a member of the court of Louis XIV, cautioned the king on the dangers of tyranny, particularly concerning – in Nakamura's report – religion and trade. Writing at the time of the Huguenot resettlement, Fénelon urged a disinterested love of God and toleration of others' beliefs as an alternative to persecution.[50] Nakamura found Fénelon's endorsement of religious liberty worth repeating; he agreed that the danger in forcing people to convert is the risk of producing hypocrites: 'A king's right does not extend to the right of the human heart and innate good conscience; and a king's power cannot easily subdue the power of the human heart and faith.' A monarch would do better to support his people in their several faiths, encouraging them to religious instruction and, presumably, moral behaviour.[51]

More important, Nakamura found in Stewart's account of Fénelon's *Telemachus* a broader endorsement of liberty and the specific principle of free trade. (Fénelon's tale concerns the travels of Ulysses' son Telemachus in search of his father, in the course of which he is instructed on superior principles of rulership.) If Fénelon, like Mill, insisted that the people be free to do what they will and that the people's welfare be based on such freedom, Nakamura concluded from Fénelon that free trade was one of the essential paths to prosperity. Nakamura quotes a scene in *Telemachus* that contrasts the people's interest in freely trading with the sovereign's desire to profit by taxing their trade. Narbal, the commander of the Phoenician fleet at Tyre, explains to Telemachus that the great prosperity of Tyre is a conse-

quence of the morality of the people and their well-regulated government, their industriousness and their good faith to strangers, and their
free trade unhindered by any avaricious and extravagant prince, and
he urges Telemachus to institute a similar policy back in Ithaca.[52]
Nakamura goes on to invoke the names of Adam Smith and Benjamin
Franklin, who comment that in contemporary conditions of trade, the
operating principle is 'to sell more to strangers yearly than we consume of theirs in value.' The nation's prosperity will grow.[53]

But again, Nakamura augments Mill's argument to push it in a
direction away from the original, for Nakamura would substitute the
national interest for Mill's point of interest, the buyer's right. Mill
argues that trade, because it is most assuredly a social act, comes
within the jurisdiction of society. Hence, governments once had a duty
to fix prices and regulate manufactures. But under the new doctrine of
free trade, restraints on trade are categorically evil and should concern
only that part of conduct that society is competent to restrain – 'as, for
example, what amount of public control is admissible for the prevention of fraud by adulteration; how far sanitary precautions, or arrangements to protect workpeople employed in dangerous occupations,
should be enforced on employers.'[54] Although Mill notes that the doctrine of free trade 'rests on grounds different from, though equally
solid with, the principle of individual liberty,' he does not discuss
those grounds but notes instead that regulation of trade raises two
sorts of questions. First, Mill's preceding examples of restraints are
those that concern the public good, which is necessarily engaged
because trade is a social act, and these examples 'involve considerations of liberty': although control is legitimate for such protective
goals, it is better to leave individuals free to do what they will. This set
of considerations raises the same set of issues that Mill addresses
throughout *On Liberty*: to the degree that individual acts are social, in
what manner and to what degree shall government intervene to assert
standards or guidelines? Mill's second set of examples concern what
he calls 'interference with trade,' such as the sale of opium to China or
the sale of poisons, which certainly have to do with individual liberty;
and in these cases he absolutely upholds the individual buyer's right
to buy. Even if we have reason to suspect that a buyer of poison may be
plotting a murder – just as we have reason to believe accidents should
be prevented, as with the person foolishly attempting to cross an
unsafe bridge – the preventive function of government is more likely
to be abused and the better path of action is to honour the individual's

liberty to buy.[55] The free circulation of commodities and the buyer's right take precedence.

In reproducing this argument in translation, Nakamura represents Mill's position not so much as an issue between the individual and society but as an opposition between the people (as buyers) and public or government control. The public interest takes precedence, and so Nakamura's addition of Fénelon's argument minimizes Mill's support of the individual buyer's right.[56] Since political economy maintains a national perspective, the national interest of prosperity is promoted when the principle of free trade is redefined by the injunction to sell more than one buys. Nakamura's addition, I believe, is a deliberate commentary on the debate surrounding national political economy in Japan in the 1870s, divided between the British doctrine of free trade (seen in Mill and Fénelon) and the national doctrine of protection, exemplified in the ideas of Friedrich List and the behaviour of the United States. Hence, Nakamura urged his readers in *Jiyū no ri* 'to sell more to strangers yearly than we consume of theirs in value.'[57]

In conclusion, when Nakamura endorsed Mill's project of a liberal society that would be based on individual liberty and rights, he attempted to go a major step further than Mill. If Mill found sufficient guarantee of the public good in each individual's effort to better himself and in the principle of tutelage exercised by those of superior education and intellect, Nakamura attempted to circumscribe the individual so as to limit his capacity for selfish and harmful behaviour: both by foregrounding the well-being of the community as the condition and goal of individual liberty, and by introducing Christian love and conscience as checks on our treatment of others in the community. We will see other such attempts to circumscribe individual liberty in the following chapter regarding Yan Fu. But at the same time, Nakamura's discussion of free trade began to supply a national goal toward which individual liberty could be directed, a project of central concern to the leaders of Meiji Japan. This raises the issue of the role of the state in securing and developing individual liberty, as well as promoting standards of behaviour, questions to which we turn in chapter 5.

CHAPTER FOUR

Yan Fu and the Moral Prerequisites of Liberty

Yan Fu (1854–1921) made a major contribution to ideas for imperial reform in China with his famous translations of Western texts at the end of the nineteenth century. But in comparison with his intellectual reputation, his life followed a sad trajectory. He was born into a family of marginal scholarly standing in China's southeastern Fujian province. Although his grandfather had attained the *juren* or entry-level civil degree and served for a time as an education official, his father practiced traditional medicine and placed his hopes on his son, for whom he hired a tutor to instruct Yan Fu in the Confucian classics and to prepare him for the civil examinations. The deaths of Yan's tutor and father abruptly ended his education and put the family in dire economic straits. Luckily for Yan, the imperial creation of Westernizing institutions provided new opportunities, and in 1867 he passed the entrance examinations to the new naval academy attached to the Fuzhou shipyard, where he specialized in navigation and studied the English language, mathematics, and science. He graduated in 1871 and served on the personal staff of Shen Baozhen, minister of naval affairs. Between 1877 and 1879, Yan pursued advanced naval studies in England at the Greenwich Naval College, where he developed a keen interest in Western politics and society.

Shortly after his return to China, he was appointed to the administration of the new Beiyang Naval Academy at Tianjin, where he eventually rose from dean to vice-chancellor (1889) and to chancellor (1890). It was during this time, in the wake of repeated public failures at attempts to reform imperial institutions and his own private failures at the official examinations, that Yan began his prominent writings on institutional and cultural reform and his translations of Western texts such as Mill's *On Liberty*, Adam Smith's *Wealth of Nations*, Herbert Spencer's *Study of Sociology*, Edward Jenks's *History of Politics*, Montesquieu's *De l'Esprit des Lois*, and his most famous, the widely read and studied translation of Thomas Huxley's *Evolution and Ethics*, which introduced the concept of evolution to China. Yan resigned from the Naval Academy in 1900 and worked in a number of advisory capacities for new Western-oriented institutions, but the chaotic wake of the revolution in 1911 left him isolated and embittered, as well as addicted to opium, and he spent the last several years of his life in retirement and at work on commentaries on Daoist texts.[1]

In translating *On Liberty* in 1898, Yan took his cue from chapter 4 of Mill's original, 'Of the Limits to the Authority of Society over the Individual,' and titled his translation *Qun ji quan jie lun*, On the boundaries of authority between the group and the self. The new emphasis on mutuality was central to his project. Where Mill made a strong case for the liberty of the individual in the face of the claims of his fellows, Yan's title accentuated instead the practical problem raised but left largely unresolved by Mill: how to best negotiate the proper spheres of authority and judgement respective to society and the individual – or, as he named the parties, the group and the self. Although Mill emphasized the individual before all, proposing the abstract individual as the starting point for a rational exercise in self-government, Yan pondered the collective consequences of such a defence of individual autonomy, and hoped to make a positive contribution to defining mutual territories of authority. To Yan, the individual was not abstract but always substantive. The self was necessarily embedded within the group, and thus the moral relations central to humanity – *rendao* or 'the way of humankind' – imposed mutual obligations on both self and group.

This is not to argue that Yan systematically altered Mill's argument; rather, he was emphasizing and expanding points already in Mill. As I observe below, if Mill mentioned in passing that human character implied a 'love of virtue,' Yan insisted at the outset that virtue was fundamental to the possession of liberty. Thus Yan's emphasis on the moral prerequisites of individual liberty point toward a solution to the conflict at the heart of Mill's essay.[2] Mill justified liberty as a two-fold explanation of, first, how individual liberties contribute to the progress of humankind, and second, why society, the public, the majority, or the state should not restrict the actions of individuals. His argument stumbled on the difficult question of what constitutes harm and thus did not adequately explain why and under what conditions the group ought to restrict individual actions.[3] Many scholars have inferred that each such case deserves its own discussion and that, moreover, the burden is on the group to justify its restrictions. Indeed, such an approach to so important a social and personal issue is not unreasonable.

However, because Yan qualified individuality with moral expectations, he treated Mill's justification as two mutually related dialectics, which he highlighted through two key terms – personal conduct and social intervention – and which promised to better resolve the struggle between the self and the group. The dialectic of personal conduct centred on the self's relations with the group and its customs; this was a moral struggle engaging personal desires and the liberty of personal conduct, the potential outcome of which would be to synthesize new group customs. Alternatively, the dialectic of social intervention centred on the group, society, or the state, and its internal relations of humaneness or reciprocity (*ren*); this ethical struggle posed private against public in an effort to better harmonize the self's moral judgements, the people's customs, and the state's law.[4] Yan's goal was greater justice in resolving conflicts between personal conduct and social intervention, but his concept of justice (or 'public principle') pointed toward the embeddedness of individuals in society and their capacity for mutual improvement. If Mill affirmed the pursuit of virtue as a utility, Yan went further and affirmed the innate moral capacity of the self, which is necessarily oriented to the group.

As scholars of Chinese culture are well aware, Yan's interpretation of liberty bears a striking resemblance to Confucian ideas of what we might call moral autonomy. Confucius taught in the *Analects* that we learn good behaviour by putting it into practice. One observes it in the world, practiced by one's parents and teachers, and then internalizes it within the self – the goal being a self-control that does not swerve. In this manner, one can succeed at actualizing in social relations what Confucius called 'the way,' the virtuous path of a genuine human being. This virtue was especially marked by a flexibility of conduct: according to *ren*, the egalitarian principle of humanity or reciprocity, one treats every other person in every encounter as a fully capable human being like oneself; at the same time, according to *li*, the hierarchical principle of ritual or propriety, one treats others in accord with the social positions brought to the encounter. Yan notes, as we will see, that the virtuous person exemplified a moral autonomy – a moral freedom of action – capable of moving others and their communities to new habits of virtue.[5]

As a practical matter, the enactment of a political system based on liberty, for both Mill and Yan, would begin with an elite minority who deemed themselves sufficiently responsible to assert their own liberty within the context of a self-governing state. These elite would serve as behavioural models for their social inferiors, who would be granted liberty in due course, as they demonstrated their responsibility, character, and commitment to self-improvement. Yan complicated this scenario somewhat by pointing out a pair of tensions that require optimal balance. First, following Mill, Yan noted the problem posed by differences of personal judgements – that my good may be what you deem bad – and concluded that these are precisely the reasons for not interfering with each other: we do better to grant each other the responsibility of liberty.[6] But what is the substance of this responsibility? And how is it to be enforced through, presumably, some combination of popular opinion and law? Yan invoked the moral claims of Confucian virtues like reciprocity to assist Mill's argument. The second tension is, by contrast, unique to Yan's text. He wanted to make the concept of liberty useful, he says, by demarcating the borders of authority between the self and the group.[7] But how do we reconnect liberty and authority – *quan* (J: *ken*), this ancient word meaning judgement, the power to judge, and the authority of judgement?[8] Yan proposes that we need to determine what is properly free from what is not and how the territories of authority relative to the self and the group are to be negotiated. To him, this was not a matter of territories possessed on the model of sovereignty or private property but an issue of physical borders: contact zones in which the group and the self are mediated.[9] In the end, Yan's ideal of justice committed him to the position that only moral uses of freedom deserve consideration in the social context of authority.

The Group and the Self

That Yan introduced Mill's argument as an attempt to differentiate between the authority of the group and that of the self is significant on two accounts. First of all, this word for 'group,' *qun*, introduces a general and abstract term for the social configurations that potentially restrict the individual's liberties; *qun* encompasses society, nation, people, clubs, communities, companies, parties, factions and so on. In employing this abstract concept, Yan found a collective term that managed to synthesize the range of groups that problematically diffused Mill's (and Nakamura's) text; where Mill vacillated in targeting the majority, society, the state, or the public as the primary threat to the individual, Yan could treat them all as groups. *Qun* is an especially astute choice: it suggests both the natural, or ascriptive, and the social, or acquired, groupings into which humans can be classified or can choose to associate themselves, for *qun* is an ancient word meaning both 'kind' or 'type' – designating a category of thing – as well as 'friends' or 'communities of people.' It is this second meaning of *qun*, particularly as a verb denoting 'to assemble into a group,' that encouraged the ancient philosopher Xun Kuang to conclude that *qun* is the activity of associating that distinguishes men from animals. Although scholars of animal behaviour may protest that Xun Kuang incorrectly assumed that animals do not choose to combine into groups, the issue is neither conscious choice nor the fact that it is we humans who categorize things like animals into groups. John Knoblock reminds us that to Xun Kuang, the human capacity to associate in groups is itself a natural process; human inventiveness enters into the process as people construct standards of morality and justice and as human communities divide into classes based on knowledge, labour, and the like.[10] Or, Yan suggests in a pair of passages from Mill, as people coalesce naturally into groups, and sufficient numbers mass to form a country, they assume the authority of law and morality.[11] In this regard, Yan was more successful than Nakamura Keiu in grasping Mill's abstract 'society.'

In the second place, by foregrounding this general term for groups, Yan sets into motion a dialectic more fundamental than that animating Mill's argument. Where Mill started with the overtly political opposition between the people and the tyrant, Yan removes to a more basic opposition between groups and the self. Asserting that the nature of humankind is social, Yan proposes groups as the fundamental units of humanity, against whom the self is forever committed to some measure of struggle. Once the child becomes aware of itself as a social being, its liberty is bounded by the liberty of others.[12] In Mill, the people and the tyrant negotiate a constitutional monarchy; in Yan's translation, this quintessentially modern political problematic becomes a general phenomenon. The self is confronted always by a vast range of potential differences between oneself and one's groups, from habits and customs, laws and public opinion, to random likes and dislikes.[13] Hence, struggle and negotiation with groups generally occupy the life of the individual. But Yan of course preserves the political thrust of *On Liberty*; his opening transition from the general concept of the group to Mill's text makes clear that apart from our families, companies, communities, or clubs, and whether we live under monarchy, aristocracy, or a representative system, government persists as the single most powerful institution opposed to the self. The problem facing liberty is, at its worst, the tension between self and government.[14]

If *qun* or the group is an abstract and general concept to Yan, the individual is not. Rather than the individual per se, Yan writes most often of the self, using either a poetic term of self-reference, *xiaoji*, the 'little self' or 'myself,' or simply *ji* or *yiji*: 'the self,' 'one self,' or 'one-self.' (In Yan's text, *ji* also assumes plural forms of self-reference such as 'themselves.') But he also uses commonplace expressions such as 'one person' (*yiren*) or 'each and every person' (*renren*), as opposed to groups such as the people or the majority. To be sure, Yan has expressions to convey the significance of individuality – which I discuss below – but unlike Mill's Japanese translator, Nakamura Keiu, who painstakingly constructed an abstract neologism for individuality, Yan primarily employs these terms of concrete reference. To put the point another way, Yan attempts to metaphorically extend the meaning of a Chinese word for self (*xiaoji*), in order to encompass the abstract English noun 'individuality' – and, in two places, he does employ an experimental but defunct neologism, *xiaoji zhuyi*, the 'principle of self-hood' or 'selfism,' to translate individuality.[15] But unlike *ziyou* for 'liberty,' for example, his use of *xiaoji* for 'individual' was not a lasting extension of meaning. In his subsequent translation of Herbert Spencer's *Study of Sociology* (*Qunxue yilun*, translated 1901–1902 and published 1903), he would adopt the neologism standardized in Japanese for 'individual,' *geren* (J: *kojin*), but he uses no such translation word in his rendition of Mill.[16] *Xiaoji* and the related terms retain their more concrete meaning of 'self.' In fact, at one point he patiently articulates the difference between this personal self (*ji*) and the more abstract or impersonal self (*zi*) of self-government (*zizhi*); the former refers to a self like 'myself,' while the latter refers to the group claiming to be self-governing. In a regime of self-government, the concrete former, myself, must submit to the abstract latter, the group.[17]

I return shortly to the issue of the individual – the self – because Yan's translation of *On Liberty*, after all, locates liberty in the self, albeit with significant conditions. But this dialectical tension with which Yan begins – that between the natural unit of the group and the conscious, mature self – is mediated in ways both identical to Mill and in novel fashions. As one might expect, Yan duly introduces the set of liberties enumerated by Mill – comprising liberty of conscience (from which follow the more celebrated liberties of thought, feeling, discussion, writing, and publishing), liberty of tastes and pursuits, and liberty of association. Yan's formulation of these liberties is, as in Mill, expressed with geographical metaphors; conscience, tastes and pursuits, and association are the three primary 'territories' of liberty, the spaces over which the self contends with the group (Mill's word is 'region'). Thus the assertion of these liberties is one of the self's attempts to resolve its dialectical tension with the group, which it does by persuading the group of the general utility of liberty to both individual and group: the liberties promote self-improvement and thus advance everyone.[18] Mill's 'one simple principle' – that self-protection is the only reason for the interference of society into the affairs of the individual – represents the group's counterargument to the individual's assertion of liberty. If utility is the rationale on which society and selves both ground their respective positions, the selves assert their liberties and society responds by reining in individual liberties in order to preserve and protect its unity. This is precisely the struggle over the territories demarcated by the liberties.

But when Yan presents Mill's 'one simple principle,' he is more willing than Mill to entertain the possibility that the utility of the majority is an equally important and valid factor. Utility – which Yan sometimes renders 'gain and loss' – is a key determinant affecting ethical relations and the liberties of people; one takes stock of one's own utility in view of the utility of the majority.[19] Although Mill's and thus Yan's discussion of utility is largely confined to a justification for the need for liberties – they benefit the progress of humankind – Yan builds on Mill to grant groups such as society and the nation more latitude. Consider, for example, Mill's introduction to the section culminating in his 'one simple principle' of self-protection: '[The] practical question, where to place the limit – how to make the fitting adjustment between individual independence and social control – is a subject on which nearly everything remains to be done. All that makes existence valuable to anyone, depends on the enforcement of restraints upon the actions of other people. Some rules of conduct, therefore, must be imposed, by law in the first place, and by opinion on many things which are not fit subjects for the operation of law. What these rules should be, is the principal question in human affairs; but if we except a few of the most obvious cases, it is one of those which least progress has been made in resolving.'[20] Mill goes on to consider custom, one's own opinions, class interests, and religion as possible bases for the imposition of limits, only to dismiss each in turn and to assert his principle of self-protection – which he also phrases as the desire 'to prevent harm to others.'

Yan, by contrast, asserts the utility of custom as a starting point in considering liberty. The ancients held that 'submitting to custom' was 'second nature'; hence, adhering to this body of long-established 'nature' affords us a point of view from which to evaluate the soundness of the degree of group control. As he noted in the context of freedom of discussion, the utility of old theories is not that they might be true or false but that most people believe them; they supply a context for evaluating liberty and progress.[21] Thus, Yan considers the possibility of still other, alternative rationales for establishing limits. Observe how he translates Mill's statement of the 'one simple principle' (I retranslate):

> In this book, my explanation of liberty is meant to clarify justice and law. Regarding the nation's treatment of its people, and society's treatment of the self, at what time can nation and society assert authority and control? Over what activities can they interfere? Or rely on superior force, as with criminal punishments? Or praise and blame, as with the rebukes and exhortations of enlightened criticism? Take this as the greatest and fairest theory: that mankind can personally interfere with others for no reason other than 'I act to protect my own life.' In this statement, 'personally' can refer to either one person or a country; 'others' also can refer to either one person or a country; 'interfere' must be based on something much more than mere desire; and 'life' means pre-eminently life and property. From the opposite point of view, this theory maintains that a nation can restrain its people only to prevent harm to people.[22]

Yan appends the series of explanatory notes here ('In this statement ...') in order to compensate for his lack of an abstract term for individual persons and, as a consequence, the rhetorical awkwardness of juxtaposing 'mankind' and 'myself.' It is clear from Yan's addition of the final line that he aknowledges – to a degree greater than does Mill – the group's need to protect itself and its property and thus control the lives of persons like 'myself.' Mill's formulation of the 'one simple principle' appeals to Yan less as 'self-protection' and more as 'to prevent harm to others' – a point to which I return in my discussion of reciprocity.

More important, this passage alerts us to the first of further points of mediation between the self and the group, which Yan has added to Mill's argument: that this book is meant to 'clarify justice and law.' In proposing such a purpose for resolving the tension between self and society, and people and government, Yan has added a significant dimension to Mill's central fight to persuade the majority in society of the benefits to accrue to individual liberty. Where Mill emphasizes the utility of liberty for all, Yan instead envisages that the conflict between the people's liberties and government laws will develop toward a solution of 'justice' – a public and principled basis for interference with personal liberty.[23] As he put the problem, in the past the king alone determined justice, or the privileged minority of an aristocracy did so. But now that the people become self-governing, who is to determine justice? The goal, says Yan, is to balance liberty and justice equitably between government and people, and he is confident that this can be done. Because the government has a monopoly on public authority, the people necessarily assert the principle of liberty, but this assertion is in the interests of government officials too, as they are part of the people. Yan recommends that in considering the opposition between self and society, and people and government, we look to justice (*gongli*) and fundamental law (*dafa*).[24]

The method for achieving this ideal balance between liberty and justice, to which Yan alerts us in his title, is the demarcation of boundaries. One way Yan interpreted the problem in Mill's text was that the social nature of man requires that in groups, my liberty is bounded by the liberty of others. Echoing the goal of one of the classical statements of Confucian thought, *Daxue* (The Great Learning) – that the way to bring peace to the world is by making distinctions and honouring reciprocity – Yan proposed that we need to distinguish between what is properly free and what is not. Moreover, in terms of the political problem that motivates Mill's text, Yan noted that the need for differentiating boundaries arises when the people revolt against their lords, for when people become masters, selves contend with society and the national group.[25] Thus the project at hand is to clarify the bounds and limits of mutual powers – the authority of judgement held by both the self and the group.[26]

Yan noted repeatedly that these questions of balancing liberty and justice, and demarcating the boundaries of power and authority, were problems unaddressed by China's ancient sages and their several theories of human morality or 'the way of humankind.'[27] In thinking practically about this project, Yan emphasized a two-fold effort recalling practices of the self in earlier forms of Confucianism. First, noting that Mill's interest in religion parallels Confucian teachings on morality and social relations, Yan proposed that the Chinese concern for virtue could help to explain liberty as a search for true principles, and that the search would aim for a substantive (rather than an abstract) understanding of liberty. Yan phrased the comparison in the very terms of traditional Confucian virtues: '[Liberty] should make the Chinese people's knowledge and virtue advance at the present time, and make certain that each person begins to cherish true principles: reciprocity, courage, wisdom, and skill; and loyalty, filiality, integrity, and honesty. Let these be the root from which liberty grows and thence assumes material form.'[28] As religious belief could produce new truth and new teachings and a Confucian's personal quest for the way could be actualized in social relations, so too true principles regarding liberty could be substantiated in interpersonal relations such as discussion and debate.[29] Because both liberty and virtue are expressed in personal conduct, they can jointly reinforce each other.

Second, in addition to sharing a common goal with virtue, the pursuit of liberty should produce personal responsibility of a magnitude found in China's sages, those paragons guiding human morality through the ages. Yan hoped not for an abstract or ideal conception of liberty based on book learning but for a concrete practice of liberty actualized in responsible, moral behaviour.[30] In a provocative explanation of sagehood, Yan quoted Aristotle on the greater importance of true principles over teachers, fathers, and other authorities: 'I love my teacher Plato better than many other things, but I love true principles better than my teacher.'[31] Liberty invites the overthrow of erroneous authority in order to establish the true principles that inform sagehood and establish human morality.

By reassessing Mill's argument in *On Liberty* as an effort to achieve a just balance between liberty and law, by means of a careful demarcation between the authority of the self and the group, Yan placed the burden of proof – much more explicitly than Mill did – on the self. In his preface to *Qun ji quan jie lun*, Yan makes clear that the self is the conditioned site of liberty and the liberties. If each self pursued his or her affairs responsibly, each would avoid the interference of society.[32] Only the moral self deserves its measure of liberty. In order to protect the concept of liberty from its misinformed detractors (who argued that 'liberty' meant licentiousness, unscrupulousness, and so on), Yan impressed on his Chinese readers this point of morality: it is not liberty that we should praise or blame but the actions that follow from decisions formed on the basis of liberty.[33]

Hence, Yan supplied three conditions to safeguard the determination of which self deserves liberty. First, as liberty is the site of personal responsibility, so only those who demonstrate their responsibility deserve liberty. Second, given the utilitarian justification for the several liberties, self-improvement is also a condition of a free self; liberty exists to improve the self and, by extension, the others in the group. And third, Yan asserts specifically that the main condition for the acquisition of liberty is character (*ren'ge*) – that measure of the mature self that can serve as a model for others. Where Mill discussed character as a balance of impulses and self-control and denigrated mindless imitation, adherence to old forms, and self-indulgence in favour of love of virtue and stern self-control, Yan accented the commitment to virtue and self-control.[34] Liberty applies only to qualified adults – not, as Mill too insists, to children, dependents, wild and stupid peoples, or barbarians, all of whom rightly deserve the tutelage of their superiors, and, in the case of the last two groups, authoritarian government.[35] Moreover, in a move far more restrictive than either Mill's position or current understandings of freedom of speech in the United States, Yan insisted that improper forms of speech such as satirizing, mocking, or cursing were excluded from liberty, properly considered.[36] With these conditions placed on the self's investment with liberty, liberty should more reliably promote the progress of the people's virtue and participate in the self's search for the true principles that guide our lives.

Yan realized that Mill's concept of liberty contained a specific epistemology of action, insofar as liberty invited us to consider the abstract individual as the source and sufficient context of action. But he cited a number of other authorities on the issue, English and Chinese, in order to stress that Mill's confidence in the progressive impulse implicit in the freedom of individual action remained firmly linked to responsibility in a group context. He quoted a passage from Herbert Spencer's *Ethics* asserting that only liberty permits us to consider individual responsibility; otherwise, behaviour ceases to issue from the individual and we are left to evaluate good and ill fortune in men's actions. Without liberty and the utility of natural selection, we cannot account for the progress of the people's virtue. Liberty justifies the location of action in the individual. Like Mill, Spencer acknowledged the existence of society and government with measured resentment; he hoped for a silencing of society on matters over which it need not busy itself and also for a cutting-back of the scope of government authority – to only that which protects people from harm. Both Mill and Spencer believed that the world and its individuals are by nature progressive – that people strive to improve themselves, to advance society, and to benefit everyone in the process. Spencer's 'law of equal freedom' (enunciated in 1851 in his first major work, *Social Statics*) imagined that we would learn daily to adapt to each other in our free interactions, so that the necessary and the conventional in human relations would in time harmonize into more progressive social relations; society would move beyond its current need for government.[37] Spencer's and Mill's resentment of government did not look to positive measures for improving government; rather, in the absence of government interference, which is usually a nuisance, individuals would flourish and all would progress.

But Yan underlined the goal of progressive self-improvement by referring to the self-transformative aspect of the free and responsible person, a process that he judged analogous to the Buddhist notion of 'transforming one's thingness' or the Western notion of the materiality of the self subject to freedom and restraint, under conditions of which greater acts of self-control and self-mastery produce the self's satisfaction of having liberty. Out of concern for personal responsibility, Yan was most interested in the self-transformative consequences of liberty.[38] Liberty might afford a new location of action in the individual, but Yan insisted that the individual was therefore accountable to the group for all of his actions. By placing personal responsibility, self-improvement, and character as conditions on those individuals who receive liberty, Yan made clear that a demonstration of a morally informed judgement precedes individual liberty.

Models of Private and Public from Chinese Antiquity

Yan shared the belief that progressive individuals dwell among us – the exceptional persons whom he called sages and heroic luminaries. But to a degree more than Spencer or Mill, he assumed that their appearance could only be contemplated within the context of groups, peoples, and states. Mill imagined the genius as the best exemplar of individuality, on the basis of his eccentric pleasures, his originality and intellectual insight. By contrast, Yan's sage or heroic luminary – each one a venerated archetype from the ancient foundations of Chinese civilization – was primarily a moral leader and founder of social and political institutions. If Mill's individual was willing to go his own way, at the risk of incurring the sanction of public opinion or, worse, ostracism from the community, Yan's moral paragon was necessarily embedded within the group and its values, and his actions were specifically intended to reform and to guide the group to better moral behaviour – even to contribute to the universal 'way of humankind.'[39]

Chinese antiquity – familiar to Yan through his education in Chinese classicism – offers a pair of quite alternative versions of sagely activity and the relation of personal behaviour to public standards. These are worth mentioning because, unlike many of Mill's critics in England, China, and Japan, Yan did not especially fear the self's capacity for private interest and selfish behaviour.[40] His concern to find some practical limits for the spheres of authority proper to the self and to the group was informed instead by an optimistic evaluation of the self; he contemplated how to best allow the moral impulses of selves to flourish and thereby have a positive effect on their fellows.[41] But before turning to Yan's translation and interpretation of individuality, let us look at two analyses of private and public in China's antiquity, in order to illuminate Yan's understanding of the relation between self and group, and to corroborate his proposal that China's sages and their quest for virtue serve as a model for understanding liberty.[42]

The first of these, a philosophical analysis by David Hall and Roger Ames, explicates the Confucian promotion of sagehood in terms of aesthetic versus rational (or logical) modes of order. Aesthetic order, which privileges particularity and the uniqueness of single objects, constructs 'an event ontology' in which disjunction and inconsistency unleash creativity.[43] To Hall and Ames, 'The focus of an aesthetic order is the way in which a concrete, specific detail discloses itself as producing a harmony expressed by a complex of such details in relationship to one another.'[44] By contrast, rational order privileges generality, substitutability, consistency, and continuity; rational order 'consists in a pattern of relatedness which is, in principle, indifferent to the elements whose mutual relatedness comprise the order.'[45] Hall and Ames argue that aesthetic order embodies especially the domain of the personal, expressed best in ritual, which permits the spontaneous exercise of harmonizing actions: 'the origins of ritual action for Confucius are personal acts of signification, and the continued justification for any given ritual lies in its power to elicit significance in its performance.'[46] By contrast, rational order is especially the domain of the public, expressed best in law, which orders external behaviour in accord with an overall pattern ideally independent of any particular instance.[47] Now, what is particularly interesting in this simple dualism is that Confucians understood that sagehood provided the foundations for human institutions in ritual, those unique and innovative actions whose replication or repetition offered signification. From the sages' personal virtue, standards of public morality developed; from the sages' rituals, patterns amenable to public law developed. Hall and Ames again: 'Obedience to ... principles involves the realization of what we have called ... rational order; the imitation of a model entails, by contrast, the realization of aesthetic order.'[48] The Confucian ideal, in other words, proposed personal grounds for public standards.

A second analysis, that of Mark Edward Lewis, is a historical account of some of the very institutions idealized by Confucius. Lewis looks at the transition from the aristocratic and lineage states of the Spring and Autumn period (721–481 BC) to the authoritarian and military states of the 'Warring States' period (ca. 481–221 BC), and argues that a profound change occurred in the relation of private and public. The earlier period was characterized by the overlap of lineage and city-state; aristocratic lineages enfoeffed sons and branches in walled towns, producing overall a 'segmentary state' composed of lineage units related through ritual enactments of lineage rules. The state was the domain of kinship; the private family was the basis of the political. Lewis argues that the breakdown of the central Zhou kingdom after 721 BC encouraged the rise of hegemons – leaders among the 'feudal' lords – who began to forge a 'public,' non-kin realm by means of blood covenants, rituals that created binding alliances among lords, states, sublineages, and the inhabitants of capitals.[49] But the disintegration of this system in the fifth century BC produced warring states that created a new public realm through the practice of registering local and rural populations for military service in exchange for land. Defined by the army, this new social order was based on peasant householders (whose new surnames had previously been owned exclusively by aristocrats) and dominated by authoritarian rulers who decreed codes of law in order to maintain the new social and military structures. As the personal event of ritual gave way to the written code of law, the public state was severed from private kinship relations.[50] Lewis shows that the creation of the new public realm required an authoritarian restriction of the private and the familial to a smaller sphere, rather than a benign and fortuitous construction of the public realm from the personal example of sages, as we find in Hall and Ames.[51] As scholars have long observed, Confucians lamented the rise of an authoritarianism based on military violence and longed for a return to the earlier age of virtue presumably informed by sagely ritual.

But the impossibility of such a re-enactment of the founding of society and state is ensured by our inability to retreat to an originating moment. Yan found himself, as we find ourselves, in the midstream of historical development, making do as we can at present. As he put it, one purpose of Mill's essay was to turn the tide of the times, not to launch what did not need to be launched.[52] In liberal fashion, his statement was intended both to offset the rising call for revolution against the imperial order and to encourage the development of some alternative to the authoritarian state.

Yan's engagement with theories of the modern Western state returns to the same interpretive dilemma we find regarding Chinese antiquity. As he noted in his translation of Mill, once aware of oneself as a social being, the self submits to the group. It is the abstract totality that tends to take precedence in the people's state, much as the warring state created an ideal public to which all personal interests were forced to yield. As Mill had noted, the French Revolution gave birth to the modern state, which was always at risk of unleashing its authoritarian impulses, so individual liberty was a necessary corrective. Yan imagined splicing onto this dualism the example of China's ancient sages: he proposed an elevation of individual liberty, properly conditioned by moral prerequisites, as the foundation for that supreme personal virtue of the sage who founded public systems of human morality.

Individuality as Moral Self-Cultivation

In translating Mill's endorsement of individuality, Yan emphasized the moral parameters of liberty and selfhood by repeating a pair of terms central to his interpretation of individuality: first, the 'liberty of conducting oneself' (*xingji ziyou*), or, to phrase it more generally and abstractly, the liberty of personal conduct; and second, 'independent integrity' (*tecao*), an archaic term that refers to one's capacity to independently will personal principles of action – that is, a stability of will in determining and acting on one's own principles.[53] Yan's description of what is required of each person makes striking parallels to statements from Chinese moral tradition: 'One must make models and rules for oneself, whereupon one's affairs engage all one's talents. One must exhaust the powers of one's eyes and ears in order to observe and listen. One must think deeply and discerningly compare in order to foresee the favourable and harmful. One must be diligent in searching broadly and consulting widely in order to observe similarities and differences. One must have insight at judgement, for then one will know what is excluded and what included, and thus determine what to exclude and to include. One must have an expansive and determined steadfastness that reaches the bounds of self-control, for then one can attain a will that does not swerve.'[54]

The effect of this interpretation of individuality was to relate Mill's rationalist project in *On Liberty* to a project like sagehood in Chinese antiquity, described by Hall and Ames above. What to Mill was a logical method of self-scrutiny and informed judgement, from which others might learn, was to Yan a cultivation of moral autonomy, which might provide a model for all. Following Mill, Yan reiterated that the difficulty facing the liberty of personal conduct was the body of habit and custom inhabited by the group. If custom tended to be conservative and was given public or official sanction through popular opinion and law, its danger to the self had reached new levels with the development of representative government, which accorded popular opinion a significant measure of political power.[55] But as Yan explained it, independent integrity could safeguard the liberty of personal conduct because the goal of independent integrity encouraged moral development and character building, which, in extraordinary and heroic persons, not only fulfilled Mill's goal of fostering reform, new customs, and progress but also, in keeping with classical Chinese goals, encouraged civilization and the development of 'the way of humankind.'[56]

Yan saw this as primarily a moral effort and contrasted the solution of independent integrity to that attempted in earlier ages, treating both in moral terms that echoed Buddhist and Confucian practices of the self. In antiquity, the self had been encouraged to suppress and control his desires, feelings, and fondnesses. Government application of punitive law had reinforced the suppression of private desires, and presumably this technique tended to reproduce obedient uniformity. In recent times, however, the preferred technique was to develop independent integrity and the people's character in all their diversity, so as to encourage them to be responsible for their liberty.[57] This development of independent integrity depended especially on a program of education – that tutelage of the immature by their social superiors – but Yan phrased it in a notably Confucian manner: each should be encouraged to perfect his or her measure of 'heaven's endowment' in the interests of both self-cultivation and 'study of the way,' and ideally this would contribute to the people's virtue, the advancement of the way, and the beautification of human morality.[58] It is striking that at one point, in specifying 'the two main elements of the way,' Yan reiterated a point in Mill that nicely dovetails with our understanding of the social vision of the Confucian *Analects*: the two elements – liberty of personal conduct, and the differences of each situation – remind us that perfect reciprocity in the *Analects* requires a flexibility of conduct that masterfully accords with the unique circumstances of the social situation in which one acts.[59]

But where classical Confucian thought imagined the sage or superior man as the paragon of accomplished virtue, and where Mill invoked the genius as the model of originality and individuality, Yan wrote instead of the 'heroic luminary' (*haojie*) as the 'extraordinary person' who would 'expand the open-mindedness of society and introduce new experience to ordinary people.'[60] This heroic luminary was the one in a myriad, the 'true person,' the gentleman of special standing, independent conduct, and exceptional ability; he began with his personal standard, demonstrated to others that their laws and ideas were unsuitable for the times, and thus established new teachings and ritual customs for the age. Progress and civilization followed from his example of independent integrity.[61] As the ancient philosopher Mencius noted during the Warring States period, common people may flourish during the time of a sage-king, but such a luminary will flourish in the absence of a king.[62] The *haojie*, in other words, undertakes the work of the sage.

Hence, as Yan translated, it is in our interests to encourage the education and liberty of personal conduct that foster the development of independent integrity. If earlier ages had more readily allowed for a man to develop his independent integrity, the present situation was much less encouraging, because the self was now overwhelmed by the national group.[63] Where Mill stressed the intellectual and hedonistic advantages of allowing the genius to pursue his own cause, however eccentric, because he contributes to the wisdom and artistic pleasures available to all, Yan placed added emphasis on the moral direction provided by the luminary and noted liberty's close relation to virtue. We tolerate what Mill calls 'constructive injuries' (Yan's apt rendering is 'connected' or 'collateral injuries') – those inconveniences we incur because of another's bad habits or irresponsibility – 'for the sake of the greater good of human freedom.' Yan adds, in return for the blessings of human morality.[64] Likewise, Yan's rephrasing of Mill's insistence on the importance of the liberty of discussion returns to the goal of virtue. Where Mill stressed the expansion of knowledge and truth, which may teach us a better way to live and afford progress for all, Yan described a process whereby ideas that spread from the self to the group develop a universal stature and participate in the expansion of human morality, contributing to the growth of goodness and its principle.[65] Conversely, he noted that without free discussion, the human heart-and-mind is not benefited, and the way becomes unclear or unpracticeable.[66]

The Boundaries of Authority: Mutual Encouragement and Local Administration

And yet the problem that Mill raises in *On Liberty* remains: on what grounds can society interfere with an individual's liberty? Or, as Yan phrased it, how do we reconcile personal conduct and social intervention?[67] As I mentioned at the start of this chapter, Yan envisages that the conflict between the people's liberties and government laws will develop toward a solution of justice. How will this be achieved?

In a striking departure from Mill's perceptions, Yan maintains an optimism that each party will look out for the interests of the other. This view is informed by the virtue of reciprocity, which enters Yan's translation at several points. In introducing the opposition of self and group, Yan notes that this is meant to be a civilized arrangement, productive of progress. Observing boundaries for both self and state is not meant either to encourage personal selfishness or to turn the encouraging of goodness into interference. Rather, boundaries are to mark a positive and mutual engagement, inspiring concerned interaction from both sides: they are more a matter of moral negotiation and less a matter of legal fixity. As Yan notes in a comment phrased more pointedly than Mill's, both speaker and listener participate in the suppression of truth, so liberty of discussion is intended to benefit both.[68] Yan also introduces reciprocity in his discussion of Mill's comments on accidents and other unsuspected harms: one warns another about walking across an unsafe bridge and may rightfully interfere with his passage, out of mutual concern for fellow members of society.[69] (As Mencius had famously insisted, one attempts to save a child about to fall into a well because one responds unthinkingly with compassion.) From Yan's account, we can infer as a general proposition two seemingly paradoxical personal activities: mutual non-interference; and mutual encouragement of each other. Rather than interfere with each other, we encourage each other's good behaviour and discourage the bad; thus, the moral way of humanity mutually matures and stabilizes.[70] Hence, as noted earlier, Yan's construction of Mill's 'one simple principle' – the self-protection of society – gravitates toward its alternative phrasing: preventing harm to others. Reciprocity would impel us to look out for the interests of others; the act more in keeping with the virtue of reciprocity is to prevent harm to others, before I selfishly worry about my own self-protection.

Such optimism that Yan introduces to Mill's argument, through this interest in reciprocity, corresponds to Yan's insistence that the self is embedded naturally within the group. In fact, this aspect of his understanding of the human condition is quite at odds with Mill's attempt to treat the abstract individual as a solitary entity. Yan notes in passing the difficulty of delimiting the self and the other, and liberty and interference; he confesses that it is difficult to balance actions in terms of person versus state.[71] The two are necessarily intertwined: the official is a person and one of the people too. Thus, the value that I derive from my life accords with the value that others derive from my life: our collective goal is not uniformity but vitality.[72]

But in light of the undercurrent of tutelage in Mill's argument, some differentiations must be made, for the fact is, middling men and women of limited knowledge (Mill's 'ordinary' persons) tend to 'lead the way' – they dominate society through representative government – and Yan's point about heroic luminaries is that, ideally, they redirect the masses to new knowledge, customs, and orthodoxies. In any event, society or the state is always faced with the need to advance the dumber and weaker in our midst, and it is not appropriate for a civilized country to treat them like children and barbarians, lacking in rational and moral qualities. In attempting to raise all to a common standard, there is always a risk of departing from principle and relying on force.[73] Yan's problem, like that of Mill's tutelage, is how to guide and encourage without interfering.

At the same time, the fact remains that some people fail. There are stupid, selfish, irrational, or otherwise defective persons living in our midst, who, for whatever perverse reasons, will not do what is expected of them or behave in a manner appropriate to their surroundings. And it is on their account that the natural processes of groups have been supplemented by law; it is the defective persons who force the state to use law for purposes of control.[74] In this context, where 'the people use their liberty but have not yet made a necessity of its principle'[75] – which, recall from above, is Yan's description of the progress of virtue – how do we reconcile the ideal of liberty of personal conduct with the necessity of social intervention?

Mill's approach, which Yan largely reproduces, is to urge caution on the group. Too often controls reflect the preferences of dominant minorities in society, as with restrictions on religion or food and drink. Too often controls have the effect of restricting the behaviour of all merely because of the defective behaviour of one, as with restrictions on the consumption of alcohol and spirits. Too often controls attempt to restrict harms before they occur – whether or not they do – as with prohibitions on the sale of poisons. And typically, controls deliberately address the consequences of human mistakes rather than their causes.[76] Mill's approach, remember, is to emphasize education. Since society has an even greater responsibility than parents for the education of children – because it is in a better position to do so, through the public financing of schools – and since society has a significant measure of control over children in their years of schooling, Mill argues that the process of youthful education is the appropriate time and place to urge rationality and responsibility on future citizens in order to get at the potential causes of mistakes before they can happen. Once children have grown into citizens, their rights and privileges of personal liberty take precedence before the control and intervention of the group.[77]

In Yan's account, however, the burden of justification is less on the group than in Mill's account. Yan repeats his point that the self is naturally embedded in society and is therefore rightly subject to its restrictions.[78] The group burdens us each with social duties, for mutual interest gives rise to our agreements and contracts, whether as formal law or informal sentiment, and both of these serve as guidelines in that they provide us with not only our duties, such as military service and police protection, but also our rights and privileges.[79] Nonetheless, following Mill, caution prevails. In examining the behaviour of persons when they fail, Yan tells us to differentiate between direct harm and intangible effects and to look to the purpose or goal of interference.[80] That is, in assessing harm, we should differentiate between harms to oneself and those that extend to others, particularly those that harm the group or the way of humanity. Are they merely private failings or public evils?[81] The tippler who nightly slumbers into dreams in the quiet of his home may be accused of private failure but is rightly left alone; it may be that he occasionally forgets to turn out the lights, but these are not direct harms to his family or to others – they are intangible effects. However, the bad drunk who provokes brawls in the streets deserves to have his liberty of personal conduct curbed – likewise the

idler who ignores his social duties and the ill-mannered fool who sub-
verts rational discussion. Likewise parents who forsake their duties to
their children, and families who forsake their elderly.[82]

But even if, as Mill would have it, we agree that these irresponsible
troublemakers deserve punishment – however effective or ineffective
it may prove in thwarting future harm – is it the case that all so-called
private or solitary behaviour that takes place in the privacy of a home
deserves to be left alone? That even behaviour reprehensible to nineteenth-century Victorians like fornication and drug use is beyond the
purview of society?[83] That activities like these, which pertain to customs and ethics, are simply beyond the capacity of the state to administer, because we simply cannot know what people do in the privacy of
their homes without a fearsome and inappropriate expansion of state
power?[84]

Although Yan does not develop the point explicitly, it is clear from
his treatment of individuality in Mill's essay that there is in fact something reprehensible in the tippler's drunken stupor. Contrary to what
is good, the tippler is not acting responsibly, seeking self-improvement, or building his character. Recall Yan's point about mutual concern and encouragement. One should try to rouse the tippler to return
to our collective pursuit of the way. One can encourage community
discussion.[85] This is not a matter of asserting 'society's rights and privileges' (what Mill calls our 'social rights') against the offending person,
for that merely invites squabbles over the conflicts between my rights
as a person and my rights as a group member – for example, my right
to consume spirits versus my right to have my community free from
my neighbour's drunken brawls, versus my community's right to
restrict the consumption of spirits, versus the wine merchant's right to
sell spirits, and so on.[86] Yan imagines a range of activity broader than
Mill's original sense of tutelage. We can counsel, instruct, and exhort
our fellows; if they prove incorrigible, we can avoid or ostracize them;
and in the worst case, we can apply the punishment of law.[87] But Yan
suggests, above and beyond Mill, that we have a responsibility of
mutuality in encouraging the failures among us to mark their self-
treatment and to undertake self-correction. He observes, 'To speak
solely of one person alone is to render impossible self-correction and
the recovery of dignity, thus putting an end to the beauty of heaven's
endowments ... Since what is called self-correction and the recovery of
dignity does not incur [direct] merit or demerit to society, how can
society snare such behaviour and prohibit or punish it?'[88] To answer

Yan's rhetorical question, it is in our interest to concern ourselves with each other, before bad behaviour does extend to others and incur the punishment of law. We must each heed the national group, but because the group cannot perfect the self's nature – because restrictions on one's heavenly-endowed capacities do not necessarily foster progress under such duress – it is better to promote virtue. Rather than undertake correction by law, it is better to have the people develop their independent integrity and to create a civilized group.[89] In other words, one way to better balance liberty and law is to engage one another, particularly our weaker fellows, in self-improvement and the development of character, with an eye to living together in a state committed to justice.

From the opposite perspective, that of the majority who might interfere with the behaviour of minorities (including the minority of one person), Mill and Yan urge us to examine the behaviour of groups in order to identify those losses and gains that become public.[90] In a manner analogous to the decisions and behaviour of one person, we look to what are in effect collective policies of groups and how these affect others in society and the state. More often than not, this is for both Mill and Yan the issue of self-government and its excesses, as when the Puritans ruled during the English revolution and outlawed dance, theatre, music, and public games, or, during the nineteenth century, when the United States prohibited alcohol and spirits or socialists agitated for equality of wealth.[91]

Yan returns, moreso than Mill, to the work of encouraging individuals to develop their intelligence, virtue, and character, because reasoned and mutually sustaining self-government depends on, first, helping private selves and their families to understand that their personal interests are those of the group and country – this is the important work of the people's training for government. And second, excellent self-government depends on the education of all, which is appropriately verified through public educational testing in order to secure qualified officials who conduct the public work of government.[92] This is not to say that the best and brightest should assemble into the ranks of government service; rather, Mill and Yan argue that talented persons must be available for service inside and outside of government: a free people create a free country. The best solution for improving self-government is more self-government: the focus should be on local administration and popular organizations, not on national bureaucracy, which threatens always to extend its authority and usurp both local administration and the people's liberty. Encouraging local organizations and administration best serves the development of a civilized society and a free people.[93]

To conclude: Yan's translation of Mill offered a new solution for mediating private and public in Chinese political thought at the turn of the twentieth century. Unlike the models available through classical learning, that of the moral sage whose personal example established models of ritual and law, and that of the authoritarian monarch who decreed law in an effort to control his subjects through threat of punishment, Yan proposed a new hybrid that combined the model of the moral paragon and that of popular government found in the West. But Yan modified Mill. Rather than reiterate Mill's proposal, in which the solitary individual possessed a nearly absolute claim of liberty against his fellows in society, who were thus charged to justify their interference with an individual, Yan imagined a moral community led by sage-like virtuous leaders who integrated communities through their personal example and their roles in local administration.

Yan hoped to improve on Mill by better aligning public principles (of interference) and public authority through a balance of liberty and law. As Mill had argued, local government – in the hands of representatives of the people – is a better site for constructing a public authority that respected individual liberty as it set about establishing law. Yan added that because force at best secures only a 'severe justice' with ill consequences, it is far better to encourage moral development with an eye to the people's internalizing a just measure of that public authority.[94] And this project, to return to a comment at the beginnings of Yan's introduction and this chapter, made a necessity of 'determining what is properly free from what is not,' by which Yan meant that 'a man must be free and must take the freedom of others as his boundary,' an axiom that accords with the principle of reciprocity in the Chinese classics.[95] Thus we make the self's affairs the responsibility of personal liberty and differentiate the boundaries between the self and the group. To observe boundaries, then, is not to demarcate what is mine from what is not, as with property rights, but rather to observe the multiple contours of responsibility: my responsibility for myself; my responsibility for others; others' responsibility toward me; and our collective responsibility for each other.

Four or five years after Yan Fu translated On Liberty, a second Chinese translation appeared in Shanghai, from a very different context. This was the work of Ma Junwu (1881–1940), who went to Japan to study in 1901 and joined the nationalist revolutionary cause there. In Japan, he was an associate of Liang Qichao and contributed to Liang's Chinese newspaper, the *Xinmin congbao*; he also became a member of the United Alliance and remained an associate of Sun Yatsen and a member of the National People's Party until his death.[96] Ma's translation of Mill, titled *Ziyou yuanli* (The fundamental principle of liberty), is an example of the passage of Chinese character terminology from Japan to China in the first decade of the twentieth century, for his translation owes apparently nothing to the translations by Nakamura Keiu and Yan Fu; instead, it resembles another translation published in Japan in 1895 by Takahashi Masajirō, as *Jiyū no kenri* (The rights of liberty).[97] Ma's vocabulary reflects a confident and stable Japanese idiom – *ziyou* for 'liberty,' *geren* for 'individual,' *shehui* for 'society,' and so on. It is singularly like language still in use in China today. Moreover, Ma's translation reflects his revolutionary interest: he highlights the conflict between government and individuals, and stresses that only when a society of individuals forms a government will such a civilized government be in a position to defend the liberty of its individuals. In that regard, it is a deliberately efficient and condensed version of Mill's text – Ma reduces Mill's long paragraphs and sentences to short, explicit paragraphs with their points highlighted in the margins; he is interested in conveying the bare essentials of Mill's text and in a manner that reduces philosophical possibilities to practical application. For example, Mill's opening line, which differentiates social or civil freedom from the liberty of the will (or philosophical necessity), is condensed to read: 'The main point of this book is to explain the public liberty of people and society, as well as the rights that society can impose upon the individual according to procedures of law; in addition, it explains the basic nature of these rights and their limits – it does not rely on the nonsense expounded by philosophers.'[98] Where Yan invoked much of Chinese traditional vocabulary and values, Ma is singlemindedly focused on Mill. Be that as it may, Ma's endorsement of individual liberty eventually succumbed to Sun Yatsen's and the National People's Party's interest in reinstating traditional values and emphasis on the state over the individual, which I describe in chapter 5.

CHAPTER FIVE

Personal Liberty and Public Virtue

As the preceding discussions of Nakamura Keiu and Yan Fu have argued, the interpretation that each presented in translating Mill's *On Liberty* directed attention to an inevitable conflict between personal liberty and the public maintenance of some collective morality. Nakamura's and Yan's concerns, however, addressed the problem of morality in a manner somewhat differently than Mill had done. Mill had asserted the existence of an oppressive and middle-class sensibility on moral questions, and this 'common morality' provided the necessary context for his defence of individual liberty from an overbearing majority. (This abstract assumption of a common morality is symptomatic of most bourgeois discussions of liberty and law – whether conservative or liberal – a historian's point of criticism against political theory, to which we return in the concluding chapter.) At the same time, Mill assumed the existence of a moral code shared by himself and his readers – that Victorian commitment to duty, hard work, and altruism. Nakamura and Yan, by contrast, could not confidently assume either such moral consensus. They understood the great contributions that free individuals might make to Westernized societies and thus approved Mill's rhetorical defence of individual liberty from the habits of an unthinking community, but they were also cognizant of the desperate and revolutionary situations in which they lived. In the face of European and American imperialism, the Chinese and Japanese nations were at risk. Nakamura and Yan feared for the maintenance of good behaviour and sought to encourage respect for some public good, lest society succumb to an anarchy generated by free but foolish agents.

From the viewpoints of Nakamura and Yan, the problem was not so much to defend individual liberty from an oppressive middle-class majority as to assert the conjoined values of individual liberty and public morality. In Japan and China, a number of Nakamura's and Yan's contemporaries perceived the problem raised by Mill – and Western liberal thought in general – in a new and surprising formulation. They faulted Japanese and Chinese traditions for a lack of any public or collective morality. In their understanding, teachings such as Confucianism or Buddhism concerned social and ethical relations between persons and overlooked the important integrative relations between persons and groups. What was needed in Japan and China, according to scholars such as Nishimura Shigeki and Liang Qichao, respectively, was a new moral system that provided ethical norms for the fundamental constituents of the future nation-state: the citizen, the family, the social group, and the nation. By embedding the individual in a systematic code of ethical relations, both individual liberty and moral duty in the public sphere could be jointly maintained.

Mill's Encouragement of Virtue

In fact, this concern with liberty and morality was not absent from Mill's thinking; according to Joseph Hamburger, Mill too had expressed the importance of both 'liberty and control' in a letter to his friend George Grote in 1854.[1] But few of Mill's readers have read *On Liberty* with an emphasis on control. Rather, as some have demonstrated, particularly John M. Robson and Bernard Semmel, Mill's oeuvre can be read in such a way that *On Liberty* becomes part of a larger plan for the improvement of humankind. One of his points in *On Liberty* and generally in his writings is that the improvement of human communities depends on an expanding project of individual internal culture (or *Bildung*) – a point emphaticallly taken up by T.H. Green: ever greater numbers of individuals must undertake that personal program of self-development and cultivation of character that corrects the selfishness both natural to the child and ascendant in the commercial society of the bourgeoisie. In Robson's analysis, Mill sought to encourage the personal development of sympathy (which Adam Smith, Herbert Spencer, and others had also singled out as the human feeling key to improvement), and this goal was best achieved through development of both the conscience and the intellect. Generally, Mill scholars have considered two paths of development: one, the formal discipline of education, which is stimulated by the example of the genius and managed by the intellectual elite – in the manner of Coleridge's 'clerisy' – and the other, the formal practice of self-government, which encourages personal involvement in the management of society. For both education and self-government, individual liberty is necessary to the free development of each person.[2]

Although these two paths of development constitute a chronological sequence, the path of self-government is circumscribed by the more prominent work of education: self-government remains secondary. As Mill makes clear in *On Liberty*, formal education is especially critical in childhood, in order to inculcate rational habits of mind and a proper concern for others in the young person. Of course, education does not cease for the responsible, independent, and thinking adult; one of the main reasons individual liberty is so useful, according to Mill, is that it encourages the intellectual debate in which we defend our positions and learn from each other. Hence, as adults, self-government is the arena in which we continue to develop conscience and intellect, for it is only in cooperation with our fellow citizens that we learn to value others' interests as our own. Mill singled out three participatory activities of particular value and utility: local government, jury duty, and the free discussion of political debate.[3]

But if Mill was committed to some form of representative system, the degree of democracy in such a system continues to be debated. Where Dennis Thompson and Nadia Urbinati, in their thoughtful analyses of Mill on representative government, would persuade us that Mill advocated a qualified form of democratic government, J.H. Burns, Maurice Cowling, and others make the negative argument – that Mill's elitism committed him to a prolonged tutelage of the underdeveloped masses and to structural limits on the expression of the popular will. In both cases, two points are salient: in the first place, as both John Robson and Urbinati have observed, when Mill concerned himself with the problem of how to structure political institutions in order to take account of individuals, he argued for both the prerequisites of education and practices like proportional voting (based on the analysis and recommendation of Thomas Hare), which would emphasize the participation of educated elites as a significant minority within the voting population.[4] In the second place, as Thompson argues, when Mill was concerned with the qualifications of individuals to participate in self-government, he stressed competence in the service of self-development: competent citizens participated in government as a consequence of their being sufficiently self-developed; as independent individuals, they could best protect their interests in self-government and educate their fellows in the process.[5]

The priority of education before self-government is consistant with the point emphasized by Semmel: to Mill, good government follows not so much from political institutions (or 'forms of government') but from individual intelligence and virtue.[6] As Semmel noted, Mill's reflections on government pointed most often to the problem of how to establish a 'regime of virtue' and yet preserve individual liberty. Clearly, education remained the predominant path of personal development and a prerequisite to political participation.

In this regard, it has been said that Mill was breaking with the approach of his father and Jeremy Bentham, who targeted not persons but institutions for reform.[7] Given that Mill was aware of the ways in which political culture, so to speak, moulds the political consciousness of agents acting within government institutions, it seems an impossible task to strictly differentiate persons and institutions, particularly where public virtue is concerned.[8] As Mill noted at the outset in *Considerations on Representative Government*, our paradoxical view of political institutions – in that they are directly received from our predecessors, and they are deliberate human constructions – complicates our efforts to improve or reform them. He was working within a liberal model that envisaged the point at which civil society constitutes a government (which Nakamura Keiu took pains to explain in his translation), but Mill discloses the point at which this theory of civil society confronts the fact of an extant government whose interests may diverge from those of civil society, or side with one or another faction within civil society. Slavery, the opium trade with China, and factory legislation were three such causes for deep fissures in nineteenth-century England. Virtuous individuals may produce good government, but if we start with the fact of a government that has its own interests to pursue, how do we ameliorate the quality of its many decisions and actions? Mill's supporters propose that we treat government action as the sum of actions of those persons who work in government. By constrast, as we will see, Chinese political theorists at the turn of the century would reject Mill's liberalism over precisely this wish to attribute the goodness of government to the capacities of individuals who represent the ruling elite.

However one construes the goodness of institutions or individuals, the immediate problem is that Mill's commitment to utilitarian justifications has rendered the collective pursuit of education, virtue, and liberty the most contentious aspect of his legacy. There are a number of ways to interpret the form of Mill's utilitarianism, and I would concede to H.J. McCloskey, C.L. Ten, and others the point that Mill is more a 'rule utilitarian' than Bentham's strict 'act utilitarian.' That is, Mill examines not merely the consequences of actions for their utility (act utilitarianism) but also a person's internal commitment to moral rules prior to action (rule utilitarianism). So, for example, I may avoid using vulgar language around my mother so that my actions do not offend her, but I may also avoid using vulgar language altogether as a general rule of action, lest I offend anyone. Thus Mill accepts and values a person's capacity for maintaining disinterested virtue.[9] In any case, when utility serves as our main criterion in conflicts over relative goods, a heirarchy of values accompanies our choices. As most scholars have agreed, Mill valued liberty because it is more useful than equality or justice in ameliorating social conflicts. (He was not much interested in rights in *Liberty.*) As Robson put the issue: because liberty is the element that contributes most to the righting of error in our collective search for truth, and because liberty is essential to each individual's realization of his or her potential and self-development, liberty is more useful than equality or justice and thus it is prior to both. Only self-dependent individuals are in a position to solve problems and guide their fellows from the present imperfect social order to a future perfect order. Thus the principles of equality and justice follow liberty.[10]

Such an argument underscores the hierarchy of values that accompanies Mill's utilitarian endorsement of higher pleasures, for central to both Mill's and Bentham's reliance on utility is the conviction that some pleasures – those of the intellect, which are categorically more responsive to higher culture, personal character, and public concerns – are superior to baser pleasures of a sensuous or frivolous nature. These higher pleasures, which include rationality, altruism, and intellectual interests such as science, literature, philosophy, and fine art, arguably promote the general and long-term happiness of all the citizens, while the base pleasures are presumably limited and personal. This is why, to Mill's mind, the intellectual elite take control of education and impress on the young the superior value of intellectual pleasures.[11]

Now, I know of no Mill scholar who challenges his preference for intellectual pleasures and promotes instead drink, recreational drugs, or fornication as a worthwhile goal. There has been, in other words, a consensus among Mill's readers that the intellectual pleasures are superior, even if the consensus leaves unexamined questions such as the relevance of intellectual pleasures to political needs or their relation to the personal wealth generated by the system of capitalism. Controversy lies instead in the tension between the normative set of pleasures that Mill prescribes and the individual liberty for self-development that he advocates. To what degree would he suspend liberty in order to coerce his fellow citizens into a 'regime of virtue'? Maurice Cowling's presentation of Mill as seeking to indoctrinate his fellows with an authoritarian liberalism remains quite controversial: Cowling argued that Mill's goal was a morally homogenous and intellectually healthy society based on these normative intellectual values.[12] Bernard Semmel subsequently presented Mill as yearning after a society in which citizens widely shared some moral code, but rejecting the coercive example of Auguste Comte's 'religion of humanity,' which Mill felt erred on the side of authoritarianism.[13] Mill's difference from Comte, I believe, is most salient in their opposing views of the role of the state: where Comte advocated state management of not merely education but all aspects of civil life and thus a comprehensive indoctrination of virtue, Mill insisted on private control of education with the state at most providing funding and institutional facilities.

Joseph Hamburger's recent posthumous work charts something of a middle course between these two views. Based on his reading of Mill's late essays on religion, Hamburger argues that Mill continued to imagine some 'religion of humanity' that he hoped would displace Christianity – Mill criticized Christianity for its contributions to a dogmatic and oppressive middle-class morality and its complicit encouragement of selfishness. Accordingly, Hamburger reads *On Liberty* as promoting moral reform at the expense of liberty – in a manner not unlike the example of Yan Fu. Or, as T.R. Wright puts it, Mill's utilitarian morality would focus on altruism, taught as a religion.[14]

The problem that Cowling, Semmel, and Hamburger engage to varying degrees is the fact that in the face of Mill's failure to adequately or convincingly explain the grounds for our interfering with an individual's putative 'other-regarding' actions, we are left with the principle of utility. And in the context of education as an initial example, utility certainly does justify interfering with an individual's actions and restricting that individual's liberty. Whether we examine the consequences of an individual's acts, or consider the moral rules orienting an individual's potential actions, the principle of utility and the interests of the higher intellectual pleasures can be invoked as grounds for collective regulation of the individual. This is particularly so, as T.H. Green and his idealist colleagues argued, and as H.J. McCloskey and C.L. Ten have convincingly shown for the case of Mill, because preventing harm to others is always a relevant consideration.[15] But it is not at all clear, from Mill's argument, at what point this utilitarian set of interests becomes what Cowling called 'moral indoctrination' or what others have criticized as Mill's authoritarianism.

One dominant shortcoming with Mill's encouragement of virtue, which Cowling has most forcefully explained, remains the question of authority in moral decisions – especially as they affect political and social actions. In the context of Mill's scheme, in which the minimal state serves the interests of civil society and the latter has control of education, Mill's criteria grounded in utility do not necessarily promote a uniform code of values. Rationality may suit the intellectual elite in charge of education, but wealth, character, and social status more often come into play with the social elite who, for better or worse, usually comprise the pool from which political leaders are selected. Societies as complex as those in our world today diverge significantly from the libertarian model that Mill advocated in his day, and thus our willingness to recognize and accept authority tends to reflect multiple and potentially exclusive values and utilities.[16]

Mill's readers, then, from among his contemporaries through today, have continued to fault him for his indifference to individual commitment and his underestimation of personal conviction. However much we might agree with Mill on the superiority of the intellectual pleasures, personal commitments and convictions within moral, religious, or political systems are not necessarily open to rational questioning, for at least two reasons. First, such convictions are not necessarily abstract matters but responses to specific and historical circumstances; accordingly, some individuals cannot be appealed to on the basis of reason, and we might pause at the point of hindering the sense of moral duty that comes from such an individual's commitment.[17] Cowling cast doubt on the rational basis of liberal motives when he asked provocatively, 'Do societies generally become free because the best minds have altruistically advocated that they should be? Or do they become free because selfish men try selfishly to preserve their interests? Have the consequences of the best men and the noblest doctrines always been what they should have been?'[18] That is, we cannot be certain in relating superior reason and selfish blindness as cause or consequence in Mill's vision, and the point is especially apt in light of his interest not in institutional but in personal reform. Cowling reminds us that free institutions are not necessary; they may be useful in promoting diversity and innovation among civilized peoples, but with uncivilized peoples, they are utterly inappropriate.[19] If Mill once endorsed obedience as a first lesson of civilization, it remains difficult to tell if the rational self-interest evident in obedience follows from an agreement among citizens or the simple threat of sanctions.[20]

A second reason convictions may not be open to rational question has to do with the superior abilities of the intellectuals who encourage the work of questioning. R.W. Church, a contemporary of Mill who shared a similar elite outlook, pointed out in 1860 that intelligent and reasoning people will make their judgements, but social opinions matter to 'common people' who do not have time for thought, or whose thought is occupied by more pressing matters of livelihood, and who take much for granted, including truth. Mill's defence of liberty is appropriate for those with powers of mind but not for those of average capability – whom Church described as 'those whose independent reason and judgment will not serve them to find their place in the world.'[21] Church concluded that the underlying problem with *On Liberty* was that Mill had failed to differentiate adequately between society and the individual, particularly since the project of education that Mill endorsed was precisely the case of society choosing to mould character in a certain way. Since we do not want mediocrities forcing their faint individuality on the superior intellects in society, Church endorsed a more authoritarian measure than Mill: it would be entirely appropriate for those committed to the higher intellectual pleasures to take the lead in maintaining society.[22] Otherwise, added their contemporary R.H. Hutton in a prescient remark, the public opinion that encourages social indifference – because it accepts any and every position – may very well promote not individual vitality but a lacklustre 'liberty of indifference.'[23]

It seems that Mill's encouragement of virtue leaves us at best with the strong theory of education enunciated in *On Liberty*: it would be reasonable to force parents – with state sanction – to turn their children over to the intellectual elite for instruction in the higher pleasures and the cultivation of character. In time, presumably, these superior values will find expression in the political elite and socio-political institutions. But Mill nonetheless warns against a centralized educational system, which he finds dangerous because it can turn education into moral instruction used to define 'the good' and to produce a uniform system that potentially contributes to the despotism of custom.[24] A tyranny of virtue may well invite a tyranny of the majority. At the least, Mill had observed well before writing *On Liberty*, a good society must achieve some degree of stability characterized by (a) its system of education, (b) a strong measure of loyalty or allegiance to something – to God, the rule of law, a person – and (c) cohesive interests characterized perhaps by values that are permanent.[25] The work that united everyone – Mill, his supporters, and his critics – was thus to carry on with education in the hope of some future improved social order.

But this question of proceeding from education to a good society neglected the very real problem, from the Chinese and Japanese point of view, of social disorder that Mill does not imagine in *On Liberty*. To many Japanese and Chinese elites, external threats and internal divisions gave precedence to the more pressing issues of social disunity and national weakness, and accordingly, attempts to educate one or another citizenry invited a variety of tyrannies over individual liberty. As we will see, a state education system in Japan took over tutelage of the people and produced what Mill would have denigrated as a despotism of custom. Persons who had supported a project of middle-class liberalism and civil society acquiesced in the government's urgent claims of national interest; and so men such as Fukuzawa Yukichi, who emphasized the development of a new class of capitalist entrepreneurs, or Niijima Jō, who fostered the growth of an independent and moral citizenry (as well as Christianity), modified instruction at their private academies in order to accommodate the government's growing domination. In China, by contrast, even the restriction of freedom to those who demonstrated the prerequisite moral standing – as Yan Fu had presented Mill – did not garner appeal for Mill's liberalism among the educated elite. To be sure, like Yan, Chinese political activists imagined educational programs that would transform the Chinese people, but they were also well aware that liberalism had provided motivation for those very Western societies involved in colonial projects the world over, particularly in China. When they visited the West, they saw the bourgeois oppression of labour, the degradations of slavery and racism, and the hypocrisy of political theories and institutions. To them it seemed that both society and individuals in the nineteenth century were greatly in need of education and reform – all the more reason to concentrate on the slow work of educating the free but foolish, particularly in light of the repeated triumphs of bourgeois and corporate self-interest. Chinese activists consequently turned their attention to the prevention of tyranny at home, insisting that freedom be subordinated to equality and that all persons equally commit themselves to the constitution's laws. These East Asian interpretations of Mill provided an occasion for scrutinizing the principle of individual liberty for the elite and the necessity of public virtue for all.

Public Virtue and the Priority of Common Interests

In both Japan and China, Mill's *On Liberty* was translated at a time of political change and social transformation: the Tokugawa shogunate had been overthrown in 1867 and a new Meiji regime announced in Japan; the Manchu Qing empire in China was in disarray; and in the face of Western imperialism, the survival of the Chinese and Japanese nations was in doubt. In this milieu, Mill's argument was received with a greater appreciation for the criteria that defined a stable society, noted above – systematic education, collective allegiance, and common interests. A great many reformers in Japan and China elevated public-mindedness and public virtue above and beyond individual liberty; while they understood the need for the latter, they faulted their own societies for having been so lacking in public morality. Nakamura Keiu's fellow educator and moralist Nishimura Shigeki insisted that Japan had no collective morality, only a number of philosophies and religions that were specific to classes in Japan, including this-worldly teachings such as Confucianism and *bushidō* (a samurai code of ethics) for the upper classes, and other-worldly religions such as Buddhism for the lower classes. The newly imported religion of Christianity and other Western philosophies, too, were partial for their appeal to specific minorities of Japanese.[26] Nishimura's goal during the 1880s and '90s was to forge a new Japanese morality for the new imperial state. Like the work of his Chinese counterparts, Confucianism provided the point of departure.

If Nishimura surprises us for his assertion that traditional Japan had no common morality, the point was reiterated by Yan Fu's contemporary and fellow reformer, Liang Qichao. Liang argued that traditional China had no public morality, by which he meant that when he examined the foundational principle of Confucian ethics, the 'five bonds,' he judged the ethical teaching promoted by this principle paltry in comparison with Western ethics, on which was based the system of ethics that Nishimura and other Japanese of the Meiji period were in the process of constructing. Western and now Japanese ethics linked personal ethics to the three branches of family ethics, social ethics, and state ethics.[27] Confucianism's 'five bonds,' by contrast, comprised little that corresponded to each: family ethics was represented by the father-son, husband-wife, and elder brother–younger brother bonds; China's social ethics noted only the friend-friend bond; and its state ethics consisted of only the ruler-subject bond. All five of these bonds were hierarchical relations in which the subordinate gave his or her loyalty and duty to the superior, who in turn was obliged to render his benevolence to those below. Hence, Liang argued, the ethical system of Confucianism concerned only individual conduct and hierarchical relations among individuals. The reform of political and social institutions required the creation of a new and expressly public morality that would encourage a broad cohesiveness among China's new citizens and would promote the collective interests of all.[28] In Japan, that new public morality was constructed in a hierarchical fashion, with personal conscience increasingly subordinated to a public sphere defined by imperial government priorities, while in China, reformers and revolutionaries proposed the construction of an egalitarian state and a regime of public virtue, the success of which would depend on the social education and reconstruction of the people.

The Japanese State and Its Subjects

Concerns over the lack of public virtue during the first decades of Meiji rule in Japan were voiced by members of the self-appointed oligarchy and its supporters among the intelligentsia. As I have argued elsewhere, the pragmatic construction of the Japanese state in response to external aggression served eventually as a pretext to organize the people and to subordinate the public sphere to the official interests of the government. Mill's liberal vision, tempered at the outset by Nakamura Keiu, fell further in disesteem. As the state took precedence before individuals and citizens were reduced to subjects, adherence to public morality came to dominate personal liberty.[29]

We can identify three developments that prompted concern over public virtue among Japanese leaders. First, the demise of the Tokugawa shogunate and, in particular, its institutions that fostered social hierarchy and segregation left a void quickly filled with a chaos of people in motion. Where the Tokugawa order of territorial domains had attached all subjects of each domain to that place and had impeded movement between domains, and the Tokugawa status system had ideally prescribed all habits of daily life for all members of each status

group, the new Meiji order allowed all Japanese the freedoms of movement, occupation, and domicile, with the result that traditional local
control of subjects was gradually removed. People from different
regions and different status groups moved and intermingled, with no
settled rules to guide their behaviour and no fixed authorities who
could command their deference and imitation as a means to establish
new patterns. Of course, the Meiji state maintained some continuity
with Tokugawa leadership and policing functions in towns and rural
villages – representatives of the state still possessed the legitimate force
to command obedience to law – but in terms of the long-standing Confucian notion of an internal basis for moral behaviour, Japanese society
had lost its bearings, and many former samurai among the new ruling
class regretted the absence of a national code for good behaviour. As
Nishimura Shigeki lamented in 1875, Confucianism was in decline, but
nothing had been introduced to replace it.[30]

A second source of concern grew out of political developments after
1874, the year when disaffected members of the ruling oligarchy, who
had broken with their fellows over the decision not to launch a military
expedition against Korea, issued their demand for a national assembly
in order to expand participation in national political decisions. Where
Itagaki Taisuke and his allies began to establish political associations
and to sponsor petition drives in an effort to influence the government,
others such as Saigō Takamori fomented rebellion among frustrated
former samurai. Although the oligarchy managed to suppress both
movements, many Japanese leaders were dismayed by this growth of
destabilizing activity. Selfish and wilful dissent was on the increase
and repeatedly threatened to disrupt the work of the new government.
Worse, this bad behaviour was arguably motivated by the Western
political theory of liberalism, which encouraged the dissidents' demand for participation in government. In response, some leaders con-
tended that Japan needed a new unifying ethics to guide behaviour as
the new state was constructed.

The third development that gave cause for concern was in fact the
overall policy directly fostered by the Meiji state: a comprehensive
Westernization. The Tokugawa order had been overthrown to introduce Western social, political, and economic forms; the oligarchy and
its allies in the intelligentsia encouraged this set of changes, but, as
some noted, with the turn to Western learning and the new emphasis
on science, technology, property, and business, morality had been
overlooked. Nishimura and his colleagues feared that if attention were

not paid to creating a Japanese moral code for Japan, Christianity might fill the gap. Some Japanese intellectuals such as Nakamura Keiu and Tokutomi Sohō argued that since Western civilization and presumably all its attributes were based on Christianity, it behooved Japan to adopt Christianity. To counter such an argument, Nishimura, Sakatani Shiroshi, and other concerned moralists undertook the production of ethics textbooks and the creation of ethics associations to foster a new morality for Japan. Because this project was conceived in a time of crisis, as foreign threats to Japan loomed on all sides, it privileged the position of the state, and after 1890, when the constitutional monarchy was formally installed, it centred on the emperor as the defining element of Japan's unique body politic.[31]

In sum, as the Japanese oligarchy and its allies among intellectuals and educators contemplated the liberal project introduced through the translations of Mill, Herbert Spencer, and others in the 1870s and '80s, they did so with a strong apprehension of the disorder produced in the wake of the overthrow of the Tokugawa regime and then by the popular agitation for political participation. Hence the 'strong' version of Mill's liberal theory suited them: it was entirely appropriate that the ruling elite manage government as it undertook the tutelage of the lower classes. In every public debate over liberties in the 1870s, from the freedom of religion to the liberty of the press, Japan's oligarchy and its supporters reasoned that the maintenance of public order justified public restrictions on individual liberty. A person might be free to personally believe whatever religion he chose, but public worship was rightly limited by the government. The Meiji regime decreed a progressive series of laws restricting the press, the publishing industry, public assemblies, membership in political associations, and so on – all in the name of public order. And it insisted on a policy of gradualism: personal liberties and political participation would be introduced only as the masses were tutored in the appropriate behaviour prerequisite to the granting of those privileges.[32]

As a contribution to that larger project of tutoring the people in preparation for representative government, members of the Meiji intelligentsia promoted ethics textbooks and ethics associations. Their goal was defined as both 'moral training' and the cultivation of 'national character.' The former was expressed as *shūshin*, 'rectifying the self,' or *dōtoku*, 'cultivating the path of virtue' (now the standard translation word for 'morality'), and these referred to an ideal of proper behaviour defined by an accepted public standard and taught by parents, teachers, and other social superiors. The latter, national character, denoted the virtues specific to the Japanese people and invited the consideration of national virtues that defined familial, social, and political roles inherited from the past – despite the overthrow of the authoritarian Tokugawa regime and the Meiji intelligentsia's initial denunciation of the thoughtless subservience that the Tokugawa shoguns had fostered among the people.[33]

It is striking that Japanese moralists immediately perceived the problem of creating a new national morality as a problem of education: the instruction of Japanese youth by means of an institutional apparatus that would be created and managed by the state. Thus, it is important to note that the development of a national morality coincided with the creation of private academies and a national school system that were intended to provide the rudiments of a Westernized education. In Japan, theories of morality received practical feedback and revision as they were implemented in the classrooms of nascent institutions. Unlike the work of Chinese political and moral theorists in the late nineteenth century, Japanese approaches to constructing a new national morality were not only theoretical but were undertaken as a practical component of a new system of national education.

We can distinguish three primary phases in the development of programs of moral training in late-nineteenth-century Japan. Initially, in the 1870s, moral education was broadly conceived as an effort to encourage those virtues conducive to Westernization and, in turn, Japan's wealth and strength. Japanese educators imported and translated what they believed were key guides to the apparent successes of the West. The two most influential of these texts were Samuel Smiles's *Self-Help*, translated by Nakamura Keiu in 1870, and Francis Wayland's *Elements of Moral Science*, which appeared in several partial translations, including an official version by the Ministry of Education in 1874. These were in fact the most widely read examples, respectively, of Anglo-American success manuals and moral philosophy texts, and they were intended for the development of character in young men, by stressing a combination of virtues appropriate for 'being good' and 'doing well' in modern entrepreneurial society.[34] Smiles stressed honesty, industry, and frugality, as well as self-discipline and self-control; Wayland emphasized veracity, chastity, and duty, suffused in an overall love of God and submission to his scriptural revelations. These and other such moral texts were widely used in a variety of public and especially private schools by former samurai educators, who not only found these values compatible with those of their own samurai upbringing – loyalty, duty, and self-control – but were also convinced by Smiles's argument that character is capital: the cultivation of virtue would be rewarded in business dealings as worldly success. Greed, extravagance, and dissolute behaviour would bring ruin.

But in the minds of some educators, these foreign texts for moral training suffered two major shortcomings. First, they were explicitly individualistic. They presented morality as a matter of individual cultivation, and no social network intervened to standardize values and to homogenize social behaviour. Although these texts in their indigenous environments largely promoted a Victorian middle-class set of virtues intended to raise the consciousnesses of working-class and farming men, in Japan they potentially exacerbated the confusion occasioned by revolutionary change. There was no national component to the values that these texts espoused: indeed, one could conclude that given the individualist perspective on the social contract that these texts asserted, they undermined the social and national context of moral behaviour by emphasizing the individual before all. Hence, they seemed to contribute to the chaos afflicting Japanese society in the 1870s. A second major drawback was the fact that many of the foreign texts were explicitly Christian. Wayland, for example, grounded all aspects of human moral behaviour in a Protestant interpretation of the Bible – from man's innate moral sense and his natural liberty to his right to property and his assent to the social contract – and this orientation gave pause to many Japanese educators. To ground moral behaviour in a foreign religion was to encourage the dissolution of Japanese society, for Japanese converts to Christianity turned away from domestic authorities to the authority of foreign missionaries in Japan and foreign churches overseas. Such a moral program promoted not social unity but greater dislocation and disorder.

As a solution to the persisting absence of a national morality, Nishimura Shigeki sponsored the creation of a national ethics association in 1876, the Tokyo Society for Moral Education, which was renamed and its operations expanded in 1887 as the Japanese Society for Extending Morality, an organization still in operation today. It undertook a range of activities – including public lectures and discussions, the writing and translating of moral pamphlets and treatises, and frequent public meetings – as an effort to encourage Japanese society to develop virtuous customs and to achieve a moral unity.[35] In conjunction with this work, Nishimura also compiled the first new, comprehensive, and official ethics textbook for the Ministry of Education in 1880, *Shōgaku shūshin kun* (Lessons in moral training for elementary education), which was designed for use in Japan's new system of elementary schools. And he wrote an influential treatise in 1887, *Nihon dōtoku ron* (On Japanese morality), in which he explained and defended these efforts for a systematic and national morality.

This second phase in the development of Japanese programs for moral training was explicitly national.[36] Nishimura's goal was a morally united people. In contrast to the fundamental values proposed by other educators – say, Fukuzawa Yukichi's emphasis on personal independence or Nakamura Keiu's emphasis on Christian duty – Nishimura argued that morality was the basis of the people's interests. And in contrast to the advocates of political participation, who insisted that a new ethics would be created out of the public cooperation of free individuals, Nishimura advocated not political society but a moral society of the national people.[37]

In many respects, Nishimura's project represents a Confucian reaction to conditions in 1870s Japan, but his was not simply a conservative project, for it was not limited to Confucianism.[38] The Meiji revolution had overturned values in Japan: 'knowledge and technique are honored while good behaviour and sincerity are left behind; law is substituted for morality; integrity is slandered as an impoverishment; and gradually grows the habit of valuing greed and unruliness as signs of wealth and nobility.'[39] Nishimura responded to this situation with terminology familiar from Confucianism: what the nation requires is the cultivation of filial children, loyal subjects, and faithful wives; friendly elder brothers and agreeable younger brothers; virtuous officials and good farmers, craftsmen, and merchants.[40] Although his language recalls Tokugawa ruling-class proposals for the moral reform of society, from its officials to its lower orders, his textbook of 1880 is an eclectic mix of several guides to moral training. He acknowledged four sources for morality: Confucianism, the moral teachings of Shintō, the binding duty of subject to sovereign, and Western ethics.[41] Accordingly, *Shōgaku shūshin kun* includes a variety of maxims, excerpted from Chinese, Western, and Japanese sources. The section on cultivating virtue, for example, includes Chinese classics like the Confucian *Analects* and the *Mencius*; Western texts like the Wisdom of Solomon and Samuel Smiles's *Self-Help*; and Japanese ethics texts from the Tokugawa past, such as *Onna daigaku* (Great learning for women) and *Yamato zokkun* (Lessons in Japanese custom). With the guidance of a teacher, students would move from maxims that encouraged the internalizing of loyalty, sincerity, and the other Confucian virtues to, for example, Smiles's pronouncement that moral behaviour is based in a heart that respects heaven and cherishes humankind, and thus the cultivation of moral behaviour is not for the self alone but for the amelioration of present social customs.[42]

The most striking point that recurs in Nishimura's many writings on morality is his unflagging insistence that morality is not religion. He took pains to differentiate morality and religion in order to guarantee that moral education remain an utterly secular enterprise. Because he believed that Western civilization was founded on Christianity, his insistence on a moral project free of religion served to differentiate Japan and the West in order to safeguard a Japanese space that authorized an indigenous Japanese civilization and the construction of its own morality. But he also wanted morality free from religion in order to forestall the influence of those who advocated the reconstruction of the Japanese imperial cult, Shintō, as a national religion for Japan. Religion of any variety was inappropriate as a basis for morality, because it too often provoked doctrinal disputes, sectarian rivalries, and general disorder; moreover, religion concerned spirits, superstitions, and irrationality, and thus did not accord with contemporary efforts at national construction. A secular morality provided a superior training, because it was based on a 'way' – a path and comprehensive program – that offered an actual practice for the people to follow. Nishimura seriously considered Comte's efforts to forge a new morality on the basis of philosophy, even if it took the form of a religion of humanity – in fact, Comte's work was one of the translation projects undertaken by the Japanese Society for Extending Morality – but he concluded that philosophy, too, was an inappropriate basis for morality. Like religion, philosophy was divided by rival schools whose contentiousness obscured potential principles of morality, and perhaps worse, Western philosophy – unlike Confucianism – offered no techniques for managing the human heart and its unruly passions.[43]

Nishimura thus rejected Mill's visions of both liberal society and a regime of virtue based on a set of values amenable to philosophical principles like utility and rationality. Rather, moral unity was fundamental to social order and was to be constructed from values consonant with national history and national character. A secular morality for Japan should be grounded in the principles of Confucianism and embrace the best of national values, and Nishimura's description of a moral project for Japan gravitated toward more rather than fewer key principles. The creed of the Japanese Society for Extending Morality was a lengthy list of exhortations invoking ten pairs of virtues: (1) intensify loyalty and filiality, and respect the gods; (2) honour the imperial house, and cherish the nation; (3) obey the nation's laws, and heed the nation's interests; (4) pursue learning with diligence, and train a strong body with exercise; (5) work hard at household enterprise, and maintain frugality; (6) be harmonious in the family, and assist one's fellows in the village; (7) maintain trust and rightness, and follow goodness; (8) never harm others, and never pursue immoral profits; (9) do not be weakened by liquor and fornication, and do not be polluted by wicked habits; and (10) be free to believe religion, but do not believe a religion that would harm the nation.[44] With this set of moral commands, Nishimura and his group worked to contain religion – reiterating Confucius's dictum to honour the gods but keep them at a distance – in order to focus on moral behaviour as it concerns oneself, one's family, one's community, and the pre-eminent nation.

The promulgation of the Japanese Constitution in 1889 and the Imperial Rescript on Education in 1890 invited a third phase of programs for a Japanese moral code.[45] The Constitution and especially the Imperial Rescript emphasized, as the basis of education and the morality of imperial subjects, the two principles of the emperor and the *kokutai*, Japan's unique 'body politic' defined by the imperial house and its descendence from the sun goddess Amaterasu. Although Nishimura supported these pronouncements, he preferred to interpret their principles in a secular fashion. The emperor and the body politic were the groundings of national morality and national history, and justified the moral principles of honouring the emperor and loving the nation. Nishimura minimized the political consequences of the Constitution and the Imperial Rescript, insisting that moral education was a project independent of political institutions, and he downplayed their religious significance in the context of Shintō, insisting that the imperial household was a historic and secular foundation for Japanese moral education – unlike the West with its moral basis in Christianity.[46]

But he noted with some ambivalence that the new official developments did in fact link the imperial house, the body politic, and the Meiji government into a stable configuration. This point was underscored by the intellectual historian and moral philosopher Inoue Tetsujirō, who supplied the official interpretation of the Imperial Rescript in 1891.[47] Inoue's approach to moral education was informed by two significant developments. In the first place, his study of philosophical idealism encouraged the situation of Japanese morality within a universal scheme of ethics. In his initial major work, *Rinri shinsetsu* (A new theory of ethics), which impressively synthesized the field of European ethics, Inoue painstakingly distinguished ethics (*rinri*) from morality (*dōtoku*) in order to identify ethics as the philosophical and universal basis of morality. Where ethics could be explained in terms of natural law, morality provided particular standards of good and bad behaviour for historical communities. Like Nishimura, he deemed religion an inappropriate basis for morality, but unlike Nishimura, he was committed to philosophy as the proper basis for morality.[48] That is because, unlike Nishimura, who understood philosophy as a collection of contending schools, Inoue regarded philosophy as an intellectual approach. Thus, his life work was to construct a new and progressive system of morality for Japan, which would both actualize the universal ideals of ethics and demonstrate the superiority of the particular ethos informing Japanese moral development.[49]

In the second place, Inoue was writing at a time of increased tensions with the foreign powers and domestic hostility to Christianity. A draft of the new civil code of law had been released in 1890, and although it was meant to assure the European powers that Japan had attained a significant measure of civility, it provoked acrimonious debate because it granted legal status to the traditional patriarchal form of the Japanese family. And an acceptable measure of civility perceived in Japan's civil code was prerequisite to European willingness to revise the unequal treaties that they had negotiated with Japan under the previous Tokugawa government. Inoue's irritability over foreign interference in Japan's affairs therefore coincided with the celebrated case of lèse-majesté on the part of Uchimura Kanzō in 1891. Uchimura, a Christian educator, had merely inclined his head toward the emperor's portrait at a school ceremony rather than offering the deep bow that many believed was the appropriate behaviour endorsed by the Imperial Rescript. Inoue's reaction was a vigorous and sustained denunciation of Christianity.[50]

Thus Inoue's contribution to the moral education of Japanese subjects sought to endorse a set of values that were specific to the Japanese nation and body politic and, at the same time, that were distinct from foreign moral theories and Christianity in particular. Inoue acknowledged in his autobiography that, at the time, the turmoil within the family system was the primary defect hindering the moral development of Japanese subjects.[51] The ill effects of industrialization, which created wage labourers from farming families and promoted cash as a new cause for mobility, were eroding Japanese families. Inoue's solution in his *Chokugo engi* (Explication of the Imperial Rescript) was to reinforce the family system by a return to four Confucian values prominent during the Tokugawa period: filiality, reverence toward superiors, loyalty, and sincerity. Moreover, the entire nation would be modelled on the family, with the emperor taking the parental role and his subjects the roles of children; this granted to both the emperor and the Japanese state the devotion of their subjects. Relations among subjects were to encourage the attitude of 'widespread affection' or 'philanthropy' (*hakuai*), which would ideally oppose selfishness and egotistic utilitarianism and encourage each person to work for the benefit of others. The consequent unity of the people's hearts would be reinforced by another prominent and fundamental value, patriotism, which Inoue endorsed both as a measure of national defence, in that patriotic Japanese subjects would fight to defend the nation, and as a measure of national conservation, in that patriotism would guard against unpremeditated changes to the body politic. As Inoue contemplated the prospect of representative government, he imagined that morality and law worked in an integrated fashion: morality served as the primary internal support for good behaviour, and law served as the primary external condition on behaviour.[52]

At the same time, Inoue utterly negated the moral vision of Nakamura Keiu and other Christians with his trenchant attack on Christianity. He argued in *Kyōiku to shūkyō no shōtotsu* (The clash between education and religion) that Christianity was essentially the antithesis of Japanese moral education: Christianity was opposed to the status of the imperial household and the continuation of Japan's body politic; it was opposed to the fundamental virtues of filiality and loyalty; it undermined patriotism; and it detracted from the goals of Japan's national progress toward wealth and strength. Moreover, Inoue insinuated that faith in Christianity was treasonous when he asserted that Christians harm Japan's body politic and oppose social peace and order because their faith places them outside the spirit of the nation. The moral education of Japanese subjects necessitated the exclusion of Christianity.[53] Indeed, with efforts to formalize 'Japanese morality' in the 1890s in such a way as to accommodate the new imperial polity, the inner space of personal freedom of conscience began to erode, and morality increasingly assumed an exclusively public nature.

By the middle of the 1890s, the liberal and universal possibilities imagined by Mill and his translator Nakamura had been largely foreclosed in Japan, for the oligarchy had opted for a regime of virtue that was aggressively authoritarian and proud of its particularity.[54] Having spurned the theory of civil society and turned instead to German theories of *Rechtsstaat* ('legal state') and *soziale Recht* ('social right'), Japanese intellectuals came to see the state as a self-justifying entity, sufficient in itself and prior to its constituent subjects. In adapting German theory, Japanese advocates claimed that state sovereignty was based legally in the Constitution and that individual rights are bestowed by the state; it was not that the citizen was 'free from the state' but 'free in the state.' Accordingly, they minimized the liberal impulse in the German model, which conferred self-government on local bodies of government according to the laws of the state.[55] Thus, the Meiji state, as an incarnation of Japan's unique body politic, became a means to advance the goals of the emperor and his officials; public virtue was made to serve the state.[56]

The Reconstruction of the Chinese People

In contrast to the construction of moral programs in tandem with state institutions in Japan, the situation in China was quite different at the time that Mill's *On Liberty* was introduced and discussions of public virtue ensued. The empire was in decline, having suffered several crises of legitimacy: the Sino-Japanese War of 1894–95, which ended with a humiliating loss to Japan; the debacle of the 1898 reform proposals, which finished with the Empress Dowager's palace coup against the Guangxu Emperor; and the disastrous Boxer Rebellion in 1900, which saw a foreign occupation of Beijing. Revolutionary groups were organizing against the imperial government, several of which joined together in 1905 as the United Alliance, whose most celebrated leader was Sun Yatsen. Thus the perceived need for public morality among Chinese scholars remained a largely theoretical component of programs for change; although most were interested in the institutional form of the state, they gave perhaps more attention to the state of the Chinese people. Public morality was embedded within the problem of the people and their political reconstruction.

As was described in the preceding chapter, Yan Fu mapped individual liberty onto a traditional understanding of personal moral autonomy. Other Chinese scholars would do the same. In the terminology typical of the neo-Confucianism more properly called 'the study of the way,' Yan emphasized the practice of 'following the way' by means of 'cultivating the human heart.' He explained this expressly as not an egotistical practice – one undertaken for the sake of personal goals – but one pursued out of consideration for others and their interests, with a mind to fostering harmony between the self and others.[57] Some of Yan's reform-minded contemporaries developed an understanding of ethics – in the effort to accommodate Western political thought – that more explicitly borrowed the inner-outer duality characteristic of the Confucian study of the way. Liu Shipei, for example, a prominent reform intellectual and anti-Manchu revolutionary who later turned to anarchism, described Chinese traditional moral development as composed of the inner cultivation of the person, which resulted in personal moral character, and the external development of social relations and institutions. Liu proposed an 'ethics of the self' that rendered this formulation compatible with a simplified version of Western ethical patterns: moral development of the Chinese citizen would undertake an inner project of self-realization in the Chinese manner in combination with the external project of developing individual autonomy, or liberty, as in the West.[58] Liu's interpretation of the relation between liberty and morality is similar to those of both Yan Fu and Nakamura Keiu, in that he too subordinates external liberty to internal moral development, thus straying from most representations of liberalism.

Similarly, Liang Qichao proposed a number of approaches to self-cultivation, invariably in the interest of developing a self-mastery that prepared the individual for a reformed social existence in a new Chinese nation. But Liang's particular significance to our argument was his enlistment of ideas familiar in Yan Fu's translation of Mill, which he used to demonstrate the need for a public or collective morality: *qun*, the group, and *gong*, the public. Like Yan, Liang used the concept of *qun* to discuss the human propensity for grouping as the natural basis for a range of social forms. Liang was especially concerned with the political practices of human groups, and grouping served to explicate the key process of integrating people into a political community, the scope of which extended to the nation-state and constitutional government, as defined and legitimized by the central work of political participation. Ideally, grouping signified a collective commitment to a national community.[59]

But in theorizing how best to encourage the moral relations that would bind the group together, both Liang and Liu turned not to the

English liberal notion of interests but to the Chinese concept of *gong*, or public-mindedness, in order to promote their respective programs of 'public virtue' or 'social ethics' (*gongde*). Together, these programs entailed a sequence of developments away from Confucian habits of self-cultivation: they initially promoted public virtue as an antidote to private selfishness and then presented the cultivation of public virtue as a practice superior to self-development. Now, we have earlier encountered *gong* in our discussion of Yan Fu's comments on 'justice,' a term that reflects long-standing connotations of *gong* as 'official' impartiality. (A title of nobility typically translated as 'duke,' *gong* reflects that moment described in chapter 4, when the family-state of ancient China was reconstructed as a more public and impartial regime – hence, its meaning as 'official' or 'imperial.') Liang Qichao's teacher, the renowned reformer Kang Youwei, had expanded the meaning of *gong* beyond its connotations of the Chinese imperial polity to express a universal human arena, so in the work of Liang and Liu *gong* has been interpreted as the ideal degree of public-mindedness that a citizen holds for the new national community. As the citizen's social arena expands beyond his village or county, he arrives at a new consideration for his national group. In thus imagining a public morality linked to the new nation-state, both Liang and Liu first had to detach the concept of virtue in relation to social custom from the enduring association between virtue and cosmic truth (typical in the study of the way). That is, in a move reversing that of Kang Youwei, they downgraded moral universalism to a scale more appropriate to a national public and offered this public virtue as a moral corrective to the private and selfish ego, insisting on an inner transformation that would invite commitments to the new national or public community.[60]

In fact, Liang's treatise of 1902–3, *Xinmin shuo* (On renovating the people), proposed a systematic moral education in both public and private virtue. Education in public virtue would promote activities that both encouraged the individual's recognition of common interests and fostered group cohesion; of particular importance to Liang were cooperation, mutual assistance, and the formation of civic associations. Education in private virtue, by comparison, promoted the moral perfection of the individual and his or her character. In a rather utilitarian fashion, Liang maintained that private virtue was best understood in terms of its serviceability to the collective interests of the group.[61] During his exile in Japan, he increasingly approved of the statist position of the Meiji oligarchy and the collectivist outlook of moral leaders like

Nishimura and Inoue. The collectivity defined by the group took precedence over the individual and his rights or liberties; and Liang began to argue, following his Japanese models, that since the state is the most sovereign body, the collective rights of the citizenry in the state precede the rights of individuals.[62] The personal moral project of inner self-cultivation as prerequisite to external autonomy began to be displaced by the greater importance of public virtue, to which all personal cultivation was beholden. Thus, we can begin to understand the commitment to constitutional monarchy among some reformers, for whom maintaining the imperial institution granted at least some connection to the traditional moral system: in the nationalist and communist phases of the Chinese revolution, the individual's moral authority would be redirected from self-cultivation to the more external grounds for legitimacy, party loyalty and ideological orthodoxy.[63]

Liang Qichao, Liu Shipei, and others of their contemporaries after the turn of the twentieth century – men such as Ma Junwu, who sided with the National People's Party – gradually turned from Mill's liberal conception of society composed of individuals, which treated the individual as the fundamental unit of society, in order to give priority to larger collectivities and the moral relations that could unite them. It is striking that this shift away from individual liberty was marked by two conceptual moves: a turn to a rudimentary populism that problematized the people of the nation-state, who, in their degraded and ignorant condition, were in need of comprehensive renovation; and a rejection of the political institutions of liberalism – especially liberal constitutionalism as the guarantor of individual rights – in favour of political structures that might guarantee an equality of participation among the people.[64]

Liu had always been critical of the Confucian traditions of the five bonds, family ethics, and filial piety and had early on urged programs of broader moral and social commitments and identifications. From his 'ethics of the self' he turned to a theory of 'public ethics,' which stressed public-mindedness as a moral commitment to the social whole and the public good. Under the influence of Mencius, who treated the people as the worldly counterpart of heaven's authority in establishing a sage as king, Liu paired that philosopher's idea of the people as the standard of legitimacy for benevolent rulers with Rousseau's theory of the social contract and the general will, and moved toward populism: the people, in their cohesiveness as the nation, were the appropriate unit of political, social, and moral concern. He began to view the state in a new light, and in the wake of his trip to Japan in 1907 Liu turned to anarchism and rejected liberalism, especially because of its utilitarian individualism, which he faulted for its encouragement of egotism and selfishness. Liu also rejected parliamentary or representative democracy because it was invariably dominated by the wealthy and encouraged a tyranny of the majority.

Liu and his fellow anarchists did not look to Mill's libertarianism for solutions. Contrary to the utilitarian theory that self-interest is the basis of public interest, or the related notion that enlightened self-interest leads to the public good, Liu insisted on a commitment to the social whole in such a way as to root out self-interested conduct – a position that would be shared by all of China's anarchist factions. Where Mill had asserted that liberty was prior to equality, on the basis of the principle of utility – as only free individuals can develop into equal individuals – Liu and his fellow anarchists would reverse the order: equality must preceed liberty, because only equal individuals could become free.[65] To be sure, Mill would subsequently, in 'Utilitarianism,' undertake to bring justice and equitability into his description. If there is a general utility in maintaining justice – which Mill defined in terms of moral and legal rights – it behooves society to protect our individual rights, one of which is a right to impartial and equal treatment. 'Utilitarianism' can be read as subordinating liberty and equality to the principle of justice. But as John Gray has noted, in this revised description of Mill's liberal project, there are still no resources for protecting equity in the distribution of liberty. Some will have more latitude than others.[66]

Thus, in Liu's anarchist vision, liberty was pre-empted by equality, for the first step was to eliminate the oppression of the lower classes by granting their equality with the rich and powerful. Liu and his comrades began to propose anarchist revolution and employed the concept of public virtue as a theory of moral education, which would serve as the means to cultural or social revolution. As one scholar has put the issue: 'The task of social ... revolution was to peel off layers of accumulated oppression to reveal the human core within, and to create the social conditions that would enable humanity to realize its "natural" propensity to cooperation.'[67] To assist in that transformation – even if it was represented as an idyllic return to some natural state – moral education offered not only truth and public-mindedness, and reciprocal love and equality, but also science, practical skills for modern industry, and the ability for self-government.[68] As with T.H. Green and the British idealists, nature is harmonious. Nonetheless, lest the moral elite subvert the equality of all the people and create new social inequalities by formally prolonging their leadership, Liu encouraged institutional safeguards to ensure the maintenance of equal conditions of labour, as well as its responsibilities and rewards.[69]

Liang Qichao, who considered the revolutionary arguments of Sun Yatsen as they crossed paths in exile in Japan, remained a reformer and nationalist in the decade of the 1900s. He too eventually reformulated his plans for public morality with a political veneer encompassing the people and, in accord with his convictions regarding the prior claims of the collectivity, the importance of the democratic participation of the people. His commitment to constitutionalism grew not in support of the liberal constitution – which serves as a legal guarantor of civil liberties – but in favour of a constitution from the point of view of the people. For Liang, the problem was how to structure a constitutional government that would ensure the people's participation. In a manner similar to Yan Fu's translation of Mill, liberty was pre-empted by self-mastery; Liang insisted that moral self-restraint and a proper perspective of one's social being and obligations to the group were prerequisite to liberty. He rejected liberalism and its utilitarian individualism for the same reasons that had appealed to the Japanese in their adaptation of the theory of the *Rechtsstaat*: the people's collective rights in the state precede individual rights and liberties, because only state sovereignty guarantees the individual's existence and his or her rights and liberties. Like Liu Shipei, Liang perceived that liberalism produced societies and governments dominated by the rich; thus, key to his understanding of liberty are the equal rights and liberties of the common people, who must be transformed into an educated citizenry to qualify for participation in the affairs of the state.[70] The state provided education for the people, and its constitution and laws guaranteed the equality of their participation.

Moral education and the cultivation of public virtue thereby took precedence over liberty in Chinese political thought in the 1900s, from the so-called left wing represented by anarchism to the so-called right wing represented by reformers sympathetic to some combination of Confucianism and Westernization. The problem, which would linger on into both the nationalist and communist phases of the Chinese revolution, remains the profound tension between the self as a moral individual and the self as a citizen with public duties and responsibilities. In China, as in Japan, the reformative and revolutionary reconstruction of the old society proceeded through the stimulation of national consciousness because in the face of Western imperialism the survival of the nation was at stake. But nationalism necessarily made a problem of the relationship between individual and society. As Arif Dirlik has so aptly explained,

> [The] reconstitution of China as a nation presupposed the reconstitution of the subjects of the Confucian order as citizens who were the ultimate source of political legitimacy and whose active participation in politics was essential to the creation of a new national order ... Everyone, not just the ruler or the ruling class, was equally obliged under the circumstances to cultivate the public morality that was the essential condition of a cohesive national community. At the same time, however, the possibility of public morality was even more of a predicament for nationalist discourse than it had been for the Confucian, because of its recognition of, or demand for, the individual as citizen – as the autonomous source of public values. The question for nationalist discourse was not whether Chinese should be transformed from subjects into citizens, but how soon they could be expected to make the transformation.[71]

In the name of renovating the people and taking their collective interests as the primary political criterion, the Chinese revolution pursued a national agenda that dispensed with Mill's liberalism. One cannot stress enough that the theoretical bases for this movement included the work of both conservative and radical intellectuals. Liang Qichao was willing to entertain a homology relating individual and society – that self-rule in a state develops from the self-rule of individuals, or again, that the individual is like a nation in its being the recipient of favour and responding in terms of duty – but he was committed to collective goals and the public duty of each to respect and support those public goals.[72] Where Liu Shipei looked to the moral authority of the revolutionary vanguard and urged the elite to institutionally limit their propensity to command power, Liang emphasized law and the creation of a constitution to which all would pledge themselves. The constitution and law formalized morality, for the benefit of a group; and such a self-governed group is like an army in which the leader is law – law made by all the group rather than just one man.[73] But much as Yan Fu had imagined with his 'heroic luminaries' and Mill with his educational elite and their higher intellectual pleasures, Liang, Liu, and their contemporaries imagined that the instigation and leadership for change and development would come from a set of moral heroes whose authority in moral decisions would be apparent to the people, who would welcome these moral heroes into positions of political authority.[74]

Ultimately, however, the path taken by China's revolution, under the leadership of Sun Yatsen and the National People's Party, resembled that of Japan. Although Sun early on advocated, in a fashion not unlike Liang or the anarchists, the creation of a good and moral society through a national transformation of society's customs, values, thinking, and structures, he was always interested less in culture and ideas and more in institutional structures. Moral values received his attention only late in his pronouncements on nationalism.[75] Sun's 'Three Principles of the People' (nationalism, democracy, and the people's livelihood), articulated in several revised forms between 1905 and 1924, focused on the gradual introduction of institutions of constitutional government and programs of socio-economic reform, which eventually included socialist plans for land redistribution and some public ownership of at least transportation and communications facilities. Sun wanted to ensure that China would never be subject to a capitalist dictatorship as in the United States and Europe. He was not opposed to capitalism; he understood well how capitalism and private entrepreneurialism encouraged industrial development. But he insisted that political power and capital had to be balanced in the national interest.[76]

As in Japan, Sun – and especially his successor, Jiang Jieshi (Kaishek) – came to emphasize the national point of view. Where, in 1905, Sun asserted that the people's rights were a goal of the revolution – which meant the establishment of equal rights for all and the abolition of inequality – by 1919 he began to dwell instead on the 'four great people's rights' pertaining to democratic political structure: election, referendum, initiative, and recall.[77] In 1924 he significantly revised the goal of individual rights; both in speaking to the graduates of the national military academy and in delivering his final version of the 'Three Principles,' he insisted that the freedom and equality of the nation had to precede that of the individual, for only a free people can offer freedom to individuals. Sun's new focus was in part a reaction to the persisting imperialism in China and the ill treatment of China at the Versailles Peace Conference, but it was also a deliberate criticism of the anarchists whom he had encountered twenty years earlier and whose selfish concerns and lack of discipline, he believed, had amounted to nothing. If he once agreed with the anarchists that the equal opportunity of all citizens to develop themselves took precedence over liberty in efforts to create a democratic China, he now privileged the position of China within its international context. He criticized Mill's theory of liberty as an endorsement of 'loose sand' – a degree of social disorganization that invited the predatory incursions of imperialist powers into China. Because the Chinese people were as disorganized as loose sand, limits had to be applied to their liberties and rights. Only when the nation could act freely, would China be strong and Chinese individuals have personal freedom. Sun urged his audiences to sacrifice their liberty for the future of the party and the nation: public service might help to equalize inequalities.[78]

At the same time, now at the end of his career, Sun retreated to the traditional morality of traditional learning as a way not only to define and maintain the character of the Chinese people but also to assist the cohesion of the Chinese nation. Traditional values had served Chinese well in the past to make them the superior people that they had been, and Sun advocated renewed attention to loyalty and filiality, kindness and affection, faithfulness and justice, and harmony and peace. These moral standards would restore the status of the Chinese nation, and the cultivation of self-development by dwelling on the classics – as Confucius had advocated – would restore individuals. And personal loyalty, the pre-eminent value, would serve to build the nation in a graduated scheme, from one's loyalty to family, to loyalty to clan, and then loyalty to the nation.[79] In much the same way that Inoue Tetsujirō had invoked traditional values in the service of the new imperial state, so Sun Yatsen encouraged the reconstruction of the Chinese people as a nation by means of traditional values so respectful of traditional hierarchies.

For those of us living in a bourgeois and liberal society, the Japanese and Chinese solutions smack of tyranny and authoritarianism when they favour the subject-citizen and his public morality well above the individual self and his private interests or rights. But such solutions shouldn't alarm us, for the history of bourgeois liberalism is similarly marked by tyranny on the part of an exclusive political class – defined over the past century by landed property owners, industrial entrepreneurs, and corporations. All political orders appear to practice exclusions that invite a propensity to tyranny. In the late nineteenth century, European and East Asian observers noted that liberal political orders typically promoted a tyranny of the wealthy, who excluded the poor and working classes from participation – and the prerequisites of education – and left the governing of the state increasingly to committees of experts operating behind closed doors. Even Yan Fu was committed to a form of exclusivity when he asserted that only the moral self deserves liberty. As was Mill with his principle of tutelage by the educated elite.

That exclusivity invites tyranny is a danger common among the proposals encountered in this book. As noted in chapter 1, the conditions that informed the relocation of Mill's theory of liberty to East Asia were marked by a common outlook on the part of self-conscious individuals that their elite education qualified them for a central role among the political class. They believed in the rightness of their position and were thus committed to a role as tutors of the common people. But they were also aware that social divisions generated by industrial capitalism had accompanied the development of liberal institutions, and accordingly, they proposed moral development as a compensatory educational strategy that might reunify society by means of a common civic morality. T.H. Green and his students certainly believed that a recommitment to public virtue might redeem the alliance of liberalism and capitalism in England. Mill and his critics such as Green, and his East Asian interpreters Nakamura and Yan, offered their projects of self-development as pragmatic models for the people and conditions on the people's political participation. Chinese and Japanese leaders, in contrast, problematized social unity and actively created programs of collective moral development that would assist their efforts to construct new societies.

As this chapter has noted, the threat of tyranny within liberalism is explained in part by the profound tension between liberty and equality. Where the liberal order in England and the United States has allowed social and political inequality at the expense of stability and the public good, the Chinese and Japanese states pursued an equality and a public good that embraced an authoritarian disregard for the individual. But can a state of any kind ever reconcile its need for stability, which people demand, with the desire for a genuine equality? If bourgeois liberal polities have generally chosen liberty, rights, and self-government for the putatively worthy few – and Japan is now among this group – the Chinese revolution pursued for the last half of the twentieth century an alternative vision of some form of equality for the many. But both appeal for their legitimacy to a principle of democracy, defined in practice by elections that are reportedly free and fair for the people who are deemed eligible to vote. And neither the liberal nor the revolutionary position represents Mill's best intentions in *On Liberty*: individuals would do well, first, to cultivate education and the moral values of sympathy, tolerance, and altruism, and second, to participate in the political practice of local self-government and reasoned debate. Both recommendations remain pertinent precautions against modern tyrannies, and both mark the necessity of some renewed commitment to a practice of public citizenship.

Conclusion

In a recent critique of the liberal order long normative in England and the United States, John Gray points to John Stuart Mill as one of the important foundations on which liberalism began to fracture in the nineteenth century. It was Mill's work, particularly *On Liberty*, that started to disengage the liberal project of universal civilization, based on the ideal of rationality, from the more mundane commitment to liberty and diversity, based on the fact of human fallibility. And it is this commitment to liberty and diversity, even as it breaks apart national and local communities, that has become the modus vivendi of contemporary lives and in the name of which toleration and pluralism are jointly advocated. Mill's error, Gray concludes, was to posit a mode of personal development that would lead us all to the same set of higher pleasures.[1]

Indeed, the liberal promise endorsed by Mill and elaborated by T.H. Green left much to good fortune, in the uncertain hope that as personal interests were balanced, goodwill would outweigh selfishness and error. Far from being a rational plan, the liberal promise depended on each individual's capacity for self-realization as a member of a community, and it advocated a system of self-government on the part of those enlightened individuals that would develop the linkage between their exercise of political power and their awareness of a common good. The state that they created would maintain a common good defined legally in terms of personal property and rights. As scholars of Euro-American colonialism have emphasized, the putative universalism of the liberal order was based on a particular form of society – bourgeois capitalism, or what C.B. Macpherson defined as 'possessive market society' – whose anonymous presentation as an abstract and rational form encouraged its partisans to forget that particular social conventions and manners have always informed liberal thought.[2] Moreover, the libertarian state defined by liberalism, one limited to protecting society from harm, was never benign or minimal: it had interests to maintain. The state itself – or control of the state – became a target of interests held by private and corporate factions. As Michel Foucault noted in his important work on governmentality, the notion of self-government allows a political system to map onto itself the power relations within society.[3]

The illusion of the liberal state as the fruition of a rational plan grew out of a misunderstanding of the state that predated Mill. In the sixteenth and seventeenth centuries – in the work of Jean Bodin and Thomas Hobbes, for example – the existence of the state or commonwealth was assumed. It was a received element of the political world into which men were born, and of course it maintained an executive power armed with an administration. By the eighteenth century – in the work of John Locke, Adam Ferguson, and Jean Jacques Rousseau – the state began to be treated as a political construction, a malleable structure built by the consent of civil society from the ground up, with administrative units added in pragmatic fashion as needs for them arose. As the liberal state grew, in reaction to the former view that informed monarchy, and in the hope of emulating the latter view that historically favoured the sovereignty of Parliament, its modus operandi was always – has always been – a project of reform. The liberal state reacts pragmatically to the status quo while at the same time it purports to act according to its ideal description as a construction based on consent.

The distance between these two perceptions of the state, which complicated nineteenth-century efforts at social and political reform, corresponds to a related ambivalence over civil society and its relation to the state – a tension that seemed obvious to some Japanese and Chinese observers in the nineteenth century. On the one hand, as Ernest Gellner has so aptly argued, civil society is an amoral order. It breaks up the 'circle of faith, power and society' in traditional communities, so that the social order becomes instrumental, no longer the guardian or agent of the absolute. Civil society thus dismisses the comfort of a moral order, which provided confidence in our ideas because they were shared by our fellows, and offers instead a functional pragmatic compromise among cosmological and moral verities.[4] The market mechanism works to reduce all values to the terms of the economic market, which mediates all things; and the state, which would theoretically act as neutral arbiter among interests, assumes an instrumental value as an economic object of partisan interests.[5] But on the other hand, civil society and notions of community are always prior to individuals, and hence references to specific cultural norms are inevitable. In Mill's ideal political regime, the higher pleasures that he assumes represent an appropriate set of community norms more important than the individual. As Uday Singh Mehta notes in his compelling assessment of liberalism's complicity with imperialism, 'some conception of community must be presupposed ... as existing prior to the consensual justification of the political community.'[6] Insofar as the liberal state claims to rest on the consent of the governed, the state necessarily reflects the values of civil society as community norms constitutive of a common good – these begin with personal property and rights. It is this claim to serve the interests of civil society that maintains in theory the state's autonomy from instrumental and partisan uses.

The problem created by this pair of ambivalent understandings, as I noted in chapter 5, is the inability to effectively attribute cause in assessing questions of social unity and social stability. In turn, this inability hinders the liberal state's plans for effective policy and action. As a project whose tactic has always sought reform rather than revolution, liberalism is rarely confident that the action it takes is rational, for it acts pragmatically – some would say blindly – on the basis of the market mechanism and self-interests it cannot predict or control. Its pretensions to scientific reason, institutionalized in our disciplines of economics and political science, are little more than revelations informed by a faith in self-interest. At best, the liberal cast of mind returns to advocating free trade and minimal state involvement into the economic affairs of civil society, dominated by that elite set of private and corporate entrepreneurs whose self-interest marks a general standard for the people. In the nineteenth century, moral appeals in favour of the poor invited the intervention of the state – to ameliorate the living conditions of the working class; to expand the voting franchise; to tend to necessary matters of education, sanitation, and water and electric supply; to set a host of standards; and to tax the ruling class of entrepreneurs in order to monitor the quality of public services. The former majority within liberalism – advocates of libertarianism, as it came to be called – rejected this use of the state. In their view, and in spite of what many considered the fact that their view had already demonstrated its failure to maintain any quality of life for the working peoples, the state had only two purposes: to maintain, first, a police force in order to protect civil society from internal violators of the peace, and second, armed forces to defend civil society from external threats. The improvement of living conditions would naturally grow with the market of self-interest, and education and public services would be best managed – efficiently and profitably – by the ruling class of entrepreneurs.

The liberal vision thus came to be associated with the class position of the bourgeoisie, and, as in earlier centuries, it was flawed by a fundamental contradiction. The seventeenth- and eighteenth-century debates over enclosure in England, and the eighteenth- and nineteenth-century debates over slavery in England and the United States, had established the absolute right of private property over its companion ideals of freedom, equality, and justice.[7] Likewise, nineteenth-century liberalism claimed this set of universal values but was reluctant to put them into practice when the lower classes demanded participation in a representative government. In order for the bourgeoisie to maintain their profitability, they require the working classes to work for minimal wages; in order to maintain their control, they require the lower classes to remain subjects of the political order. The rule of law, historically committed to private property, has typically remained at odds with a social order committed to a common good.

As this book has undertaken to demonstrate, liberal theory creates a problem of values generally and of morality (or virtue) in particular. Social theorists as diverse as Immanuel Kant, Karl Marx, and John Stuart Mill observed that the creation of a moral social order depended on the coincidence of the private interests of each constituent individual with the general interests of society – if not humanity in general. But by the end of the nineteenth century, it seemed clear to some observers in Europe, China, and Japan that the commitment of bourgeois liberal society to the natural law of economic advantage had foreclosed such a harmony of interests.[8] As any number of critics have pointed out, liberalism typically treats morality in the negative, so that the dominant ethos understands each of us as a sovereign individual whose freedom inhabits a clearly defined territory, independent of others' domains – the very notion Yan Fu worked hard to revise in 1890s China, with his translation of On Liberty. Accordingly, the state is not to interfere with our individual lives – particularly moral questions that, increasingly, are said to reflect personal interests or preferences. Theodor Adorno once noted that the concept of morality had been degraded into a notion of moral rigour associated with sexuality; this in turn had been superseded by psychoanalysis and psychological theory.[9] But as Bhikhu Parekh so aptly argued, liberal society removes ever larger areas of social life from the jurisdiction of morality: economic life is the pursuit of a self-interest regarded as natural and inevitable; calculations of profit or efficiency have no bearing on their ill effects to workers, tenants, and so on. Politics is the process of making decisions on the basis of pressures exerted by contending parties, and each is so committed to negotiating from a position of strength that partisans resort to any available means of exerting pressure. The result, Stuart Hampshire has observed, is a 'draining of moral significance from ceremonies, rituals, manners and observances,' which 'leaves morality incorporated only in a set of propositions and computations.'[10] That is to say, both collective social moralities (such as Mill's Victorian ethos) and particular normative views belonging to minorities (such as one or another Christian sect) are gradually eroded by the calculus of self-interest that dominates social life. All are left with a utilitarian sort of 'computational morality.'

And this computational morality is the residue of the failures of nineteenth-century liberalism, both its libertarian and constructive forms, represented to the 'right' and 'left' of Mill by Herbert Spencer and T.H. Green respectively. As one might well imagine, political reform without the prerequisite of tutelage produced an expanded electorate ill-prepared for participation. Or, as English critics within the Liberal Party may have complained, 'What was the use of reforming institutions at home if the decline of any true sense of social discipline made it impossible for them to work effectively?'[11] Brian Harrison, John Roach, and other historians have recounted that the stresses provoked by reform caused the Liberal Party to crack in the 1880s, with the result that 'old liberals' (or libertarians) shifted to conservatism, and the more insistent of constructive liberals shifted to radical or socialist positions. The conservatives lost interest in social reforms such as those to ameliorate poverty and to raise the status of women, political reforms such as suffrage, and moral reforms such as temperance; they were instead committed to maintaining faith in God and the ruling-class values that had built the empire and brought Britain to its pre-eminent position.[12] Socialists, by contrast, went on to advocate fundamental economic reforms that would have altered the bourgeois composition of civil society.

That is to say, computational morality is the functional compromise that remained in the wake of the failures of both libertarian and constructive liberalism, when they substituted political-moral solutions, such as electoral participation and public debate, for justice within the political-economic reality of class conflict. Scholars have noted three reasons for the inadequacy of the substitution. First, negative liberty and liberal individualism can only perpetuate the libertarian status quo. Whatever our identities, allegiances, or preferences, the negative conception of liberty would have us remain sovereign individuals free from the interference of others. And with the failure of liberalism to locate goodness in social life, moral values are reduced to such categories of individualism as will, personality, or nature. Second, concepts of positive liberty propose some notion of social unity that cannot withstand either the fact of class conflict in existing society or the alienation and fragmentation that has been the result of an amoral civil society. The little that citizens hold in common constitutes an inadequate basis for the self-development prerequisite to self-government. And third, the political-moral substitute offered by liberalism cannot reconcile ethical egalitarianism with the existing inequalities and divisions within society. That is, slogans pertaining to equality of opportunity or equality before the law belie the fact of structural inequalities.[13] Unwilling to address the fundamental economic inequalities created by the entrepreneurial ruling class and its ranks of bureaucracy, constructive liberals acquiesced in the status quo, which has remained dominated by the libertarian (and eventually, conservative) commitment to a normative self-interest. And such interests do not speak to morality; rather, they ignore and thus undermine it.[14]

The obverse of this computational morality is the persisting problem of social unity in local or national communities. What seems to be the theoretical solution added to the liberal compromise on 'morality' – that is, the tacit agreement to remove morality from public consideration – is the ubiquitous set of assumptions made by liberal writers of diverse positions concerning the nature of individuals and communities. That is to say, liberal approaches to the problem of liberty in the absence of morality assume an abstract social whole that is concretely filled with overlapping communities, some of which are 'natural,' such as neighbourhoods or racial or gender groups, and some of which are 'constructed' on the basis of economic interests, such as homeowner or business associations. (The nature of others – for instance, gay and lesbian organizations – is disputed, seen by some as natural and by others as constructed.) Liberal writers routinely assume that the nature of individuals and their groups in civil society is to communicate and cooperate – we are ready partners to discussion. This is because we implicitly agree on basic procedural rules in order to maintain the political process that mediates interests – we share social interests in maintaining our institutions.[15] Thus, once given their right to participate, individuals and groups can and do adequately represent their interests in political processes. As Rolf Sartorius puts the point, in utilitarian fashion, people at least implicitly understand that it is in their interests to respect a principle of reciprocity so that social and political institutions continue to function.[16]

But can we assume the existence of a society of fellows who share these political values? A noteworthy rubric for this problem, raised intermittently since T.H. Green's lectures in the nineteenth century, has been the question of 'political obligation.' How is it that we obey the law and continue to agree to the rules by which our political process works? Most liberal writers fall back on the set of assumptions outlined in the preceding paragraph. Alternative views seem to be limited to those critical of market capitalism or commited to Marxist analyses, who emphasize the class conflicts within industrial societies or the structural limits of market society. C.B. Macpherson, for example, argued in his well-known examination of the origins of market society that for Hobbes political obligation was based on a perception of equal insecurity and hence the collective commitment to support a sovereign who would uphold the law – provided that he recognize an equality of political rights before the law. But the systematic inequalities of class eventually undermined market rationality and the commitment to a sovereign power, so political obligation is no longer based on a cohesion of self-interests. Rather, political obligation has expired.[17]

At the same time, the fundamental unit of liberalism, the enlightened individual, has been degraded. The individual assumed in the work of liberal political theorists such as John Rawls – one characterized by rationality and benevolence – is no more. The individual assumed in many other writers – the responsible and participating citizen – is no longer a working model.[18] Rather, self-interest and the putative claims of 'natural' identities and their attendant personal values define the individual's socio-political relations. Meanwhile, the pressures on capitalism to maximize profit and thus to merge, divest, and restructure – regardless of the effects of such processes on workers – perpetuate computational morality and the fragmentation of communities. As V.S. Naipaul once remarked, in observing that strong family relations among South Asian emigrants to the Caribbean accounted for their relative success vis-à-vis the descendants of African slaves in the same struggling nations, 'Three hundred years of slavery had taught him only that he was an individual and that life was short.' A community of such individuals, wholly committed to personal interests, is not a viable community.[19] L.T. Hobhouse, whose oeuvre constitutes a trenchant and comprehensive critique of liberalism at the turn of the last century, pleaded that expediency be checked and that greater value be accorded to the moral right of the community to maintain its common life. But backsliding and reaction in his day tended to sacrifice collective commitments to justice to the individual's achievement of his ends.[20] At best, the individual is an autonomous creature of his own making, with society a means to the satisfaction of his personal goals. Worse, the individual has been degraded as such by the primacy of his private existence, and his new identity as a consumer represents a further erosion of what had once been an individual.[21]

The result is that liberal civil society, as a self-governing body of rational and reponsible individuals, has lost its constituency. In the United States, liberal–libertarian ideology since the 1980s repeats its claims to offer the solution of increased prosperity for all by insisting that the state rescind costly regulations and leave civil society and the capitalist market to the rational self-interest of entrepreneurs. On those occasions when the entrepreneurial ruling class levels complaints against the moral state of the people, which it finds decadent and undisciplined, it has turned to 'family values,' seemingly unaware that the possiblity of such values is undermined by economic policies that ensure that both parents are working rather than raising their children.[22] Not until recently in the United States have libertarians within the Republican Party allied themelves with fundamentalist Christian groups who would use the state to further the latter's creeds of religion. In order to encourage a regime of standard behaviour and belief, the state has begun to sponsor a national moral project. Under the second Bush presidency, for example, efforts shifted from 'family values' to military discipline and the virtue of patriotism. The spectre of an undisciplined population acting on its own autonomy and without a thought for the authority of the ruling class has provoked the latter to undertake an instrumental use of the state more often associated with Lenin's Bolshevik party or Mao Zedong's Chinese communists: based on their superior position, the ruling clique produces a pragmatic ethics that serves to impose order on the mass of autonomous citizens; some of the latter, in turn, embrace this ethics as their inheritance.[23]

Although such trends appear to mimic nineteenth-century solutions in Japan and China, the contrast with East Asia could not be more striking. As this book has explained, the moral argument against liberalism in Japan and China preceded the political-economic argument in its favour. There is an obvious reason for the difference: economic development preceded the ideology of liberty in England, whereas the two arrived simultaneously in East Asia. As governments and entrepreneurs set about developing industrial capitalism in Japan and China, scholars such as Nakamura Keiu and Yan Fu introduced liberal ideas through their translations of ideological works such as John Stuart Mill's *On Liberty*, which justified the liberal order. If we accept the evidence provided by the translations of Mill into Japanese and Chinese, and the reaction to liberal theory among Japanese and Chinese leaders, it is clear that the appeal to liberty was repeatedly an object of suspicion. Some readers were sceptical that good would come of freeing the individual to chart his own way independent of his fellows in society. Without some commitment to public morality or standards of virtue, the free individual risked becoming mired in his natural state of selfishness and egotism, and society risked a descent into decadence and disorder. Hence Mill's Japanese and Chinese interpreters added a measure of public virtue to Mill's work in order to assuage the scepticism of their fellows regarding liberal models of society.

To their credit, Nakamura's and Yan's translations of Mill attempted to solve some of these problems within liberal theory. Yan Fu in particular offered a more coherent version of Mill's theory than perhaps had Mill. Because Yan adhered to the older view of the state as a received element of the political world, his attitude of reform toward the status quo undertook a rational plan continuous with his view of the Chinese state and society. His elevation of virtue to one of the higher pleasures – and making it prerequisite to liberty – was intended to pre-empt the spectre of self-interest selfishly understood. With his belief that mature individuals would understand themselves as embedded within a moral society, he attempted to foreclose the possibility of a civil society degenerating into an amoral order of men motivated by a computational morality.

Nakamura Keiu, by contrast, offered a perhaps less successful version of liberal theory, for his conception of self-governing civil society granted the group a great deal of authority over the individual, and his enlistment of Christianity as the finest expression of individual liberty substituted an other-worldly ground of faith for what Mill presented as a secular arena for reasoned debate. In that regard, it is remarkable that subsequent moralists such as Inoue Tetsujirō would reproduce Nakamura's socio-moral ethos with a similarly divine teleology and a social authority that surpassed the prerogatives of individuals. In spite of both Yan's and Nakamura's best efforts, governments in both China and Japan would produce 'despotisms of custom' that prescribed common values for all the people.

In the nineteenth century, neither Japan nor China was a bourgeois regime, so Nakamura and Yan were able to propose Mill's theory of liberty as a novel approach to social possibilities. In Japan, capitalism preceded representative government, while in China, equality and ideological reform preceded economic development. In neither country were social or political conflicts marked by the struggles between libertarian defenders of personal rights and constructive moralists seeking to ameliorate conditions for the working poor. Instead, the state took charge in both nations, and in each the state was motivated to secure its autonomy, stability, and self-defence. Thus, the state necessarily defined some form of common good, which, for better or worse, included a commitment to national goals that mimicked the economic values of bourgeois ruling classes after the manner of Lenin's redefinition of socialism as state capitalism. The state set goals and assigned the masses to their tasks – with an important exception: in both Japan and China, national goals made a necessity of national unity, so the path to economic development proceeded through projects of state education systems and a national program for public virtue that made some attempt to ratify values such as equality and justice.

Liberal positions in China and Japan during much of the twentieth century did not accrue to the entrepreneurial class but were more often than not represented by groups in political opposition to the government. The Japanese state was in a position to command the entrepreneurial class to work on behalf of the state and coopted it for the duration of the war, the 'economic miracle' of the 1960s, and, to some analysts, continues to do so today. The problem in the Japanese context was an oligarchy's effort to industrialize and to organize a national people for its economic and geopolitical end versus the resistance of those who wanted to democratically expand the oligarchy's narrow constituency. The liberal position in Japan was often assumed by those who advocated, first, a national assembly that would undertake the promise of equality under self-government, and in time, public spaces free from the domination of imperial ideology. In China, by contrast, the National People's Party attempted to follow the model of Japan, especially during the 1920s and 1930s, but the state was never strong enough to fulfil its goals. Thus, the Chinese Communist Party revolution eventually eliminated the bourgeois class, accusing it of serving foreign colonial interests, and claimed instead to be acting in the interests of the well-being of the peasant class who comprised the great majority of the people. Throughout that long revolutionary period, liberal positions advocated greater participation in self-government and, increasingly, structural alternatives to the Leninist single-party state.

The advent of 'neoliberalism' in East Asia in the 1980s, which has recommended the opening of domestic markets to foreign goods and foreign investment in the interests of globalization, has pointedly eroded the state management of economies in Japan and China. But neoliberalism has also eroded the moral consensus that once provided a measure of social unity in each country – that altruistic regard for one's fellows in society that the state had especially fostered as the foundation for national virtue. If Japanese citizens have largely become like their Western peers, alienated consumers of late capitalism, such seems to be the destiny of the Chinese people as well. There are several laments for the passing of socialist morality in China, but in his masterful account of the dialectic of utopianism and hedonism in the Chinese revolution, Jiwei Ci argues that the deferred hedonism at the heart of Mao's utopian experiments has now been freed to develop into a crude hedonism that reflects the unchecked satisfaction of individual desires. Under conditions prompted first by Deng Xiaoping's reforms of the 1980s and then by the neoliberalism of the 1990s, the 1989 failure of the democratic movement at Tiananmen Square removed the sociopolitical possibilities for a liberal individualism and, in turn, duly sanctioned the hedonistic individual consumer as a legitimate alternative.[24] If neoliberalism has produced an economic order characterized by state manipulation, official corruption, vast profits, and new social inequalities, liberal theory at best remains a potent position for those opposed to authoritarian government and corporate control – recalling less the nineteenth-century context represented by Mill and more the eighteenth-century situation addressed by Hobbes and Locke: the basic attempt to assert security of person and property, and equal justice in legal and political processes, in the face of near absolute powers.[25] If neoliberalism and globalization confer such new powers on states and their international corporate allies, liberal theory seeks a new course that surpasses its bourgeois beginnings, one grounded not only in liberty and property rights but in equality and human rights as well.

Notes

Introduction

1 There are two previous comparisons of Nakamura Keiu's and Yan Fu's translations of *On Liberty*, neither of which is germane to my purposes: Ishida Takeshi, 'J. S. Miru *Jiyū ron* to Nakamura Keiu oyobi Gen Fuku,' in his *Nihon kindai shisōshi ni okeru hō to seiji* (Tokyo: Iwanami shoten, 1976), 1–46; and Wang Kefei, *Zhong-Ri jindai dui xifang zhengzhi zhexue sixiang de shequ: Yan Fu yu Riben qimeng xuezhe* (Beijing: Zhongguo shehui kexue chubanshe, 1996), 81–144. Ishida announces his work as an exercise in the comparative history of thought and goes on to compare the biographies of Mill, Nakamura, and Yan, their parallel interests in classical learning, the respectively intemperate times in which each lived, and ends with random comparisons of the two translations of *Liberty* – the respective treatments of public opinion and so on. Likewise, Wang compares Nakamura's and Yan's biographies and contrasts their translation techniques and views of liberty; he concludes (based not on the translation of *Liberty* but on a survey of Yan's many works) that Yan treats liberty as a mark of democracy and progress, and that Nakamura links it to Western morality. These are not the conclusions that I draw in this book.

2 John Stuart Mill, *On Liberty*, in *The Collected Works of John Stuart Mill*, vol. 18, *Essays on Politics and Society*, Part 1 (Toronto: University of Toronto Press, 1977), 220–1, 226–7. On Mill's relationship with Mrs. Taylor, see Nicholas Capaldi, *John Stuart Mill: A Biography* (Cambridge: University of Cambridge Press, 2004), 82–4, 102–17, 227–32.

3 See Stefan Collini, *Public Moralists: Political Thought and Intellectual Life in Britain, 1850–1930* (Oxford: Clarendon, 1991), 30, 60–5, 99, 109–10; George Watson, *The English Ideology: Studies in the Language of Victorian Politics* (Lon-

don: Allen Lane, 1973), 48–53, 59–60; Earl H. Kinmonth, 'Nakamura Keiu and Samuel Smiles: A Victorian Confucian and a Confucian Victorian,' *American Historical Review* 85 (1980): 535–56; and J.W. Burrow, *The Crisis of Reason: European Thought, 1848–1914* (New Haven: Yale University Press, 2000), 152–6, 170–5, 192. See also Peter Berkowitz, 'Mill: Liberty, Virtue, and the Discipline of Individuality,' in *Mill and the Moral Character of Liberalism*, ed. Eldon J. Eisenbach (University Park: Pennsylvania State University Press, 1998), 13–47.

4 David L. Hall and Roger T. Ames, *Thinking Through Confucius* (Albany: State University of New York Press, 1987), 169, 216–23; and Jonathan Riley, 'Individuality, Custom, and Progress,' *Utilitas* 3.2 (1991): 217–44. See also Mill, *On Liberty*, 267.

5 See, for example, the formative work of Hao Chang, *Chinese Intellectuals in Crisis: Search for Order and Meaning (1890–1911)* (Berkeley: University of California Press, 1987), and *Liang Ch'i-ch'ao and Intellectual Transition in China* (Cambridge: Harvard University Press, 1971). See also Kinmonth, 'Nakamura Keiu and Samuel Smiles,' 549–52; Liu Zhengtan, et al., *Hanyu wailaici cidian / A Dictionary of Loan Words and Hybrid Words in Chinese* (Shanghai: Shanghai cishu chubanshe, 1984), 216; and Lydia H. Liu, *Translingual Practice: Literature, National Culture, and Translated Modernity: China, 1900–1937* (Stanford: Stanford University Press, 1995), 316. Although Chinese scholars readily identify *rinri* (C: *lunli*) as a Japanese neologism borrowed back into Chinese, it is unclear why they do not acknowledge *dōtoku* (C: *daode*) as such, since the two Japanese neologisms were paired in the 1880s.

6 Douglas Howland, *Translating the West: Language and Political Reason in Nineteenth-Century Japan* (Honolulu: University of Hawai'i Press, 2002), 96–107. See also Xiong Yuezhi, '"Liberty," "Democracy," "President": The Translation and Usage of Some Political Terms in Late Imperial China,' in Michael Lackner, et al., eds., *New Terms for New Ideas: Western Knowledge and Lexical Change in Late Imperial China* (Leiden: Brill, 2001), 69–93.

7 C.B. Macpherson, *Democratic Theory: Essays in Retrieval* (Oxford: Clarendon, 1973), 17–18, 24–31.

8 See W.H. Greenleaf, *The British Political Tradition*, vol. 2, *The Ideological Heritage* (London: Methuen, 1983), 263–308; Stefan Collini, *Liberalism and Sociology: L.T. Hobhouse and Political Argument in England, 1880–1914* (Cambridge: Cambridge University Press, 1979), 13–17; and Thomas Mackay, ed., *A Plea for Liberty: An Argument against Socialism and Socialistic Legislation* (New York: Appleton, 1891).

9 See Stefan Collini, 'Liberalism and the Legacy of Mill,' *Historical Journal* 20, no. 1 (1977): 237–54; John Gray, *Liberalisms: Essays in Political Philosophy* (London: Routledge, 1989), 4–6; John Gray, 'The Light of Other Minds,'

Times Literary Supplement, no. 5054 (11 Feb. 2000): 12–13; and Joseph Hamburger, *John Stuart Mill on Liberty and Control* (Princeton: Princeton University Press, 1999), xi–xv.

10 H.J. McClosky, 'Mill's Liberalism,' *Philosophical Quarterly* 13, no. 51 (1963): 143–56; and John Stuart Mill, *Principles of Political Economy,* in *Collected Works of John Stuart Mill* (Toronto: University of Toronto Press, 1965), 2: 203–14; 3: 800–4, 936–70.

11 Collini, *Public Moralists*, 121–69; and Capaldi, *John Stuart Mill: A Biography,* 321–31.

12 Watson, *The English Ideology*, 168–72.

13 Irwin Scheiner, *Christian Converts and Social Protest in Meiji Japan* (Berkeley: University of California Press, 1970), 221–6.

14 Paul A. Cohen, *Discovering History in China: American Historical Writing on the Recent Chinese Past* (New York: Columbia University Press, 1984), 57–61, 97–111; Judith B. Farquhar and James L. Hevia, 'Culture and Postwar American Historiography of China,' *positions: east asia cultures critique* 1, no. 2 (1993): 486–525; Harry Harootunian, *History's Disquiet* (New York: Columbia University Press, 2000), 33–6, 61–4; Howland, *Translating the West*, 16–21; and Stefan Tanaka, 'Objectivism and the Eradication of Critique in Japanese History,' in *Learning Places: The Afterlife of Area Studies*, ed. Masao Miyoshi and H.D. Harootunian (Durham: Duke University Press, 2002), 80–102.

15 Andrew J. Nathan, *Chinese Democracy* (Berkeley: University of California Press, 1985), 226.

16 Andrew J. Nathan, *China's Transition* (New York: Columbia University Press, 1997), 136–51, 198–216; and 'Redefinitions of Freedom in China,' in *The Idea of Freedom in Asia and Africa*, ed. Robert H. Taylor (Stanford: Stanford University Press, 2002), 148–9. For an alternative example that emphasizes not culture but institutions, yet remains within this approach of democratization, see Barrett L. McCormick and David Kelly, 'The Limits of Anti-Liberalism,' *Journal of Asian Studies* 53, no. 3 (1994): 804–31. On Japan, see Iwao Hoshii, *Japan's Pseudo-Democracy* (New York: New York University Press, 1993); and Nobutaka Ike, *A Theory of Japanese Democracy* (Boulder, CO: Westview, 1978).

17 Observe how Andrew Nathan, for example, represents the West in a recent discussion of democracy in China: 'What Li [Honglin] seeks is liberation of the individual, to be sure, but *for*, not against ... the creation of a modernized ... society and a strong state. Thus Li still expresses a distinctively Chinese-liberal, as opposed to Western-liberal, conception of what freedom is and why it is to be valued.' (Nathan, 'Redefinitions of Freedom in China,' 270.) Yet Nathan ignores the fact that Li's notion of a 'positive' liberty is quite compatible with that of T.H. Green and the 'new liberals' of the late

nineteenth century in England. He finally concedes: 'What we have been calling a Chinese liberal ideal of freedom is almost closer to a republican ideal, so closely linked is it with notions of responsibility and citizenship instead of finding its basis in an affirmation of individual selfishness or hedonism.' (Ibid., 272.) But again, this idea is central to classical liberal theories like Mill's, which advocated not democracy but republicanism.

18 See, for examples, the many essays gathered in the prominent symposium 'Will China Democratize?' in the *Journal of Democracy* 9, no. 1 (1998): 3–64; and a follow-up thereto, 'Liberal Voices from China,' *Journal of Democracy* 9, no. 4 (1998): 3–23; as well as *China and Democracy: Reconsidering the Prospects for a Democratic China*, ed. Suisheng Zhao (New York: Routledge, 2000).

1. *On Liberty* and Its Historical Conditions of Possibility

1 Excellent introductions to the field include Susan Bassnett-McGuire, *Translation Studies* (London: Methuen, 1980); Mary Snell-Hornby, *Translation Studies: An Integrated Approach* (Amsterdam: John Benjamins, 1988); *The Routledge Encyclopedia of Translation Studies*, ed. Mona Baker, assisted by Kirsten Malmkjær (London: Routledge, 1995); and Lawrence Venuti, *The Translator's Invisibility: A History of Translation* (London: Routledge, 1995). Two monumental texts in English are *On Translation*, ed. Reuben A. Brower (Cambridge: Harvard University Press, 1959); and George Steiner, *After Babel: Aspects of Language and Translation* (London: Oxford University Press, 1975). What Snell-Hornby calls the new approach to translation is evident in recent studies of East Asia, including Douglas Howland, *Translating the West: Language and Political Reason in Nineteenth-Century Japan* (Honolulu: University of Hawai'i Press, 2002); Lydia H. Liu, *Translingual Practice: Literature, National Culture, and Translated Modernity: China, 1900–1937* (Stanford: Stanford University Press, 1995); and Naoki Sakai, *Translation and Subjectivity: On 'Japan' and Cultural Nationalism* (Minneapolis: University of Minnesota Press, 1997). See also Douglas Howland, 'The Predicament of Ideas in Culture: Translation and Historiography,' *History and Theory* 42, no. 1 (2003): 45–60.

2 Benjamin Schwartz, *In Search of Wealth and Power: Yen Fu and the West* (Cambridge: Harvard University Press, 1964), 92, 95–6, 134–5.

3 See, for example, Tadashi Aruga, 'The Declaration of Independence in Japan: Translation and Transplantation, 1854–1997,' *Journal of American History* 85, no. 4 (March 1999), 1409–31, who compares the core message of the Declaration to the inaccuracies of Japanese translations; Frank Li, 'East Is East and West Is West: Did the Twain Ever Meet? The Declaration of Inde-

pendence in China,' ibid., 1432–48, who rejects erroneous Chinese translations of the Declaration within the narrow confines of absolute conceptual
differences and incompatibility or incomprehension; and Willi Paul Adams,
'The Historian as Translator: An Introduction,' ibid., 1283–98, who differentiates the 'timeless' from the 'timebound' aspects of translations in an effort
to encourage historians to become more careful translators.

4 See Howland, *Translating the West*, 18–25.

5 Schwartz, *In Search of Wealth and Power*, 96.

6 Lydia H. Liu, 'Translingual Practice: The Discourse of Individualism
between China and the West,' *positions: east asia cultures critique* 1, no. 1
(Spring 1993): 160–93; and James R. Pusey, *China and Charles Darwin* (Cambridge: Harvard University, Council on East Asian Studies, 1983).

7 Roman Jakobson, 'On Linguistic Aspects of Translation,' in *On Translation*,
ed. Brower, 233.

8 Ibid., 236.

9 Henry Schogt, 'Semantic Theory and Translation Theory,' in *Theories of
Translation: An Anthology of Essays from Dryden to Derrida*, ed. Rainer Schulte
and John Biguenet (Chicago: University of Chicago Press, 1992), 192–203.

10 See Eric Jacobsen on the Roman construction of grammar, commentary, and
translation: *Translation: A Traditional Craft* (Copenhagen: Gyldendalske
Boghandel; Nordisk Forlag, 1958), 29–56; and Naoki Sakai on the Japanese
'reading' (reciting) of Chinese books: *Voices of the Past: The Status of Language in Eighteenth-Century Japanese Discourse* (Ithaca: Cornell University
Press, 1991), 211–39.

11 For a concise survey of humanistic, sociological, and Marxist opposition to
contemporary or 'autonomous' linguistics, see Frederick J. Newmeyer, *The
Politics of Linguistics* (Chicago: University of Chicago Press, 1986), 99–126;
see also Naoki Sakai, *Translation and Subjectivity*, 2–11, 51–9. On the inter-
penetration of the Chinese and Japanese languages in the nineteenth century, see Douglas Howland, *Borders of Chinese Civilization: Geography and
History at Empire's End* (Durham: Duke University Press, 1996), 43–68, 236–
41.

12 See Tony Bennett, *Formalism and Marxism* (London: Methuen, 1979), 3–9;
and Raymond Williams, *Marxism and Literature* (Oxford: Oxford University
Press, 1977), 158–64.

13 See the important 1929 work of the Bakhtin circle, V.N. Vološinov, *Marxism
and the Philosophy of Language*, trans. Ladislav Matejka and I.R. Titunik
(New York: Seminar Press, 1973), 45–98; and Pierre Bourdieu, *Language and
Symbolic Power*, ed. John B. Thompson, trans. Gino Raymond and Matthew
Adamson (Cambridge: Harvard University Press, 1991), 37–65. Especially

pertinent to the issue at hand is Sakai, *Voices of the Past*, 217–22, 311–19, and *Translation and Subjectivity*, 11–15, 27–9.

14 See Theodora Bynon, *Historical Linguistics* (Cambridge: Cambridge University Press, 1977, 1983), 217. Bynon acknowledges that we 'oversimplify reality' when we begin to speak of the 'interlingual' by acknowledging two distinct languages.

15 See the formative work of Eugene Nida, *Towards a Science of Translating* (Leiden: Brill, 1964); Eugene Nida and Charles R. Taber, *The Theory and Practice of Translation* (Leiden: Brill, 1969); and Gideon Toury, both *In Search of a Theory of Translation* (Tel Aviv: Tel Aviv University, The Porter Institute for Poetics and Semiotics, 1980), and *Descriptive Translation Studies and Beyond* (Amsterdam: John Benjamins, 1995).

16 Noam Chomsky, *Language and Responsibility* (New York: Pantheon, 1979), 54–8.

17 See Ferdinand de Saussure, *Course in General Linguistics*, trans. Roy Harris (La Salle: Open Court, 1986), 65–70.

18 Chinese and Japanese linguists do not treat the phenomena of word translation in a symmetric manner. Japanese distinguish between loanwords, termed *gairaigo* ('words of foreign derivation'), and translation words, termed *hon'yakugo* (or simply *yakugo*). Chinese linguists, by contrast, indicate both with the general term *wailaici* ('words of foreign derivation'), and differentiate them as either 'phonetic transfers' (*yiyin*) or 'semantic transfers' (*yiyi*). In addition, they use the term *hunheci* ('hybrid word' or 'calque') to describe a special class of translation words that are structured after source-language terms, like *dianshi* ('electric viewing') for the English *television*. In English, see Roy Andrew Miller, *The Japanese Language* (Chicago: University of Chicago Press, 1967), 235–67; Masayoshi Shibatani, *The Languages of Japan* (Cambridge: Cambridge University Press, 1990), 142–53; Federico Masini, *The Formation of the Modern Chinese Lexicon and Its Evolution Toward a National Language*, published as *Journal of Chinese Linguistics, Monograph Series*, no. 6 (1993): 121–45; Ping Chen, *Modern Chinese: History and Sociolinguistics* (Cambridge: Cambridge University Press, 1999), 100–5; and Jerry Norman, *Chinese* (Cambridge: Cambridge University Press, 1988), 16–22. See also Sakakura Atsuyoshi, et al., *Kōza kokugoshi*, vol. 3, *Goi shi* (Tokyo: Taishūkan, 1971), 347–58; Hida Yoshifumi, ed., *Eibei gairaigo no sekai* (Tokyo: Nan'undō, 1981), 129–64, 282–8; and Liu Zhengtan, et al., *Hanyu wailaici cidian / A Dictionary of Loan Words and Hybrid Words in Chinese* (Shanghai: Shanghai cishu chubanshe, 1984). By contrast, discussions of loanwords among European languages, because they historically share a common (set of) alphabet(s), are much more complex; see Bynon, *Historical*

Linguistics, 216–39; and Frans van Coetsem, *Loan Phonology and the Two Transfer Types in Language Contact* (Dordrecht: Foris, 1988).

19 I use *denotatum* here, rather than *referent*, following John Lyons, who would discuss semiotic relations among lexemes (or words) as 'denotation' and restrict discussions of 'reference' to the pragmatic dimension of utterances. See *Semantics* (Cambridge: Cambridge University Press, 1977), vol. 1: 208. I note, however, that Lyons cautions us that unlike concrete things (including one as imaginary as *unicorn*), abstract words – like *liberty, society,* and the others at issue in this book – may lack denotation; it may be preferable to speak of the 'sense' or meaning of such words; see pp. 198–200, 212–14. Readers familiar with C.S. Peirce's semiotic theory will recall that instead of *denotatum*, he uses *interpretant*; see 'Logic as Semiotic: The Theory of Signs,' *Philosophical Writings of Peirce* (New York: Dover, 1955), 99.

20 Saussure, *Course*, 114.

21 Adrienne Lehrer, *Semantic Fields and Lexical Structures* (Amsterdam: North-Holland, 1974), 1–45; and Lyons, *Semantics*, vol 1: 230–69.

22 Morioka Kenji, *Kaitei kindaigo no seiritsu: goi hen* (Tokyo: Meiji shoin, 1991), 96–106. Lobscheid's dictionary, titled in Chinese *Ying-Hua zidian* (J: *Eika jiten*), was first published in Shanghai, 1847–48, and reprinted in Edo, 1866–69.

23 The lexicographic approach to translation is prominent in Chinese work as well; see Liu Zhengtan, et al., *Hanyu wailaici cidian / A Dictionary of Loan Words and Hybrid Words in Chinese*; and Lydia H. Liu, *Translingual Practice*, 260–2, 265–378.

24 See Douglas Howland, 'Nishi Amane's Efforts to Translate Western Knowledge: Sound, Written Character, and Meaning,' *Semiotica* 83, no. 3/4 (1991): 283–310.

25 See Howland, *Translating the West*, 25–30, 61–89. As a number of linguists have argued, the study of semantic fields both reveals the degree to which language mediates the human subject and the objective world and will allow us to examine the culturally and/or linguistically determined units of such mediations. See Harold Basileus, 'Neo-Humboldtian Ethnolinguistics,' *Word* 8, no. 2 (1952): 95–105; van Coetsem, *Loan Phonology and the Two Transfer Types in Language Contact*, 25–46, 77–81; and Stephen Ullmann, *The Principles of Semantics* (Oxford: Blackwell; Glasgow: Jackson, Son & Co., 1951, 1957), 152–7, 171–7, 220–40.

26 On incongruence, see Lyons, *Semantics*, vol. 1, 235–8.

27 Saitō Tsuyoshi, *Meiji no kotoba: higashi kara nishi e no kakehashi* (Tokyo: Kodansha, 1977), 177; see also Florian Coulmas, 'Language Adaptation in Meiji Japan,' in *Language Policy and Political Development*, ed. Brian Wein-

stein (Norwood: Ablex, 1990), 69–86; and Howland, *Translating the West*, 153–82.

28 Brian A. Porter, 'The Social Nation and Its Futures: English Liberalism and Polish Nationalism in Late Nineteenth-Century Warsaw,' *American Historical Review*, 101, no. 5 (1996): 1470–92.

29 Rebecca West, *Black Lamb and Grey Falcon: A Journey through Yugoslavia* (repr. New York: Penguin, 1994), 567–87.

30 On the issue of readership, see Wang Kefei, *Zhong-Ri jindai dui xifang zhengzhi zhexue sixiang de shequ: Yan Fu yu Riben qimeng xuezhe* (Beijing: Zhongguo shehui kexue chubanshe, 1996), 122–31; Wang describes the 'influence' of Nakamura's and Yan's translations in terms of their being cited in prominent journals such as *Dongfang zazhi* and in the works of intellectuals such as Liang Qichao, Li Dazhao, Lu Xun, Hu Shi, and Cai Yuanpei.

31 John Lyons addresses this problem within the discipline of linguistics as 'cultural salience' – the integration between culture and language, insofar as lexical structure reflects the changing distinctions that are important in a culture; see *Semantics*, 1: 248.

32 See Emile Benveniste, *Problems in General Linguistics*, trans. Mary Elizabeth Meek (Coral Gables: University of Miami Press, 1971), 217–30; Oswald Ducrot and Tzvetan Todorov, *Encyclopedic Dictionary of the Sciences of Language*, trans. Catherine Porter (Oxford: Blackwell Reference, 1981), 247–59, 323–38; William F. Hanks, *Language and Communicative Practices* (Boulder: Westview, 1996), 140–225; R.A. Hudson, *Sociolinguistics* (Cambridge: Cambridge University Press, 1980), 128–37; and John Lyons, *Semantics* (Cambridge: Cambridge University Press, 1977), vol. 2: 636–46. See also Kamei Hideo, *Transformations of Sensibility: The Phenomenology of Meiji Literature*, trans. ed. Michael Bourdaghs (Ann Arbor: Center for Japanese Studies, The University of Michigan, 2002), xxx–xxxvii, xlvi, 103; Jerry Norman, *Chinese* (Cambridge: Cambridge University Press, 1988), 117–21, 195–6; Masayoshi Shibatani, *The Languages of Japan* (Cambridge: Cambridge University Press, 1990), 312–14, 371–4; and David L. Hall and Roger T. Ames, *Thinking from the Han: Self, Truth, and Transcendence in Chinese and Western Culture* (Albany: SUNY Press, 1998), 3–43.

33 Yanabu Akira has made similar observations: 'Fukuzawa Yukichi ni okeru "individual" no hon'yaku,' in *Hon'yaku*, ed. Zasshi *Bungaku* henshūbu (Tokyo: Iwanami shoten, 1982), 276–93. J.C. Hepburn, in the first edition of *A Japanese and English Dictionary* (1867) (repr. Rutland, VT: Tuttle, 1983), describes *jiko* as literary and obsolete (p. 154), but in the third edition, *A Japanese-English and English-Japanese Dictionary* (Tokyo: Maruya, 1886), he calls it a standard word for 'oneself' (p. 222). By comparison, Hori Tatsuno-

suke, in *A Pocket Dictionary of the English and Japanese Language / Ei-Wa tai-yaku shūchin jisho* (Edo: n.p., 1862), used *waga* for 'I,' *waga o* or *waga ni* for 'me,' *waga no* for 'my,' *ware jishin* for 'myself,' and *jibun* for 'oneself' (pp. 381, 489, 523, 726). Fukuzawa Yukichi, in his phrasebook *Zōtei kaei tsūgo* (1860), used *watakushi* for the sentence subject 'I'; see *Fukuzawa Yukichi zenshū* (Tokyo: Iwanami shoten, 1958), vol. 1: 220.

34 On Chinese conceptions of the self, see Lydia H. Liu, 'Translingual Practice,' 167–8.

35 I note for the benefit of some readers that Nakamura's and Yan's work in translating Mill does not figure in the creation of literary conventions in the development of modern Chinese and Japanese fiction: first-person narrative, subjectivity, inner voice, and so on; their lexical choices for representing I and the self were not reused for fictional purposes. See Shu-mei Shih, *The Lure of the Modern: Writing Modernism in Semicolonial China, 1917–1937* (Berkeley: University of California Press, 2001), 105–7, 349–66; Karatani Kōjin, *Origins of Modern Japanese Literature*, trans. and ed. Brett de Bary (Durham: Duke University Press, 1993), 61–5, 157–60; Yanabu Akira, *Hon'yaku bunka o kangaeru* (Tokyo: Hōsei daigaku shuppankyoku, 1978), 64–72; and Tomiko Yoda, 'First Person Voice and Citizen-Subject: The Modernity of Ogai's "Maihime,"' unpub. mss.

36 See Ma Xiaoquan, 'Local Self-Government: Citizenship Consciousness and the Political Participation of the New Gentry-Merchants in the Late Qing,' in *Imagining the People: Chinese Intellectuals and the Concept of Citizenship, 1890–1920*, ed. Joshua A. Fogel and Peter Zarrow (Armonk, NY: M.E. Sharpe, 1997), 183–211; Tu-ki Min, *National Polity and Local Power: The Transformation of Late Imperial China*, ed. Timothy Brook and Philip Kuhn (Cambridge: Harvard University Council on East Asian Studies, 1989); and Mary Backus Rankin, *Elite Activism and Political Transformation in China: Zhejiang Province, 1865–1911* (Stanford: Stanford University Press, 1986). See also the debate over a Chinese 'public sphere': William T. Rowe, 'The Public Sphere in Modern China,' *Modern China* 16, no. 3 (1990): 309–29; 'Symposium: "Public Sphere" / "Civil Society" in China?,' *Modern China* 19, no. 2 (1993); and *Civil Society in China*, ed. Timothy Brook and B. Michael Frolic (Armonk, NY: M.E. Sharpe, 1997).

37 Saitō, *Meiji no kotoba*, 176–80. For a comparison with the similar situation in China, see Peter Zarrow, 'Introduction: Citizenship in China and the West,' in *Imagining the People*, ed. Fogel and Zarrow, 3–38.

38 Irwin Scheiner, *Christian Converts and Social Protest in Meiji Japan* (Berkeley: University of California Press, 1970), 110–26.

39 Thomas L. Haskell, 'Persons as Uncaused Causes: John Stuart Mill, the

Spirit of Capitalism, and the "Invention" of Formalism,' in *The Culture of the Market: Historical Essays*, ed. Thomas L. Haskell and Richard F. Teichgraeber III (Cambridge: Cambridge University Press, 1993), 441–502.

40　John Stuart Mill, *On Liberty*, in *The Collected Works of John Stuart Mill*, vol. 18, *Essays on Politics and Society*, Part 1 (Toronto: University of Toronto Press, 1977), 277, 282, 301–2. See also Nakamura Keiu, *Jiyū no ri* (Suruga: Kihira Keiichirō, 1871), repr. in *Meiji bunka zenshū*, vol. 5, *Jiyū minken hen* (Tokyo: Nihon hyōronsha, 1927), 59–60, 64–6, 76–8; and Yan Fu, trans., *Qun ji quan jie lun* ([Shanghai]: Shangwu yinshuguan, n.d.), 90–1, 96–7, 124–5.

41　Mill's father, James Mill, had early on identified the 'middle ranks' as the most intelligent segment of the community whose opinion deserved greatest representation; see his *Essay on Government*, in *Political Writings*, ed. Terence Ball (Cambridge: Cambridge University Press, 1992), 41. See Asa Briggs, 'The Language of "Class" in Early Nineteenth-Century England,' in *Essays in Labour History*, ed. Asa Briggs and John Saville (London: Macmillan, 1960), 40–73; Stefan Collini, *Public Moralists: Political Thought and Intellectual Life in Britain, 1850–1930* (Oxford: Clarendon, 1991), 29–37, 224–30; and Harold Perkin, *The Origin of Modern English Society, 1780–1880* (London: Routledge & Kegan Paul, 1969), 208–17, 252–70, 281–2, 308–19.

42　As Max Weber emphasized in his seminal work on bureaucracy, the formation of a bureaucratic class historically predated a money economy; many early bureaucratic governments administered largely agrarian economies. Moreover, the stability of the bureaucratic institution depends on a reliable system of taxation, and, as a political form, bureaucracy is the product of the long-term work of centralizing and rationalizing state administration. See Max Weber, 'Bureaucracy,' *From Max Weber: Essays in Sociology*, trans. H.H. Gerth and C. Wright Mills (New York: Oxford University Press, 1946), 204–9.

43　See Karl Marx, *Critique of Hegel's Doctrine of the State*, sections 290–7, in *Early Writings*, trans. R. Livingstone and G. Benton (New York: Vintage, 1975), 105–16.

44　Arno J. Mayer, *The Persistence of the Old Regime: Europe to the Great War* (New York: Pantheon, 1981), 152–6, 176–80, 253–7; see also Frans Gosses, *The Management of British Foreign Policy Before the First World War: Especially During the Period 1880–1914*, trans. E. C. Van der Gaaf (Leiden: Sijthoff, 1948), 19–39; and for an extended example, see Raymond A. Jones, *The British Diplomatic Service, 1815–1914* (Waterloo, ON: Wilfrid Laurier University Press, 1983). See also Collini, *Public Moralists*, 37–8; and George Watson, *The English Ideology: Studies in the Language of Victorian Politics* (London: Allen Lane, 1973), 13.

45 Thomas C. Smith, 'Japan's Aristocratic Revolution,' *Native Sources of Japanese Industrialization, 1750–1920* (Berkeley: University of California Press, 1988), 134. On the historiographical grounding of the samurai as both a legally defined status group and as a socioeconomic class, see Douglas Howland, 'Samurai Status, Class, and Bureaucracy: A Historiographical Essay,' *Journal of Asian Studies* 60, no. 2 (2001): 353–80.

46 John W. Hall, 'Rule by Status in Tokugawa Japan,' *Journal of Japanese Studies* 1, no. 1 (1974): 45–7; and Bitō Masahide, 'Society and Social Thought in the Tokugawa Period,' *Japan Foundation Newsletter*, 9, no. 2–3 (June–September 1981), 1–6. On the imposition of a rational political form on rural Japan, based on the new administrative unit, the *mura* or 'village,' see Hitomi Tonomura, *Community and Commerce in Late Medieval Japan: The Corporate Villages of Tokuchin-ho* (Stanford: Stanford University Press, 1992), 170–87.

47 John W. Hall, 'Rule by Status,' 48.

48 For specific reference to Nakamura Keiu, see Earl H. Kinmonth, 'Nakamura Keiu and Samuel Smiles: A Victorian Confucian and a Confucian Victorian,' *American Historical Review* 85 (1980): 552–4.

49 Howland, *Translating the West*, 114–21.

50 Mill, *On Liberty*, 305–8; Nakamura, *Jiyū no ri*, 80–2.

51 See R.P. Dore, *Education in Tokugawa Japan* (Berkeley: University of California Press, 1965), 176–213; H.D. Harootunian, 'Jinsei, Jinzei, and Jitsugaku: Social Values and Leadership in Late Tokugawa Thought,' in *Modern Japanese Leadership: Transition and Change*, ed. Bernard Silberman and H.D. Harootunian (Tucson: University of Arizona Press, 1966), 83–119; and Thomas C. Smith, 'Merit as Ideology in the Tokugawa Period,' *Native Sources*, 156–72.

52 Maruyama Masao, 'Chūsei to hangyaku,' *Chūsei to hangyaku: tenkeiki Nihon no seishinshiteki isō* (Tokyo: Chikuma, 1992), 38–45; Tōyama Shigeki, 'Reforms of the Meiji Restoration and the Birth of Modern Intellectuals,' *Acta Asiatica* 13 (1967): 55–99. See also Scheiner, *Christian Converts and Social Protest in Meiji Japan*, 193–208.

53 See *Civil Society before Democracy: Lessons from Nineteenth-Century Europe*, ed. Nancy Bermeo and Philip Nord (Lanham, MD: Rowman and Littlefield, 2000).

54 Benjamin A. Elman, *A Cultural History of Civil Examinations in Late Imperial China* (Berkeley: University of California Press, 2000), 110–19, 221–37, 371–2, 421–32, 519.

55 For a succinct synthesis, see Lloyd E. Eastman, *Family, Field, and Ancestors: Constancy and Change in China's Social and Economic History, 1550–1949* (New York: Oxford University Press, 1988), 3–14, 128–9, 160–1, 192–4.

56 Weber, 'Bureaucracy,' 240–4.
57 Thomas C. Smith, 'The Right to Benevolence: Dignity and Japanese Workers,' *Native Sources*, 240–1.
58 Hoyt Cleveland Tillman, 'Yan Fu's Utilitarianism in Chinese Perspective,' in *Ideas Across Cultures: Essays on Chinese Thought in Honor of Benjamin I. Schwartz*, ed. Paul A. Cohen and Merle Goldman (Cambridge: Harvard University Press, 1990), 78–80.

2. Mill and His English Critics

1 John Stuart Mill, *On Liberty*, in *The Collected Works of John Stuart Mill*, vol. 18, *Essays on Politics and Society*, Part 1 (Toronto: University of Toronto Press, 1977), 223.
2 Mill, *On Liberty*, 219–20. On the development of Mill's ideas regarding the middle class, see Eileen P. Sullivan, 'A Note on the Importance of Class in the Political Theory of John Stuart Mill,' *Political Theory* 9, no. 2 (1981): 248–56.
3 J.S. Mill, *Autobiography*, in *Collected Works of John Stuart Mill*, vol. 1, *Autobiography and Literary Essays* (Toronto: University of Toronto Press, 1981), 259–61; J.C. Rees, *Mill and His Early Critics* (Leicester: University College, 1956), 1–2, 9–10. See the testimony of the novelist and poet Thomas Hardy, reprinted in J.S. Mill, *On Liberty*, ed. Edward Alexander (Peterborough, Ontario: Broadview, 1999), 184; as well as *The Cambridge Companion to Mill*, ed. John Skorupski (Cambridge: Cambridge University Press, 1998), 1, 466–8, 490n6–7; William Thomas, *Mill* (Oxford: Oxford University Press, 1985), 123–6; and M.W. Taylor, *Men Versus the State: Herbert Spencer and Late Victorian Individualism* (Oxford: Clarendon Press, 1992), 44–5. On Mill's legacy and reputation, see Stefan Collini, 'From Sectarian Radical to National Possession: John Stuart Mill in English Culture, 1873–1945,' in *A Cultivated Mind: Essays on J.S. Mill Presented to John M. Robson*, ed. Michael Laine (Toronto: University of Toronto Press, 1991), 242–72.
4 See Rees, *Mill and His Early Critics*, 17–20.
5 Mill, *On Liberty*, 276.
6 Ibid., 276.
7 Ibid., 292.
8 Ibid., 224.
9 Robert Bell, 'Spiritual Freedom,' *Westminster Review*, no. 142 (1859); repr. in Andrew Pyle, *Liberty: Contemporary Responses to John Stuart Mill* (Bristol: Thoemmes, 1994), 127, 132–3.
10 [R.H. Hutton], 'Mill on Liberty,' *National Review* 8 (1859); repr. in John

Stuart Mill, *On Liberty: Annotated Text, Sources and Background, Criticism*, ed. David Spitz (New York: Norton, 1975), 133–4. N.B. Where Spitz treats this essay as 'anonymous,' Andrew Pyle has identified the writer as R.H. Hutton; see *Liberty: Contemporary Responses to John Stuart Mill*, v, xiv.

11 Herbert Cowell, 'Liberty, Equality, Fraternity: Mr. John Stuart Mill,' *Blackwood's Edinburgh Magazine* 114 (1873); repr. in Pyle, *Liberty: Contemporary Responses to John Stuart Mill*, 303, 305–6.

12 Rees, *Mill and His Early Critics*, 23, 36–7. Elsewhere, Rees famously attempted to justify Mill's distinctions by arguing a meaningful difference between his use of 'rights' in chapter I and 'interests' in chapter V: where interests depend on social recognition and are related to prevailing standards regarding what one can legitimately expect from others, rights are constituted by law. We are responsible to others to the degree that we must respect their constituted rights, and accordingly, the burden is on society to assess the advantages and disadvantages of social intervention into violations of others' rights. See J.C. Rees, 'A Re-Reading of Mill *On Liberty*,' *Political Studies* 8, no. 2 (1960): 113–29; and the critique of Rees, 'The Wood and the Trees,' *Times Literary Supplement*, 10 March 1961: 153. Among the best subsequent discussions of the issues are R.J. Halliday, 'Some Recent Interpretations of John Stuart Mill,' *Philosophy* 43 [No. 163] (1968), repr. in *Mill: A Collection of Critical Essays*, ed. J.B. Schneewind (Notre Dame: University of Notre Dame Press, 1969), 354–78; and C.L. Ten, *Mill on Liberty* (Oxford: Oxford University Press, 1980), 10–67.

13 Mill, *On Liberty*, 279–82.

14 Ibid., 233, 259, 278. See also the pair of essays by H.J. McCloskey and D.H. Monro, both entitled 'Liberty of Expression: Its Ground and Limits,' *Inquiry* 13, no. 3 (1970): 219–37 and 238–53 respectively.

15 An anonymous and untitled review in the *British Quarterly Review* 31 (1860); repr. in J.S. Mill, *On Liberty*, ed. Edward Alexander (Peterborough, Ontario: Broadview, 1999), 206–14. See also Ten, *Mill on Liberty*, 103–7, 134–6; and Jeremy Waldron, 'Mill as a Critic of Culture and Society,' in John Stuart Mill, *On Liberty*, ed. David Bromwich and George Kateb (New Haven: Yale University Press, 2003), 224–45.

16 James Fitzjames Stephen, *Liberty, Equality, Fraternity*, ed. Stuart D. Warner (Indianapolis: Liberty Fund, 1993), 245–8.

17 See chapter 5 below. Stephen's critique of Mill was introduced to Japan by Inoue Tetsujirō, 'Miru no *Jiyū no ri* o hakusu,' *Tōyō gakugei zasshi* 9 (1883): 13–17. I am grateful to Richard Reitan for bringing this text to my attention.

18 Mill, *On Liberty*, 230.

19 Ibid., 267–8.

20 Maurice Cowling, *Mill and Liberalism* (Cambridge: Cambridge University Press, 1963), 98.
21 Mill, *On Liberty,* 282.
22 Rees, *Mill and His Early Critics,* 20, 31–2.
23 See Cowling, *Mill and Liberalism,* 103–5.
24 See Lynn Zastoupil, *John Stuart Mill and India* (Stanford: Stanford University Press, 1994), 51–86, 126–68; and John Stuart Mill, 'Coleridge,' in *Collected Works,* vol. 10, *Essays on Ethics, Religion, and Society* (Toronto: University of Toronto Press, 1969), 140–1.
25 Mill, *Considerations on Representative Government,* in *Collected Works of John Stuart Mill,* vol. 19, *Essays on Politics and Society,* Part 2 (Toronto: University of Toronto Press, 1977), 377–8, 395–6, 401–2.
26 Mill, *On Liberty,* 219–20, 253–4, 268–9. See also Jon Roper, *Democracy and Its Critics: Anglo-American Democratic Thought in the Nineteenth Century* (London: Unwin Hyman, 1989), 3–23, 145–52.
27 Mill, *On Liberty,* 305–7; and *Considerations on Representative Government,* 390.
28 See, for example, Gertrude Himmelfarb, *On Liberty and Liberalism: The Case of John Stuart Mill* (1974; repr. San Francisco: Institute for Contemporary Studies, 1990), 24–6.
29 Stephen, *Liberty,* 55–6.
30 Thomas, *Mill,* 100–3; and Robert Paul Wolff, *The Poverty of Liberalism* (Boston: Beacon Press, 1968), 9–10, 15–20.
31 But see the analysis of G.W. Smith, who draws synthetically from all of Mill's works to argue that we construe Mill's presentation of liberty in *On Liberty* in a positive manner, in that Mill's statement 'warrants interference with others' freedom on the condition that it is only for self-protection'; see 'J.S. Mill on Freedom,' in *Conceptions of Liberty in Political Philosophy,* ed. Zbigniew Pelczynski and John Gray (New York: St Martin's Press, 1984), 182–216. On the difference of positive and negative conceptions of liberty, see Isaiah Berlin, 'Two Concepts of Liberty,' in *Four Essays on Liberty* (Oxford: Oxford University Press, 1969), 118–72; John Gray, *Liberalisms: Essays in Political Philosophy* (London: Routledge, 1989), 45–68; Charles Larmore, 'Liberal and Republican Conceptions of Freedom,' in *Republicanism: History, Theory, and Practice,* ed. Daniel Weinstock and Christian Nadeau (London: Frank Cass, 2004), 96–119; William A. Parent, 'Some Recent Work on the Concept of Liberty,' *American Philosophical Quarterly* 11, no. 3 (1974): 149–67; Quentin Skinner, 'The Idea of Negative Liberty: Philosophical and Historical Perspectives,' in *Philosophy in History: Essays on the Historiography of Philosophy,* ed. Richard Rorty, et al. (Cambridge: Cambridge University Press, 1984), 193–221; and Charles Taylor, 'What's Wrong With Negative

Liberty,' in *Philosophical Papers*, vol. 2, *Philosophy and the Human Sciences* (Cambridge: Cambridge University Press, 1985), 211–29.

32 Rees, *Mill and His Early Critics*, 15.

33 See the anonymous and untitled review from *Saturday Review* 7 (19 February 1859), repr. in J.S. Mill, *On Liberty*, ed. Edward Alexander, 191–3; Robert Bell, 'Spiritual Freedom,' repr. in Pyle, *Liberty: Contemporary Responses to John Stuart Mill*; and Henry Thomas Buckle, 'Mill on Liberty,' *Fraser's Magazine* 59, no. 353 (May 1859), repr. in Pyle, *Liberty: Contemporary Responses to John Stuart Mill*, 76–9.

34 [Hutton], 'Mill on Liberty,' repr. in Mill, *On Liberty: Annotated Text, Sources and Background, Criticism*, ed. David Spitz, 123–42.

35 Mill, *On Liberty*, 288.

36 Skinner, 'The Idea of Negative Liberty,' 202–15; Benjamin Constant, 'The Liberty of the Ancients Compared with That of the Moderns,' in *Political Writings*, ed. Biancamaria Fontana (Cambridge: Cambridge University Press, 1988), 307–28; J.G.A. Pocock, 'Virtues, Rights, and Manners: A Model for Historians of Political Thought,' *Political Theory* 9, no. 3 (1981): 353–68; Bernard Semmel, 'John Stuart Mill's Coleridgean Neoradicalism,' in *Mill and the Moral Character of Liberalism*, ed. Eldon J. Eisenbach (University Park: Pennsylvania State University Press, 1998), 49–76; and Nadia Urbinati, *Mill on Democracy: From the Athenian Polis to Representative Government* (Chicago: University of Chicago Press, 2002), 5, 158–72.

37 Stephen, *Liberty*, 8, 11–12, 35–40, 96–7, 111, 233.

38 See Franz Neumann, 'The Concept of Political Freedom,' in his *The Democratic and the Authoritarian State: Essays in Political and Legal Theory*, ed. Herbert Marcuse (Glencoe, IL: Free Press, 1957), 160–200; and Carl Schmitt, *The Crisis of Parliamentary Democracy*, trans. Ellen Kennedy (Cambridge, MA: MIT Press, 1985), 42–50.

39 Berlin, 'Two Concepts,' 131–4.

40 Wilhelm von Humboldt, *The Limits of State Action*, ed. J.W. Burrow (Indianapolis: Liberty Fund, 1993), 32–3.

41 W.L. Weinstein, 'The Concept of Liberty in Nineteenth-Century English Political Thought,' *Political Studies* 13, no. 2 (1965): 145–62. Also see Richard Bellamy, 'T.H. Green, J.S. Mill, and Isaiah Berlin on the Nature of Liberty and Liberalism,' in *Jurisprudence: Cambridge Essays*, ed. Hyman Gross and Ross Harrison (Oxford: Clarendon, 1992), 257–85.

42 H.J. McCloskey, 'A Critique of the Ideals of Liberty,' *Mind* 74 (1965): 483–508. But see Parent's critique of McCloskey in 'Some Recent Work,' 161–3.

43 Weinstein, 'The Concept of Liberty in Nineteenth-Century English Political Thought,' 153–5.

44 Andrew Vincent and Raymond Plant, *Philosophy, Politics, and Citizenship: The Life and Thought of the British Idealists* (Oxford: Basil Blackwell, 1984), 1–5; Peter P. Nicholson, *The Political Philosophy of the British Idealists: Selected Studies* (Cambridge: Cambridge University Press, 1990), 157–65. See also Sandra M. Den Otter, *British Idealism and Social Explanation: A Study in Late Victorian Thought* (Oxford: Clarendon Press, 1996), 10–51.

45 Nicholson, *Political Philosophy of the British Idealists*, 163. On the problematic identification of the British Idealists with the Liberal Party and 'New Liberalism' of the 1890s, see Vincent and Plant, *Philosophy, Politics, and Citizenship*; Eugenio F. Biagini, *Liberty, Retrenchment, and Reform: Popular Liberalism in the Age of Gladstone, 1860–1880* (Cambridge: Cambridge University Press, 1992); Peter Clarke, *Liberals and Social Democrats* (Cambridge: Cambridge University Press, 1978); Michael Freeden, *The New Liberalism: An Ideology of Social Reform* (Oxford: Clarendon, 1978); and Peter Weiler, *The New Liberalism: Liberal Social Theory in Great Britain, 1889–1914* (New York: Garland, 1982).

46 John Stuart Mill, 'Utilitarianism,' in *Collected Works*, vol. 10, *Essays on Ethics, Religion, and Society* (Toronto: University of Toronto Press, 1969), 229–32. See also the useful comparisons of Mill and Green by Gerald F. Gaus, *The Modern Liberal Theory of Man* (London: Croom Helm; New York: St Martin's Press, 1983), 15–74 passim, 270–1; I.M. Greengarten, *Thomas Hill Green and the Development of Liberal-Democratic Thought* (Toronto: University of Toronto Press, 1981), 131–41; W.H. Greenleaf, *The British Political Tradition*, vol. 2, *The Ideological Heritage* (London: Methuen, 1983), 103–41; and Ben Wempe, *Beyond Equality: A Study of T.H. Green's Theory of Positive Freedom* (Delft: Eburon, 1986), 248–57.

47 See C.B. Macpherson, *Democratic Theory: Essays in Retrieval* (Oxford: Clarendon, 1973), 31–2, 172–7; Melvin Richter, *The Politics of Conscience: T.H. Green and His Age* (Cambrige: Harvard University Press, 1964), 193–7, 204, 210; and Geoffrey Thomas, *The Moral Philosophy of T.H. Green* (Oxford: Clarendon, 1987), 28–31, 227–9, 235–6.

48 Bellamy, 'T.H. Green, J.S. Mill, and Isaiah Berlin,' 258–61, 273–8; Greengarten, *Thomas Hill Green*, 12–37; and Richter, *The Politics of Conscience*, 165–90.

49 T.H. Green, 'Liberal Legislation and Freedom of Contract,' in *Lectures on the Principles of Political Obligation and Other Writings*, ed. Paul Harris and John Morrow (Cambridge: Cambridge University Press, 1986), 199. See also Green's *Lectures on the Principles of Political Obligation*, in ibid., 92, 169–70, and 'On the Different Senses of Freedom as Applied to Will and to the Moral Progress of Man,' in ibid., 228–34, as well as Nicholson, *Political Philosophy of the British Idealists*, 116–22; and Wempe, *Beyond Equality*, 149–74, 197.

50 Green, *Lectures on the Principles of Political Obligation*, 89–90, 108, 159–61;
    Bellamy, 'T.H. Green, J.S. Mill, and Isaiah Berlin,' 278–81; Greengarten, *Tho-
    mas Hill Green*, 37–47, 53–8; Nicholson, *Political Philosophy of the British Ideal-
    ists*, 54–64, 83–95; Richter, *The Politics of Conscience*, 210–12; John Roberts,
    'T.H. Green,' in *Conceptions of Liberty in Political Philosophy*, ed. Zbigniew
    Pelzynski and John Gray (New York: St. Martin's Press, 1984), 243–62; and
    Craig A. Smith, 'The Individual and Society in T.H. Green's Theory of Vir-
    tue,' *History of Political Thought* 2, no. 1 (1981): 187–201.
51 Green, *Lectures on the Principles of Political Obligation*, 89–90, 97.
52 Ibid., 98–9, 102–5; also see Richter, *The Politics of Conscience*, 231–8.
53 Green, *Lectures on the Principles of Political Obligation*, 110–11.
54 Green, 'Liberal Legislation and Freedom of Contract,' 196–208. Two excep-
    tionally helpful discussions of liberal ideas and reform are Brian Harrison,
    'State Intervention and Moral Reform in Nineteenth-Century England,' in
    Pressure from Without in Early Victorian England, ed. Patricia Hollis (London:
    Edward Arnold: 1974), 289–322; and Peter Nicholson, 'T.H. Green and State
    Action: Liquor Legislation,' in *The Philosophy of T.H. Green*, ed. Andrew Vin-
    cent (Aldershot: Gower, 1986), 76–103. Stuart Hampshire justifies such
    work of reform as a desirable aspect of liberal societies in *Justice as Conflict*
    (Princeton: Princeton University Press, 2000), 28–9, 82–3, 88–91.
55 Richard Bellamy, 'T.H. Green and the Morality of Victorian Liberalism,' in
    Victorian Liberalism: Nineteenth-Century Political Thought and Practice, ed.
    Richard Bellamy (London: Routledge, 1990), 142–4; Greengarten, *Thomas
    Hill Green*, 90–8; Richter, *The Politics of Conscience*, 338–43; and Wempe,
    Beyond Equality, 211–20.
56 Green, *Lectures on the Principles of Political Obligation*, 130.
57 Ibid., 170, 174–8. Especially useful is the exchange between Phillip Hansen,
    'T.H. Green and the Moralization of the Market,' *Canadian Journal of Political
    and Social Theory* 1, no. 1 (Winter 1977): 91–117; and Andrew Lawless, 'T.H.
    Green and the British Liberal Tradition,' *Canadian Journal of Political and
    Social Theory* 2, no. 2 (Spring–Summer 1978): 142–55. See also Bellamy, 'T.H.
    Green and the Morality of Victorian Liberalism,' 144–7; Greengarten, *Tho-
    mas Hill Green*, 71–89; Nicholson, *Political Philosophy of the British Idealists*,
    95–115; and Richter, *The Politics of Conscience*, 269–80.
58 L.T. Hobhouse, *Democracy and Reaction* (1904), quoted in Vincent and Plant,
    Philosophy, Politics, and Citizenship, 68.
59 Bernard Bosanquet, *The Philosophical Theory of the State*, 4th ed. (London:
    Macmillan, 1923), 52.
60 Ibid., 57–60; David G. Ritchie, *The Principles of State Interference: Four Essays
    on the Political Philosophy of Mr. Herbert Spencer, J.S. Mill, and T.H. Green*

(London: Swan Sonnenschein, 1902), 83–4; and Thomas, *Moral Philosophy of T. H. Green*, 227–9.

61 Bosanquet, *Philosophical Theory of the State*, 62–7, 72–3; Ritchie, *Principles of State Interference*, 6–8, 22, 53–5, 65, 98–102.

62 See John Morrow, 'Liberalism and British Idealist Political Philosophy: A Reassessment,' *History of Political Thought* 5, no. 1 (1984): 91–108.

63 Bosanquet, *Philosophical Theory of the State*, 32–7.

64 Ritchie, *Principles of State Interference*, 68–9; David G. Ritchie, *Studies in Political and Social Ethics* (London: Swan Sonnenschein, 1902), 54–5. Elsewhere Ritchie equated general will with public opinion; see Den Otter, *British Idealism and Social Explanation*, 166–7.

65 Bernard Bosanquet, *Aspects of the Social Problem* (London: Macmillan, 1895), 290, 331.

66 Bosanquet, *Philosophical Theory of the State*, 99–114, 146–60. See also Nicholson, *Political Philosophy of the British Idealists*, 198–230; and J.W. Burrow, *The Crisis of Reason: European Thought, 1848–1914* (New Haven: Yale University Press, 2000), 122–32.

67 Ritchie, *Principles of State Interference*, 101–2; Ritchie, *Studies in Political and Social Ethics*, 58; and Bosanquet, *Philosophical Theory of the State*, 178, 182.

68 Bosanquet, *Aspects of the Social Problem*, 16–25, 290, 302–7; Ritchie, *Principles of State Interference*, 108–9; Ritchie, *Studies in Political and Social Ethics*, 62–3. On the reform activities of Bosanquet and Ritchie, see Vincent and Plant, *Philosophy, Politics, and Citizenship*, 94–161; on Bosanquet's involvement with the London Ethical Society and other such organizations bridging academic and general audiences, see Den Otter, *British Idealism and Social Explanation*, 133–41; and on the linkage of the idealists' reform activities with the Liberal Party and 'new liberalism,' see Freeden, *The New Liberalism*, 171–5, 200–38.

69 Bosanquet, *Philosophical Theory of the State*, 253–60.

70 Bosanquet, *Aspects of the Social Problem*, 329; Bosanquet, *Philosophical Theory of the State*, 267–71.

71 Ritchie, *Principles of State Interference*, 49–50; and Ritchie, *Studies in Political and Social Ethics*, 1–29. See also Stefan Collini, *Liberalism and Sociology: L.T. Hobhouse and Political Argument in England, 1880–1914* (Cambridge: Cambridge University Press, 1979), 162–7; Den Otter, *British Idealism and Social Explanation*, 91–8; and Freeden, *The New Liberalism*, 90, 98.

72 Den Otter, *British Idealism and Social Explanation*, 98–101. Far more controversial has been Ritchie's and Bosanquet's interest in eugenics; see Freeden, who pronounces it an illiberal trend that was ultimately rejected by liberalism (*The New Liberalism*, 179–94); and Morrow, for whom it is indubitable

evidence of the anti-liberal and anti-individual positions of Bosanquet and Ritchie ('Liberalism and British Idealist Political Philosophy,' 102–4, 106–8).

73 Den Otter, *British Idealism and Social Explanation*, 199–204; see also Collini, *Liberalism and Sociology*, 128–9.

74 Ritchie, *Studies in Political and Social Ethics*, 30–4, 58–60 (quote on p. 34); see also David G. Ritchie, *Natural Rights: A Criticism of Some Political and Ethical Concepts* (London: Allen & Unwin, 1894), 244–62.

75 Ritchie, *Studies in Political and Social Ethics*, 40–2; and Ritchie, *Natural Rights*, 255–8.

76 David G. Ritchie, *Darwinism and Politics* (1889), as paraphrased in Morrow, 'Liberalism and British Idealist Political Philosophy,' 104.

77 Ritchie, *Natural Rights*, 159–60; and D.G. Ritchie, *The Moral Function of the State* (London: Women's Printing Society, 1887).

78 Bosanquet, *Philosophical Theory of the State*, lvi; Ritchie, *Studies in Political and Social Ethics*, 191–2.

3. Nakamura Keiu and the Public Limits of Liberty

1 Aside from routine mention in discussions of the Meiji 'civilization' movement, the Meiji Six Society (Meirokusha), and Christianity in the Meiji period, there are only two sustained discussions of Nakamura Keiu in English, and both concern his translation of Samuel Smiles's *Self Help*: Earl H. Kinmonth, 'Nakamura Keiu and Samuel Smiles: A Victorian Confucian and a Confucian Victorian,' *American Historical Review* 85 (1980): 535–56; and Sarah Metzger-Court, 'Economic Progress and Social Cohesion: Self-Help and the Achieving of a Delicate Balance in Meiji Japan,' *Japan Forum* 3, no. 1 (1991): 11–21. The most important works in Japanese are Shōwa Joshi Daigaku Kindai Bungaku Kenkyūshitsu, ed., *Kindai bungaku kenkyū sōsho* (Tokyo: Kōyōkai, 1956), vol. 1: 405–58; Takahashi Masao, *Nakamura Keiu* (Tokyo: Yoshikawa kōbunkan, 1966); Ogihara Takashi, *Nakamura Keiu kenkyū: Meiji keimō shisō to risōshugi* (Tokyo: Waseda Daigaku shuppanbu, 1990); and Matsuzawa Hiroaki, '*Saikoku risshi hen* to *Jiyū no ri* no sekai: bakumatsu jugaku – bikutoria-chō kyūshinshugi – bunmeikaika,' *Nihon seijigakkai nenpō* (1975): 9–53. On Nakamura's membership in the overseas student group to England (1866–1868), see Andrew Cobbing, *The Japanese Discovery of Victorian Britain: Early Travel Encounters in the Far West* (Richmond, Surrey: Japan Library, 1998), 105–7, 142–3, 158, 162–9; Hara Heizō, 'Tokugawa bakufu no Eikoku ryūgakusei,' *Rekishi chiri* 79, no. 5 (1942): 21–50; Ishizuki Minoru, *Kindai Nihon no kaigai ryūgaku shi* [rev. ed.] (Tokyo: Chūōkōron sha, 1992), 115–26; and Miyanaga Takashi, *Keiō ninen bakufu*

Igirisu ryūgakusei (Tokyo: Shinjinbutsu ōraisha, 1994). In a centennial reminiscence, Inoue Tetsujirō praised Nakamura for his role as an educator but chose to emphasize Nakamura's translation of *Self-Help* and writings on moral education and to ignore *On Liberty* and Nakamura's political activism; see Inoue Tetsujirō, 'Kyōikusha to shite no Nakamura Masanao,' *Kyōiku* 1, no. 5 (8/1933): 71–81.

2 Nakamura Keiu, *Jiyū no ri* (Suruga: Kihira Keiichirō, 1871), repr. in *Meiji bunka zenshū*, vol. 5, *Jiyū minken hen* (Tokyo: Nihon hyōronsha, 1927), 6. Hereafter *JYNR*. In point of fact, *Jiyū no ri* actually appeared in February 1872, being the twelfth lunar month of Meiji 4 (1871); see Takahashi, *Nakamura Keiu*, 103, 286.

3 W.G. Beasley, 'Political Groups in Tosa, 1858–68,' *Bulletin of the School of Oriental and African Studies* 30, no. 2 (1967): 382–90, and 'Politics and the Samurai Class Structure in Satsuma, 1858–1868,' *Modern Asian Studies* 1, no. 1 (1967): 47–57; Bitō Masahide, 'Bushi and the Meiji Restoration,' *Acta Asiatica* 49 (1985): 78–96; H.D. Harootunian, 'Jinsei, Jinzei, and Jitsugaku: Social Values and Leadership in Late Tokugawa Thought,' in *Modern Japanese Leadership: Transition and Change*, ed. Bernard Silberman and H.D. Harootunian (Tucson: University of Arizona Press, 1966), 83–119; Thomas M. Huber, *The Revolutionary Origins of Modern Japan* (Stanford: Stanford University Press, 1981); 3–4, 209–31; Sakata Yoshio, 'Meiji ishin to kaikyū shikan,' *Jimbun gakuhō*, no. 1 (1950): 43–60; Bernard S. Silberman, *Cages of Reason: The Rise of the Rational State in France, Japan, the United States, and Great Britain* (Chicago: University of Chicago Press, 1993), 159–222; and Takahashi Kamekichi, *Nihon kindai keizai keiseishi* (Tokyo: Tōyō keizai shinpōsha, 1968), 2: 44–57.

4 Roger W. Bowen, *Rebellion and Democracy in Meiji Japan: A Study of Commoners in the Popular Rights Movement* (Berkeley: University of California Press, 1980), 217; Matsuo Shōichi, *Jiyūminken shisō no kenkyū*, rev. and expanded ed. (Tokyo: Nihon keizai hyōronsha, 1990), 16–17; Ōkubo Toshiaki, *Meiji no shisō to bunka* (Tokyo: Yoshikawa kōbunkan, 1988), 4; and Shimoide Junkichi, '*Jiyū no ri* kaidai,' in *Meiji bunka zenshū*, vol. 5, *Jiyū minken hen* (Tokyo: Nihon hyōronsha, 1927), 2–5.

5 *Seifu* referred quite literally to the council chamber within Edo Castle or the Imperial Palace in Kyoto; by metaphorical extension, it came to mean the Council of State (which met in the chamber) and in turn the 'government' generally. On the background of translation words for society, see Florian Coulmas, 'Language Adaptation in Meiji Japan,' in *Language Policy and Political Development*, ed. Brian Weinstein (Norwood, NJ: Ablex, 1990), 69–86; and Douglas Howland, *Translating the West: Language and Political Reason*

in Nineteenth-Century Japan (Honolulu: University of Hawai'i Press, 2002), 153–71. Nakamura's 'confusion' of society and government has been noted by Wang Kefei, *Zhong-Ri jindai dui xifang zhengzhi zhexue sixiang de shequ: Yan Fu yu Riben qimeng xuezhe* (Beijing: Zhongguo shehui kexue chubanshe, 1996), 113–14; see also Yamashita Shigekazu, 'Nakamura Keiu yaku *Jiyū no ri* ni tsuite,' *Kokugakuin daigaku Tochigi tanki daigaku kiyō*, no. 6 (1972): 61–75.

6 G.W.F. Hegel, *Philosophy of Right*, trans. T.M. Knox (Oxford: Clarendon Press, 1957), x–xi, 110, 123.

7 In contrast to the situation described in this paragraph, the subsequent Japanese translation of *On Liberty* systematically employs terminology still current today: *shakai* for 'society,' *kojin* for 'individual,' and so on; see *Jiyū no kenri*, trans. Takahashi Masajirō (Tokyo: Miyamoto insatsujo, 1895).

8 Nakamura, *JYNR*, 7–8. The material in parentheses is parenthetical in Nakamura's original.

9 For an explication of the meanings of *ken*, see Howland, *Translating the West*, 124–9.

10 For a second example, the substitution of 'government' for 'social group' (*nakama-kaisha*), see Nakamura, *JYNR*, 65.

11 Dan Fenno Henderson discusses *nakamagoto* as 'mutual affairs,' the lowest of four categories of legal claims treated by Tokugawa courts (after land and water claims, main suits, money suits); see 'Contracts in Tokugawa Villages,' *Journal of Japanese Studies* 1, no. 1 (1974): 70. Albert Craig discusses *nakama* in terms of commercial 'guilds' in *Chōshū in the Meiji Restoration* (Cambridge: Harvard University Press, 1961), 32–3, and Appendix, xxxi.

12 See Alexis de Tocqueville, *Democracy in America*, ed. J.P. Mayer and Max Lerner, trans. George Lawrence (New York: Harper & Row, 1966), 335.

13 Adam Ferguson, *An Essay on the History of Civil Society*, ed. Fania Oz-Salzberger (Cambridge: Cambridge University Press, 1995), 7–24, 131–41; Hegel, *Philosophy of Right*, 122–55; Raymond Plant, *Hegel: An Introduction*, 2d ed. (Oxford: Basil Blackwell, 1983), 21–5; and Steven B. Smith, *Hegel's Critique of Liberalism: Rights in Context* (Chicago: University of Chicago Press, 1989), 104–5, 140–5. Tocqueville, too, saw the basis of civil society in political associations; see *Democracy in America*, 225.

14 John Stuart Mill, *On Liberty*, in *The Collected Works of John Stuart Mill*, vol. 18, *Essays on Politics and Society*, Part 1 (Toronto: University of Toronto Press, 1977), 217–18; Nakamura, *JYNR*, 8. A subsequent and public discussion of liberty by Mitsukuri Rinshō similarly stressed one's right to participate in government, but made no mention of representative institutions: Mitsukuri Rinshō, '*Riberuchii* no setsu,' *Meiroku zasshi*, no. 9 (1874): 2b–4b. Cf. 'Liberty,'

in *Meiroku Zasshi: Journal of the Japanese Enlightenment*, trans. William Braisted (Cambridge: Harvard University Press, 1976), 117–19.

15 Mill, *On Liberty*, 219; Nakamura, *JYNR*, 9.

16 Maruyama Masao, *Studies in the Intellectual History of Tokugawa Japan*, trans. Mikiso Hane (Princeton: Princeton University Press; Tokyo: University of Tokyo Press, 1974), 249–64.

17 In the same way, Nakamura misses the point of what it might mean for a self-governing country to be composed of multiple villages, and how, for example, conflict might be resolved; the adjudication of criminal cases could no longer be solved by exile or ostracism, as was practiced in the Tokugawa period.

18 Nakamura, *JYNR*, 10. Cf. Mill, *On Liberty*, 219–20.

19 See Roman Jakobson, 'On Linguistic Aspects of Translation,' in *On Translation*, ed. Reuben A. Brower (Cambridge: Harvard University Press, 1959), 232–9.

20 Irwin Scheiner, *Christian Converts and Social Protest in Meiji Japan* (Berkeley: University of California Press, 1970), 121.

21 Henry Maine, *Lectures on the Early Histories of Institutions*, 7th ed., ([1914], repr. Port Washington, NY: Kennikat Press, 1966), 76–90, 226–33; J.W. Burrow, '"The Village Community" and the Uses of History in Late Nineteenth-Century England,' in *Historical Perspectives: Studies in English Thought and Society in Honour of J.H. Plumb*, ed. Neil McKendrick (London: Europa, 1974), 255–84; J.W. Burrow, *The Crisis of Reason: European Thought, 1848–1914* (New Haven: Yale University Press, 2000), 113–21; and Alfons Dopsch, *The Economic and Social Foundations of European Civilization* (New York: Howard Fertig, 1969), 1–29, 93–131.

22 Henry Maine, *Village Communities in the East and West*, 3d ed. (New York: Henry Holt, 1889); Louis Dumont, 'The "Village Community" from Munro to Maine,' *Contributions to Indian Sociology*, no. 9 (1966): 67–89; Clive Dewey, 'Images of the Village Community: A Study in Anglo-Indian Ideology,' *Modern Asian Studies* 6, no. 3 (1972): 291–328; Ronald Inden, *Imagining India* (London: Routledge, 1990), 131–61; and J.B. Peires, *The Dead Will Arise: Nongqawuse and the Great Xhosa Cattle-Killing Movement of 1856–7* (Bloomington: Indiana University Press, 1989), 246–61, 290–6.

23 Nakamura, *JYNR*, 3.

24 See Otis Cary, *A History of Christianity in Japan* (1909; repr. Rutland, VT: Tuttle, 1976), I: 274–335; II: 11–88; and Scheiner, *Christian Converts and Social Protest*, 11–25.

25 From 1856, tolerance for Christianity was a point of diplomatic pressure on the part of especially the United States and France; the experience of the

Iwakura Mission convinced the Japanese government that it had to lift the ban, which it did on the return of the mission in 1873. See Cary, *A History of Christianity in Japan*, I: 317–26, II: 37–40, 80–2. On the history of Christianity in Meiji Japan, see Yamaji Aizan, *Essays on the Modern Japanese Church: Christianity in Meiji Japan*, trans. Graham Squires (Ann Arbor: Center for Japanese Studies, The University of Michigan: 1999), and especially the introduction by A. Hamish Ion, '*Essays* and Meiji Protestant Christian History,' 25–42.

26 On E.W. Clark in Japan and Nakamura's early advocacy of Christianity, see two articles by A. Hamish Ion, 'Edward Warren Clark and Early Meiji Japan: A Case Study of Cultural Contact,' *Modern Asian Studies* 11, no. 4 (1977): 557–72; and 'Edward Warren Clark and the Formation of the Shizuoka and Koishikawa Christian Bands (1871–1879),' in *Foreign Employees in Nineteenth-Century Japan*, ed. Edward R. Beauchamp and Akira Iriye (Boulder, CO: Westview, 1993), 171–89. See also E.W. Clark, *Life and Adventure in Japan* (New York: American Tract Society, 1878), 8–52; Ōkubo Toshiaki, 'Meiji shoki bunka shijō ni okeru Shizuoka: Shizuoka no bunmeikaika,' *Rangaku shiryō kenkyūkai kenkyū hōkoku*, no. 217 (1969): 4–24; Ōta Aito, *Meiji Kirisutokyō no ryūiki: Shizuoka bando to bakushintachi* (Tokyo: Tsukiji shokan, 1979), 16–60; Ozawa Saburō, *Nihon purotesutanto shi kenkyū* (Tokyo: Tōkai daigaku, 1964), 228–50; Neil Pedlar, *The Imported Pioneers: Westerners Who Helped Build Modern Japan* (New York: St Martin's Press, 1990), 121–5; Takahashi, *Nakamura Keiu*, 85–102; and Yoshino Sakuzō, 'Shizuoka gakkō no kyōshi Kurāku sensei,' *Shinkyū jidai*, 3, no. 2 (1927): 18–25. Nakamura's memorial, 'Gi taiseijin jōsho,' is reprinted in *Meiji keimō shisō shū*, ed. Ōkubo Toshiaki (Tokyo: Chikuma, 1967), 281–3; for the history of the essay, see Howland, *Translating the West*, 222n50.

27 Nakamura's turn to Christianity is a topic of occasional scholarly interest; the typical strategy is to draw links between Confucian and Christian (or Western) concepts, such as equating *xing-er-xia* (J: *keijika*, 'that within the world of form') with science, and *xing-er-shang* (J: *keijijō*, 'that above the world of form') with the world of thought, morality, and the spirit, or again, equating heaven and God. See Kobayashi Toshihiro, *Meiji zenki shisō* (Tokyo: Sanwa shobō, 1988), 118–21, 128; Ishizuki, *Kindai Nihon no kaigai ryūgaku shi*, 116; Maeda Ai, *Bakumatsu – Ishinki no bungaku* (Tokyo: Hōsei daigaku shuppankyoku, 1972), 271–4; and Ogihara Takashi, who equates Confucian 'principle' with Nakamura's 'truth,' 250–5. Takahashi Masao proposes that Nakamura redefined Confucian 'mutuality' as Christian love, in *Nakamura Keiu*, 63; and that Nakamura explained God and Christianity with Chinese concepts informed especially by W.A.P. Martin's treatise *Tiandao suyuan*, 67–71.

28 Mill, *On Liberty*, 235–41, 254–7.
29 Mill, *On Liberty*, 235–6, 238–9, 265–6. See also Eldon J. Eisenach, 'Mill and Liberal Christianity,' and Robert Devigne, 'Mill on Liberty and Religion: An Unfinished Dialectic,' both in *Mill and the Moral Character of Liberalism*, ed. Eldon J. Eisenach (University Park: Pennsylvania State University Press, 1998), 191–229 and 231–56.
30 See Howland, *Translating the West*, 94–107.
31 Nakamura, *JYNR*, 18. Maeda Ai suggested that Nakamura's endorsement of love was related to the ancient Chinese concept of 'universal love' (C: *boai* / J: *hakuai*), in *Bakumatsu – Ishinki no bungaku*, 282. See also Kobayashi, *Meiji zenki shisō*, 112–13.
32 E.W. Clark, Introduction to Nakamura, *JYNR*, 3–4. Clark's introduction was originally in English.
33 Nakamura, *JYNR*, 18–19. This point has been noted by Ōta, *Meiji Kirisutokyō no ryūiki*, 48.
34 Mill, *On Liberty*, 222.
35 Ibid., 247–8, 254–5; Nakamura, *JYNR*, 33–6, 40–1.
36 Ogihara Takashi claims that for Nakamura, morality and religion are interchangeable; but I would argue that Nakamura advocated collective morality yet remained committed to the freedom of the individual to select his religion; see *Nakamura Keiu kenkyū*, 145, 150.
37 Ibid., 256–9.
38 Compare Mill, *On Liberty*, 231–2, and Nakamura, *JYNR*, 21–2.
39 Nakamura, *JYNR*, 1.
40 Compare Mill, *On Liberty*, 262; and Nakamura, *JYNR*, 46. Nakamura had earlier established the concept of 'experience' (*keiken*) in his 1870 translation of Samuel Smiles's *Self-Help* as *Saikoku risshi hen*.
41 On the Confucian elements in Nakamura's liberalism, see Ogihara, *Nakamura Keiu kenkyū*, 117–22, 130–4.
42 See Shimoide Junkichi's account of Kōno Hironaka, in '*Jiyū no ri* kaidai'; and Ōkubo Ichiō's personal story in his preface to Nakamura, *JYNR*, 5.
43 Nakamura, *JYNR*, 33, 46. Compare Mill, *On Liberty*, 246. Where Mill's purpose is to differentiate Catholic and Protestant views of the soul's development, and he criticizes the Catholic elite who have sole access to the scripture, Nakamura presents the two as different but nonetheless legitimate approaches.
44 Nakamura, *JYNR*, 4.
45 Mill, *On Liberty*, 260–3; Nakamura, *JYNR*, 44–8.
46 Scheiner, *Christian Converts and Social Protest*, 160, 165–6. Scheiner's analysis deals especially with the psychological dimensions of conversion to Chris-

tianity, invoking alienation and the impact of modernization on the individual, as in the analyses of Max Weber and Robert Bellah.

47 F.G. Notehelfer, *American Samurai: Captain L.L. Janes and Japan* (Princeton: Princeton University Press, 1985), 192–3.

48 Scheiner, *Christian Converts and Social Protest*, 153–4, 159, 182–3.

49 See ibid., 188–247; and Takeda Kiyoko, 'Japanese Christianity: Between Orthodoxy and Heterodoxy,' in *Authority and the Individual in Japan: Citizen Protest in Historical Perspective*, ed. J. Victor Koschmann (Tokyo: University of Tokyo Press, 1978), 82–107.

50 See Patrick Riley, Introduction to François de Fénelon, *Telemachus, Son of Ulysses* (Cambridge: Cambridge University Press, 1994), xiii–xxxi.

51 Nakamura, *JYNR*, 18.

52 Compare Nakamura, *JYNR*, 17–18, and Fénelon, *Telemachus*, 36–8. Later in the tale (pp. 161–71), Fénelon records a similar but more extensive discussion at the city of Salente.

53 Nakamura, *JYNR*, 18.

54 Mill, *On Liberty*, 293.

55 Ibid., 293–4. But several scholars have noted Mill's admission that the principle of individual liberty is not involved in free trade; see, for example, Jonathan Riley, 'Individuality, Custom, and Progress,' *Utilitas* 3, no. 2 (1991): 217–44.

56 Hence, Nakamura also differed from Mill's contemporaries, the Protestant Dissenters, who advocated both free trade and individual liberty, especially as concerned the removal of state support for the Anglican Church; see J.P. Ellens, 'Which Freedom for Early Victorian Britain?' in *Freedom and Religion in the Nineteenth Century*, ed. Richard Helmstadter (Stanford: Stanford University Press, 1997), 87–119 (esp. 112–17).

57 See Nishimura Shigeki's contribution to the *Meiroku zasshi*, 'On Free Trade,' translated by Braisted, 356–8, which advocates the national and protectionist position.

4. Yan Fu and the Moral Prerequisites of Liberty

1 Standard works for Yan's biography include Guo Zhengzhao, *Yan Fu* (Taibei: Taiwan shangwu yinshuguan,1978); Benjamin Schwartz, *In Search of Wealth and Power: Yen Fu and the West* (Cambridge: Harvard University Press, 1964); Elizabeth Sinn, 'Yan Fu,' in *An Encyclopedia of Translation: Chinese-English, English-Chinese*, ed. Chan Sin-wai and David E. Pollard (Hong Kong: Chinese University Press, 1995), 429–47; Wang Quchang, *Yan Jidao nianpu* (Shanghai: Shangwu yinshuguan, 1936); Wang Shi, *Yan Fu*

zhuan (Shanghai: Renmin chubanshe, 1975); Wang Shi and Yu Zheng, *Yan Fu* (Shanghai: Jiangsu guji chubanshe, 1984); and Xiong Yuezhi, *Xixue dongjian yu wanqing shehui* (Shanghai: Renmin chubanshe, 1994), 679–701. The great majority of work on Yan concerns his contribution of the concept of evolution to modern Chinese thought and his translation of Thomas Huxley's *Ethics and Evolution* as *Tianyan lun*; in addition to the preceding works, see Masuda Wataru, *Chūgoku bungakushi kenkyū: bungaku kakumei to zen'ya no hitobito* (Tokyo: Iwanami, 1967), 173–201; Onogawa Hidemi, *Shinmatsu seiji shisō kenkyū* (Tokyo: Misuzu shobō, 1969), 251–7, 277–8; James R. Pusey, *China and Charles Darwin* (Cambridge: Harvard University, Council on East Asian Studies, 1983), 16–79, 155–72; Takata Atsushi, 'Gen Fuku no Ten'en ron no shisō,' *Tōkyō Jōshidaigaku fuzoku hikakubunka kenkyūjo kiyō* 20 (1965): 1–61; and Zhou Zhenfu, *Yan Fu sixiang shuping* (Taibei: Taiwan Zhonghua shuju, 1964), 24–75.

2 Among previous readings of Yan's translation of *On Liberty*, Benjamin Schwartz noted in *In Search of Wealth and Power* that Yan emphasizes 'virtue' before Mill's 'well-being,' but Schwartz treated *Qun ji quan jie lun* in the context of Yan's evolutionism – that liberty contributes to the power of the group and the survival of the best ideas. Several Chinese and Japanese scholars treat *Qun ji quan jie lun* as a step in the development of Yan's concepts of liberty and democracy, or liberalism broadly construed: see Huang Ko-wu, *Ziyou de suoyiran: Yan Fu dui Yuehan Mier ziyou sixiang de renshi yu pipan* (Taibei: Yunchen wenhua, 1998); Imamura Yoshio, 'Jiyū no keifu,' in *Kōza Chūgoku*, vol. 3, *Kakumei no tenkai*, ed. Nohara Shirō (Tokyo: Chikuma shobō, 1967), 155–99 (esp. 163–8); Lin Anwu, 'Gexing ziyou yu shehui quanxian,' *Si yu yan* 27, no. 1 (1989): 1–18; Lin Caijue, 'Yan Fu dui ziyou de lijie,' *Donghai Daxue lishi xuebao*, no. 5 (1982): 85–159; Yang Yiyin and Tang Xinglin, 'Yan Fu bing fei tianfu ziyouzhe bian,' *Chongqing shiyuan xuebao (zhe she ban)*, no. 56 (1994): 106–11; and Zhang Zhijian, *Yan Fu sixiang yanjiu* (Guilin: Guangxi shifan daxue chubanshe, 1989).

3 On the issue of harm, see Joel Feinberg, *The Moral Limits of the Criminal Law*, vol. 1, *Harm to Others* (New York: Oxford University Press, 1984); and John Gray, *Two Faces of Liberalism* (New York: New Press, 2000), 85–8.

4 *Ren* is often translated as benevolence or humanity. In light of Yan's discussion of the relation between the self and the group, and following Herbert Fingarette, I would emphasize the reciprocal good faith implicit in *ren*. See Herbert Fingarette, *Confucius – The Secular as Sacred* (New York: Harper & Row, 1972), 37–56; Raymond Dawson, *Confucius* (Oxford: Oxford University Press, 1981), 37–44; Hao Chang, *Chinese Intellectuals in Crisis: Search for Order and Meaning (1890–1911)* (Berkeley: University of California Press,

1987), 80–4; David L. Hall and Roger T. Ames, *Thinking Through Confucius* (Albany: State University of New York Press, 1987), 110–27; and Zhang Dainian, *Key Concepts in Chinese Philosophy*, trans. and ed. Edmund Ryden (New Haven: Yale University Press, 2002), 285–310.

5 Irene Bloom, 'The Moral Autonomy of the Individual in Confucian Tradition,' in *Realms of Freedom in Modern China*, ed. William C. Kirby (Stanford: Stanford University Press, 2004), 19–45.

6 Yan Fu, trans., *Qun ji quan jie lun* ([Shanghai]: Shangwu yinshuguan, n.d.), 'Yi fanli,' 4–5. (In the series *Yan yi mingzhu congkan*.) Hereafter *QJQJL*. When citing from Yan's additional preliminary matter, as in this footnote, I cite the section by name ('Yi fanli'); otherwise page numbers refer to the body of the translation of Mill.

7 Ibid., 'Yizhe xu,' 1.

8 Although *quan* is now a component of the Chinese translation word for 'right' (*quanli*), it does not always mean that in *Qun ji quan jie lun*, in which Yan tends to use *quanli* for the nineteenth-century notion of 'right and privilege' or 'rights and interests,' and in which he introduced *minzhi* as a deliberate translation for 'people's right,' a neologism that did not last (see pp. 2, 90). This expression *minzhi* for 'right' is complicated by an analogous term *tianzhi* or 'heavenly uprightness' (pp. 80–1), which does not mean 'natural right' to Yan; see Huang, *Ziyou de suoyiran*, 123n5, 166–9. On the development of *quanli* for 'right,' see Stephen C. Angle, 'Did Someone Say "Rights"? Liu Shipei's Concept of *Quanli*,' *Philosophy East and West* 48, no. 4 (1998): 623–51; idem., 'Should We All Be More English? Liang Qichao, Rudolf von Jhering, and Rights,' *Journal of the History of Ideas* 61, no. 2 (2000): 241–61; Douglas Howland, *Translating the West: Language and Political Reason in Nineteenth-Century Japan* (Honolulu: University of Hawai'i Press, 2002), 122–9; Mizoguchi Yūzō, 'Zhongguo minquan sixiang de tese,' in *Zhongguo xiandaihua lunwenji*, ed. Zhongyang yanjiuyuan jindaishi yanjiusuo (Taibei: Zhongyang yanjiuyuan jindaishi yanjiusuo, 1991), 343–62; and Rune Svarverud, 'The Notions of "Power" and "Rights" in Chinese, Political Discourse,' in Michael Lackner, et al., eds., *New Terms for New Ideas: Western Knowledge and Lexical Change in Late Imperial China* (Leiden: Brill, 2001), 125–43.

9 See, by comparison, the instructive effort by Albert William Levi to identify levels of analysis related to individual and society in Mill and his critics: 'The Value of Freedom: Mill's Liberty (1859–1959),' *Ethics* 12 (1959): 37–46.

10 Xun Kuang, *Xunzi: A Translation and Study of the Complete Works*, [by] John Knoblock (Stanford: Stanford University Press, 1988–1994), I: 225; and II: 103–5. Yan translates 'flock' of sheep with *qun* in *QJQJL*, 72, 81. On Yan's use of *qun* for 'society,' see Wah K. Cheng, 'Citizenry, Nationhood, and the Chi-

nese State: Yan Fu and the Question of National Strength,' unpub. ms., 8–10, 23–5; and Pusey, *China and Charles Darwin*, 63–8. For the use of *qun* among Yan and his contemporaries, see Hao Chang, *Chinese Intellectuals in Crisis*, 109–12; idem., *Liang Ch'i-ch'ao and Intellectual Transition in China* (Cambridge: Harvard University Press, 1971), 98–103; Chen Shude, '"Qunxue" yiming kaoxi,' *Shehuixue yanjiu*, no. 6 (6/1988): 74–8, Rebecca E. Karl, *Staging the World: Chinese Nationalism at the Turn of the Twentieth Century* (Durham: Duke University Press, 2001): 89–101; Pusey, *China and Charles Darwin* 63–6, 107–12; Suzuki Shūji, *Bunmei no kotoba* (Hiroshima: Bunka hyōron, 1981), 85–97; Xiaobing Tang, *Global Space and Nationalist Discourse of Modernity: The Historical Thinking of Liang Qichao* (Stanford: Stanford University Press,1996), 63–8; and Wang Fan-shen, 'Evolving Prescriptions for Social Life in the Late Qing and Early Republic: From *Qunxue* to Society,' in *Imagining the People: Chinese Intellectuals and the Concept of Citizenship, 1890–1920*, ed. Joshua A. Fogel and Peter Zarrow (Armonk, NY: M.E. Sharpe, 1997), 258–78.

11 Yan, *QJQJL*, 89, 115.
12 Ibid., 'Yi fanli,' 1–2.
13 Ibid., 5, 7.
14 Ibid., 1–2.
15 Ibid., 86, 88. On the relation between 'self' and 'individual' in the rise of national China, see especially Lydia H. Liu, 'Translingual Practice: The Discourse of Individualism between China and the West,' *positions: east asia cultures critiqe* 1, no. 1 (Spring 1993): 160–93; see also Lin Anwu, 'Gexing ziyou yu shehui quanxian'; Wang Kefei, *Zhong-Ri jindai dui xifang zhengzhi zhexue sixiang de shequ: Yan Fu yu Riben qimeng xuezhe* (Beijing: Zhongguo shehui kexue chubanshe, 1996), 114; and David L. Hall and Roger T. Ames, *Thinking from the Han: Self, Truth, and Transcendence in Chinese and Western Culture* (Albany: SUNY Press, 1998), 3–43 [p. 5].
16 On the development of *geren zhuyi* as 'individualism,' see Lydia H. Liu, 'Translingual Practice,' 169.
17 Yan, *QJQJL*, 4. See also p. 3, where Yan differentiates 'self-governing people' (*zizhi zhi min*) from the concrete task of the people 'governing themselves' (*zhiji*). For a useful contextualization of 'self-governing,' see Roger R. Thompson, *China's Local Councils in the Age of Constitutional Reform, 1898–1911* (Cambridge: Council on East Asian Studies, Harvard University, 1995), 3–20.
18 Yan, *QJQJL*, 12–13.
19 Ibid., 11.
20 John Stuart Mill, *On Liberty*, in *The Collected Works of John Stuart Mill*, vol. 18, *Essays on Politics and Society*, Part 1 (Toronto: University of Toronto Press, 1977), 220.

21 Yan, *QJQJL*, 6, 24.
22 Ibid., 9. The quoted material ('I act ...') is introduced with the Chinese verb of quotation, *yue*.
23 Yan's 'Notes on the Translation' begin with a discussion of the difference between liberty, justice, and equitability; see *QJQJL*, 'Yi fanli,' 1.
24 Ibid., 6, 8–9. In light of what follows, and for the benefit of readers familiar with Mill, I note that Mill, too, undertook in a subsequent essay, 'Utilitarianism' (1861), to coordinate utility and justice. But Mill analysed justice as legal and moral rights, which he discussed in terms of duties and obligations in order to leave justice (and thus morality) largely grounded in utility. For Yan, moral relations are paramount, which may be justified according to utility, but which explicitly give rise to justice. See John Stuart Mill, 'Utilitarianism,' in *Collected Works*, vol. 10, *Essays on Ethics, Religion, and Society* (Toronto: University of Toronto Press, 1969), 240–59; and F.R. Berger, 'John Stuart Mill on Justice and Fairness,' *Canadian Journal of Philosophy*, Supp. Vol. 5 (1979): 115–36.
25 Yan, *QJQJL*, 'Yi fanli,' 1, 3.
26 Ibid., 1.
27 Ibid., 1, 5.
28 Ibid., 'Yi fanli,' 4.
29 Ibid., 40, 43.
30 Ibid., 'Yi fanli,' 4. Yan justified his choice of Chinese characters for his translation word for 'liberty,' *ziyou*, as an effort to produce a concept more 'substantial' than the alternative form used in Japan (and now standard in China). Where the Japanese *ziyou* (J: *jiyū*) employed an abstract term, *you* (the preposition 'from,' which thus attributed a reason or agent, and which Yan deemed 'insubstantial'), Yan chose instead a concrete but ancient homonym that meant 'thread' or 'string' – not to be pedantically archaic but to emphasize a concrete connectedness that he perceived in the Western precedent; see *QJQJL*, 'Yi fanli,' 3. See also Wang Kefei, *Zhong-Ri jindai dui xifang zhengzhi zhexue sixiang de shequ*, 97–104; and Zhang Foquan, *Ziyou yu renquan* (Hong Kong: Yazhou chubanshe, 1955), 21–3.
31 Yan, *QJQJL*, 'Yi fanli,' 4.
32 Ibid., 'Yi fanli,' 3.
33 Ibid., 'Yi fanli,' 4–5.
34 Mill, *On Liberty*, 262–4.
35 Yan, *QJQJL*, 10. But note that elsewhere, in the discussion of restricting the group's interference, Yan doubts that we can impose civilized law on barbarians; by comparison, Mill doubts that, in the manner of a crusade, 'one community has a right to force another to be civilized'; see *QJQJL*, 109, and *On Liberty*, 291.

36 Yan, *QJQJL*, 'Yifan li,' 4.
37 Herbert Spencer, *Social Statics* (New York: Schalkenbach Foundation, 1995), 77–8, 95. See also Douglas Howland, 'Society Reified: Herbert Spencer and Political Theory in Early Meiji Japan,' *Comparative Studies in Society and History* 42, no. 1 (2000): 67–86.
38 Yan, *QJQJL*, 'Yi fanli,' 2–3.
39 For a different evaluation of Yan's commitment to traditional concepts of sagehood, see Charlotte Furth, 'Intellectual Change: From the Reform Movement to the May Fourth Movement, 1895–1920,' in *The Cambridge History of China*, vol. 12, *Republican China 1912–1949*, Part 1, ed. John K. Fairbank (Cambridge: Cambridge University Press, 1983), 336.
40 Yan's term for 'selfish,' *si*, can also mean 'personal,' 'partial' or 'private.' In *QJQJL*, *si* figures especially as selfish intent in conflicts – that which inhibits a person's or a faction's reciprocity (pp. 61, 63–4, 99) – and as a personal or private form of authority (p. 99) or virtue (p. 94).
41 See Huang Ko-wu's argument that Yan's 'epistemological optimism' was incompatible with Mill's 'epistemological pessimism' – on the point of human fallibility – and hence Yan missed many of the correctives implicit in Mill's text: *Ziyou de suoyiran*, 6, 26–30, 117–19, 148–51, 186–9.
42 For an excellent discussion of the conceptual development of private and public in Chinese history, see Mizoguchi Yūzō, 'Chūgoku no kō-shi,' *Bungaku* 56 (9/1988): 88–102 and (10/1988): 73–84.
43 Hall and Ames, *Thinking Through Confucius*, 158–9.
44 Ibid., 136.
45 Ibid., 135.
46 Ibid., 170.
47 Ibid., 169, 171.
48 Ibid., 179. The public dimension of the sage's virtue is also discussed by Wm. Theodore de Bary, *The Liberal Tradition in China* (Hong Kong: Chinese University Press; New York: Columbia University Press, 1983), 48–52; and Mizoguchi Yūzō, 'Chūgoku ni okeru kō-shi gainen no tenkai,' *Shisō*, no. 669 (3/1980): 20.
49 Mark Edward Lewis, *Sanctioned Violence in Early China* (Albany: State University of New York Press, 1990), 8–9, 28–9, 33–4, 43–50.
50 Ibid., 9–10, 50, 53, 55–60, 62.
51 Lewis offers a number of interesting examples in support of his thesis: the ritual uttering of oaths became the written oath that served as a model for law (pp. 24, 67–72); the term *mie zu* shifted in meaning from the utter destruction of a lineage and state to the principle of the collective punishment of families within the legal code (pp. 10, 49, 91–2); and most intrigu-

ingly, the problem of vengeance: it was initially a family (private) and state point of honour, and remained in the later period, when the state asserted itself as the sole commander of public violence, an element of families' moral codes (pp. 80–92). Revenge remained a point of contradiction, a sign that the conversion of the private to public forms was not complete; see Michael Dalby, 'Revenge and the Law in Traditional China,' *American Journal of Legal History* 25 (1981): 267–307.

52 Yan, *QJQJL*, 13.

53 On *xingji*, see Confucius, *The Analects*, trans. D.C. Lau (Harmondsworth: Penguin, 1979), 78 (V.16.) and 121 (XIII.20.); and *Sishu jizhu*, ann. Zhu Xi (Taibei: Xuehai chubanshe, 1979), 29, 91. On *tecao*, see *Zhuangzi* II.11 ('Qiwu lun,' sect. 7); e.g., *Zhuangzi jinzhu jinyi*, ann. Chen Guying (Taibei: Taiwan shangwu yinshuguan, 1975), I: 100; *Complete Works of Chuang Tzu*, trans. Burton Watson (N.Y.: Columbia University Press, 1968), 49; and *Chuang-tzu: The Seven Inner Chapters*, trans. A.C. Graham (London: Allen & Unwin, 1981), 61. See also Huang, *Ziyou de suoyiran*, 162.

54 Yan, *QJQJL*, 69. Compare Mill's terse original, the point of which is logic: 'He who chooses his plan for himself, employs all his faculties. He must use observation to see, reasoning and judgment to foresee, activity to gather materials for decision, discrimination to decide, and when he has decided, firmness and self-control to hold to his deliberate decision.' Mill, *On Liberty*, 262–3.

55 Yan, *QJQJL*, 83, 88. Mill's expression 'public opinion' is interpreted in various ways in Yan's translation. As Huang Ko-wu has argued, Yan sometimes uses *yulun*, or 'popular opinion' – what many people think (e.g, pp. 78, 88) – but more often he uses *qingyi*, or 'enlightened criticism,' righteous criticism that officials and the educated could level as a corrective measure against their superiors in government. The latter has a very different meaning from Mill's original; see Huang, *Ziyou de suoyiran*, 139–47.

56 Yan, *QJQJL*, 69, 74–6, 83–6.

57 Ibid., 71, 75.

58 Ibid., 66–7, 70–1, 76. Cf. Wm. Theodore de Bary's discussion of 'neo-Confucian individualism' in *The Liberal Tradition in China*, 43–66.

59 Yan, *QJQJL*, 67. On Confucian virtues in the *Analects*, see Fingarette, *Confucius*, 37–56; and Fung Yu-lan, *A History of Chinese Philosophy*, trans. Derk Bodde (Princeton: Princeton University Press, 1952–53), I: 66–73.

60 Yan, *QJQJL*, 78.

61 Ibid., 76–7. Cf. p. 40, for an analogous description of the religious leader.

62 *Mencius*, trans. D.C. Lau (London: Penguin, 1970), 183 (VII.A.10.). In later

centuries, *haojie* took on the meaning of military hero, emphasizing martial aspects of his character.

63 Yan, *QJQJL*, 78–9.
64 Ibid., 97; Mill, *On Liberty*, 282.
65 Yan, *QJQJL*, 19–23, 90–1.
66 Ibid., 45, 49.
67 Ibid., 111.
68 Ibid., 30; Mill, *On Liberty*, 238–9.
69 Yan, *QJQJL*, 90, 114.
70 Ibid., 91.
71 Ibid., 91, 94, 95, 116. The point has been noted by Huang, *Ziyou de suoyiran*, 188.
72 Yan, *QJQJL*, 75, 83.
73 Ibid., 91, 98, 120.
74 Ibid., 71, 90.
75 Ibid., 8.
76 Ibid., 96, 97, 99, 105, 113, 119. Yan adds to Mill the shockingly erroneous example – given documented Chinese knowledge of epidemics – that illness is a condition that does not interfere with others' behaviour (p. 90). And – surely galling to Chinese readers – he reproduces Mill's defence of the (Chinese) buyer's right to purchase opium and hence the (English) right to sell opium to China (p. 113).
77 Ibid., 98, 124.
78 Ibid., 1, 95, 104, 115.
79 Ibid., 89–90, 98.
80 Ibid., 95.
81 Ibid., 93–4, 96–7.
82 Ibid., 96–7, 116, 123–4.
83 Ibid., 117–18.
84 Ibid., 104–5. It is surely on the basis of comments like this that a number of scholars have argued that Yan reduces Mill's concerns for society, humanity, the group, and so on to simply concern for the state, an argument with which I disagree. See Hoyt Cleveland Tillman, 'Yan Fu's Utilitarianism in Chinese Perspective,' in *Ideas across Cultures: Essays on Chinese Thought in Honor of Benjamin I. Schwartz*, ed. Paul A.Cohen and Merle Goldman (Cambridge: Harvard University Press, 1990), 63–84 (esp. p. 81); and Xu Gaoruan, 'Yan Fu xing de quanwei zhuyi ji qi tongshidai ren dui cixing sixiang zhi piping,' in *Jindai Zhongguo sixiang renwu lun*, vol. 3, *Ziyou zhuyi*, ed. Zhou Yangshan and Yang Xiaoxian (Taibei: Shibao wenhua chuban, 1980), 137–64 (esp. p. 147).

85 Yan, *QJQJL*, 104–5.
86 Ibid., 105.
87 Ibid., 93–5. Nonetheless, Yan follows Mill in not defining what sort of offences would necessarily deserve legal punishment; see Joseph Hamburger, *John Stuart Mill on Liberty and Control* (Princeton: Princeton University Press, 1999), 16.
88 Yan, *QJQJL*, 94. Yan's expression, 'self-correction,' displaces what Mill called 'duties to oneself.' See Mill, *On Liberty*, 279.
89 Yan, *QJQJL*, 5, 70–1, 74–5.
90 Ibid., 111.
91 Ibid., 102–5.
92 Ibid., 126, 128–30.
93 Ibid., 128–30, 132–4.
94 Ibid., 75.
95 Ibid., 'Yifan li,' 1.
96 For an account and chronology of Ma's life, see Mo Shixiang, Introduction to Ma Junwu, *Ma Junwu ji*, ed. Mo Shixiang (Wuhan: Huazhong shifan daxue chubanshe, 1991), 1–16, 478–90; and Huang Jiamo, 'Ma Junwu de zaoqi sixiang yu yanlun,' *Zhongyang yanjiuyuan jindaishi yanjiusuo jikan* 10 (1981): 303–49.
97 Takahashi Masajirō, *Jiyū no kenri* (Tokyo: Miyamoto insatsujo, 1895).
98 Ma Junwu, *Ziyou yuanli*, in *Ma Junwu ji*, 30.

5. Personal Liberty and Public Virtue

 1 Joseph Hamburger, *John Stuart Mill on Liberty and Control* (Princeton: Princeton University Press, 1999), 3.
 2 John M. Robson, *The Improvement of Mankind: The Social and Political Thought of John Stuart Mill* (Toronto: University of Toronto Press; London: RKP, 1968), 23–5, 71–2, 149–51; and Bernard Semmel, *John Stuart Mill and the Pursuit of Virtue* (New Haven: Yale University Press, 1984), 28–34, 46–7, 169. See also Don A. Habibi, *John Stuart Mill and the Ethics of Human Growth* (Dordrecht: Kluwer Academic, 2001), 26–48, 136–42, 217–51; Dennis F. Thompson, *John Stuart Mill and Representative Government* (Princeton: Princeton University Press, 1976), 14–28; Alan S. Kahan, *Aristocratic Liberalism: The Social and Political Thought of Jacob Burckhardt, John Stuart Mill, and Alexis de Tocqueville* (New York: Oxford University Press, 1992), 5, 100–7; and Maurice Cowling, *Mill and Liberalism* (Cambridge: Cambridge University Press, 1963), 15–17, 35–9.
 3 Robson, *Improvement of Mankind*, 190–5; Thompson, *John Stuart Mill and Representative Government*, 28–30, 44, 91–135.

4 J.H. Burns, 'J.S. Mill and Democracy, 1829–1861,' *Political Studies* 5 (1957), reprinted in *Mill: A Collection of Critical Essays*, ed. J.B. Schneewind (Notre Dame: University of Notre Dame Press, 1969), 280–328; Stephen Holmes, *Passions and Constraint: On the Theory of Liberal Democracy* (Chicago: University of Chicago Press, 1995), 178–201; Robson, *Improvement of Mankind*, 186–8, 190, 195; Nadia Urbinati, *Mill on Democracy: From the Athenian Polis to Representative Government* (Chicago: University of Chicago Press, 2002), 76–89; and George Watson, *The English Ideology: Studies in the Language of Victorian Politics* (London: Allen Lane, 1973), 158–63. Mill discusses Hare's theory in *Considerations on Representative Government*, in *Collected Works of John Stuart Mill*, vol. 19, *Essays on Politics and Society*, Part 2 (Toronto: University of Toronto Press, 1977), 454–66; see also Thompson, *John Stuart Mill and Representative Government*, 102–12.

5 Thompson, *John Stuart Mill and Representative Government*, 13–28, 30, 37, 54–5; see also Urbinati, *Mill on Democracy*, 42–59.

6 Mill, *Considerations on Representative Government*, 375–82; see also Peter Berkowitz, 'Mill: Liberty, Virtue, and the Discipline of Individuality,' in *Mill and the Moral Character of Liberalism*, ed. Eldon J. Eisenbach (University Park: Pennsylvania State University Press, 1998), 13–47; and Semmel, *John Stuart Mill and the Pursuit of Virtue*, 115.

7 Hamburger, *John Stuart Mill on Liberty and Control*, 18.

8 See Mill, *Considerations on Representative Government*, 381.

9 H.J. McCloskey, *John Stuart Mill: A Critical Study* (London: Macmillan, 1971), 73–84; Semmel, *John Stuart Mill and the Pursuit of Virtue*, 85–9; C.L. Ten, *Mill on Liberty* (Oxford: Oxford University Press, 1980), 19–28; and J.O. Urmson, 'The Interpretation of the Moral Philosophy of J.S. Mill,' *Philosophical Quarterly* 3 (1953), repr. in *Mill: A Collection of Critical Essays*, ed. J.B. Schneewind (Notre Dame: University of Notre Dame Press, 1969), 179–89. See also John Gray, *Mill on Liberty: A Defence* (London: RKP, 1983), 14, 38–46, for his related argument on 'indirect utilitarianism'; and Rolf E. Sartorius, *Individual Conduct and Social Norms: A Utilitarian Account of Social Union and the Rule of Law* (Encino, CA: Dickenson, 1975), 9–19, for a survey of utilitarian approaches.

10 Robson, *Improvement of Mankind*, 184.

11 Mill's fullest explanation of the higher pleasures and justification is in 'Utilitarianism,' in *Collected Works*, vol. 10, *Essays on Ethics, Religion, and Society* (Toronto: University of Toronto Press, 1969), 209–23.

12 Cowling, *Mill and Liberalism*, 28–31, 45–6.

13 Semmel, *John Stuart Mill and the Pursuit of Virtue*, 17, 82–93, 178.

14 Hamburger, *John Stuart Mill on Liberty and Control*, 43–4, 86–7, 108–39, 166;

see also Terence R. Wright, *The Religion of Humanity: The Impact of Comtean Positivism on Victorian Britain* (Cambridge: Cambridge University Press, 1986), 40–50.

15 H.J. McCloskey, 'Mill's Liberalism,' *Philosophical Quarterly* 13, no. 52 (April 1963): 143–56; Ten, *Mill on Liberty*, 62–3. See also John Gray, 'The Light of Other Minds,' *Times Literary Supplement*, no. 5054 (11 Feb. 2000): 12–13; and Robson, *Improvement of Mankind*, 202–3.

16 Cowling, *Mill and Liberalism*, 108–12. But see Lord Devlin's famous defense of morality in response to the 1957 Wolfenden Report that would decriminalize homosexuality: 'Mill on Liberty in Morals,' *University of Chicago Law Review* 32, no. 2 (1965): 215–35.

17 Cowling, *Mill and Liberalism*, 139; and Jean Bethke Elshtain, 'Mill's Liberty and the Problem of Authority,' in John Stuart Mill, *On Liberty*, ed. David Bromwich and George Kateb (New Haven: Yale University Press, 2003), 203–23.

18 Cowling, *Mill and Liberalism*, 146.

19 Ibid., 159.

20 Mill, *Considerations on Representative Government*, 384–5, 415–16. See also Uday Singh Mehta on British justifications for excluding Indians from self-governing representative institutions, in *Liberalism and Empire: A Study in Nineteenth-Century British Liberal Thought* (Chicago: University of Chicago Press, 1999), 64–76 (esp. p. 73).

21 R.W. Church, 'Mill on Liberty,' *Bentley's Quarterly Review* 2 (1860): 434–73, reprinted in John Stuart Mill, *On Liberty*, ed. Edward Alexander (Peterborough, Ontario: Broadview, 1999), 226.

22 Ibid., 230–2.

23 [R.H. Hutton], 'Mill on Liberty,' *National Review* 8 (1859): 393–424; repr. in John Stuart Mill, *On Liberty: Annotated Text, Sources and Background Criticism*, ed. David Spitz (New York: Norton, 1975), 128–9.

24 John Stuart Mill, *On Liberty*, in *The Collected Works of John Stuart Mill*, vol. 18, *Essays on Politics and Society*, Part 1 (Toronto: University of Toronto Press, 1977), 220–1. E.G. West has argued that Mill never resolved this dilemma between necessary education and a state mandate: 'Liberty and Education: John Stuart Mill's Dilemma,' *Philosophy* 40 (1965): 129–42.

25 Hamburger, *John Stuart Mill on Liberty and Control*, 117, 194–6; Ten, *Mill on Liberty*, 92–3; and John Stuart Mill, 'Coleridge,' in *Collected Works*, vol. 10, *Essays on Ethics, Religion, and Society* (Toronto: University of Toronto Press, 1969), 133–6.

26 Nishimura Shigeki, *Nihon dōtoku ron* (Tokyo: Iwanami shoten, 1936), 10–12.

27 See, for example, the translation of an anonymous American work by the

Japanese Ministry of Education in its journal for teachers: 'Shōgaku ni kōyō aru shūshin kyōiku,' *Kyōiku zasshi*, no. 22 (23 December 1876): 1–16.

28 Liang Qichao, *Xinmin shuo* (Shanghai: Zhonghua shuju, 1936), 12–13.

29 Douglas Howland, *Translating the West: Language and Political Reason in Nineteenth-Century Japan* (Honolulu: University of Hawai'i Press, 2002).

30 Nishimura Shigeki, 'Shūshin chikoku futamichi arazu ron,' *Meiroku zasshi*, no. 31 (1875): 3b-6. Cf. 'Government and Ethics Are Not Separate Paths,' in *Meiroku Zasshi: Journal of the Japanese Enlightenment*, trans. William R. Braisted (Cambridge: Harvard University Press, 1976), 379–82.

31 See Richard M. Reitan, '*Rinrigaku*: The Emergence of Ethics in Meiji Japan' (PhD Dissertation, University of Chicago, 2002).

32 Howland, *Translating the West*, 94–121.

33 Some useful introductions to moral education in Meiji Japan include Furukawa Tetsushi, *Nihon dōtoku kyōiku shi* (Tokyo: Kadokawa shoten, 1961), 199–294; Kaigo Tokiomi, *Nihon kyōkasho taikei – kindai hen*, vol. 1 [*Shūshin*, part 1] (Tokyo: Kōdansha, 1961), 1–36; Karasawa Tomitarō, *Kyōkasho no rekishi* (Tokyo: Sōbunsha, 1956), 49–74, 103–20, 149–64, 191–269; Sasaki Akira, *Dōtoku kyōiku no kenkyū to jissen* (Tokyo: Kyōiku kaihatsu kenkyūjo, 1996), 325–56; and E. Patricia Tsurumi, 'Meiji Primary School Language and Ethics Textbooks: Old Values for a New Society,' *Modern Asian Studies* 8, no. 2 (1974): 247–61.

34 See Judy Hilkey, *Character Is Capital: Success Manuals and Manhood in Gilded Age America* (Chapel Hill: University of North Carolina Press, 1997), 62–73, 126–41.

35 Takahashi Masao, *Nishimura Shigeki* (Tokyo: Yoshikawa kōbunkan, 1987), 92–5, 143–61; see also Masako Gavin, *Shiga Shigetaka, 1863–1927: The Forgotton Enlightener* (Richmond, Surrey: Curzon, 2001), 16–19; and Donald H. Shively, 'Nishimura Shigeki: A Confucian View of Modernization,' in *Changing Japanese Attitudes Toward Modernization*, ed. Marius B. Jansen (Princeton: Princeton University Press, 1965), 193–241.

36 See Wilbur M. Fridell, 'Government Ethics Textbooks in Late Meiji Japan,' *Journal of Asian Studies* 29, no. 4 (1970): 823–33; and Kyoko Inoue, *Individual Dignity in Modern Japanese Thought: The Evolution of the Concept of* Jinkaku *in Moral and Educational Discourse* (Ann Arbor: Center for Japanese Studies, 2001), 12–51.

37 Takahashi, *Nishimura Shigeki*, 112, 118; and Nishimura, *Nihon dōtoku ron*, 3.

38 On Confucianism in Meiji Japan, see Motoda Eifu, 'Lectures Delivered in the Presence of His Imperial Majesty the Emperor of Japan,' trans. N. Asaji and J.C. Pringle, *Transactions of the Asiatic Society of Japan* 40 (1912): 45–113; Donald H. Shively, 'Motoda Eifu: Confucian Lecturer to the Meiji Emperor,'

in *Confucianism in Action*, ed. David S. Nivison and Arthur F. Wright (Stanford: Stanford University Press, 1959), 302–33; and Warren W. Smith Jr., *Confucianism in Modern Japan: A Study of Conservatism in Japanese Intellectual History* (Tokyo: Hokuseido Press, 1959), 41–102.

39 Nishimura, quoted in Takahashi, *Nishimura Shigeki*, 92.

40 Ibid., 95.

41 Nishimura Shigeki, 'Nihon dōtokugaku no shurui,' repr. in *Meiji keimō shisō shū*, ed. Ōkubo Toshiaki (Tokyo: Chikuma shobō, 1967), 359–60.

42 Nishimura Shigeki, *Shōgaku shūshin kun*, repr. in *Nihon kyōkasho taikei – kindai hen*, vol. 2 [*Shūshin*, part 2], ed. Kaigo Tokiomi (Tokyo: Kōdansha, 1962), 6–37. See also his comments on Smiles in *Nihon dōtoku ron*, 88–92.

43 Nishimura, *Nihon dōtoku ron*, 11–12, 26–32; and Takahashi, *Nishimura Shigeki*, 102, 132–8, 153–4.

44 'Nihon kōdō kai yōryō,' reprinted on the first page of every issue of *Nihon kōdō sōki*, the journal of the Japanese Society for Extending Morality; see also Takahashi, *Nishimura Shigeki*, 159–60.

45 An excellent context of the issues is Kenneth B. Pyle, *The New Generation in Meiji Japan: Problems of Cultural Identity, 1885–1889* (Stanford: Stanford University Press, 1969), 118–43.

46 Nishimura, *Nihon dōtoku ron*, 17, 43, 100–1; Takahashi, *Nishimura Shigeki*, 162–5, 176–83; and Yamaji Aizan, *Essays on the Modern Japanese Church: Christianity in Meiji Japan*, trans. Graham Squires (Ann Arbor: Center for Japanese Studies, The University of Michigan, 1999), 156–64.

47 Inoue had earlier introduced to Japan Fitzjames Stephen's critique of Mill, to the effect that Mill was unable to establish the boundaries between the individual and society or government: 'Miru no *Jiyū no ri* o hakusu,' *Tōyō gakugei zasshi* 9 (1883): 13–17.

48 Inoue Tetsujirō, *Rinri shinsetsu* (1883), repr. in *Meiji bunka zenshū*, vol. 23, *Shisō hen* (Tokyo: Nihon hyōronsha, 1968), 413–14. Cf. Nishimura Shigeki, 'Shūshin kyōkasho no setsu' [1890], in *Hakuō sōsho* (Tokyo: Nihon kōdōkai, [1912]), vol. 2: 536–43.

49 See Masakazu Yanazaki and Tōru Miyakawa, 'Inoue Tetsujirō: The Man and His Works,' *Philosophical Studies of Japan* (Japan Society for the Promotion of Science), vol. 7 (1966), 117–19; Winston Davis, 'The Civil Theology of Inoue Tetsujirō,' *Japanese Journal of Religious Studies* 3.1 (1976): 18–19; and Reitan, '*Rinrigaku.*'

50 See Notto R. Thelle, *Buddhism and Christianity in Japan: From Conflict to Dialogue, 1854–1899* (Honolulu: University of Hawai'i Press, 1987), 119–26; and Gavin, *Shiga Shigetaka*, 110–13.

51 Inoue Tetsujirō, *Inoue Tetsujirō jiden* (Tokyo: Fuzanbō, 1973), 34.

52 Inoue Tetsujirō, *Chokugo engi* (1891), repr. in *Meiji shisō shū*, ed. Matsumoto Sannosuke (Tokyo: Chikuma shobō, 1977), vol. 2: 85–7, 100, 109–10. See also Klaus Antoni, 'Inoue Tetsujirō (1855–1944) und die Entwicklung der Staatsideologie in der zweiten Hälfte der Meiji-Zeit,' *Oriens Extremus* 33, no. 1 (1990): 99–115.

53 Inoue Tetsujirō, *Kyōiku to shūkyō no shōtotsu* (1893), repr. in *Meiji tetsugaku shisō shū*, ed. Senuma Shigeki (Tokyo: Chikuma shobō, 1974), 124–32. See also Inoue, *Inoue Tetsujirō jiden*, 35–9; Gavin, *Shiga Shigetaka*, 110–16; Thelle, *Buddhism and Christianity in Japan*, 126–34; Yamaji, *Essays on the Modern Japanese Church*, 165–72; and Yanazaki and Miyakawa, 'Inoue Tetsujirō,' 120–4. On the Christian defence of private conscience, see Irwin Scheiner, *Christian Converts and Social Protest in Meiji Japan* (Berkeley: University of California Press, 1970), 192.

54 On these same grounds, Japanese moralists eventually rejected T.H. Green's moral project; see Hirai Atsuko, 'Self-Realization and Common Good: T.H. Green in Meiji Ethical Thought,' *Journal of Japanese Studies* 5, no. 1 (1979): 107–36.

55 According to Joseph Pittau, the Japanese adaptation of *Rechtsstaat* derived from the imperial adviser Rudolf von Gneist, and *soziale Recht* from the adviser Herman Roesler; see *Political Thought in Early Meiji Japan, 1868–1889* (Cambridge: Harvard University Press, 1967), 133–57. See also Ernst-Wolfgang Böckenförde, *State, Society and Liberty: Studies in Political Theory and Constitutional Law*, trans. J.A. Underwood (Providence: Berg, 1991), 47–70, 87–114; Leonard Krieger, *The German Idea of Freedom: History of a Political Tradition* (Chicago: University of Chicago Press, 1957), 252–61, 356–8, 367–70, 459–60; Franz Neumann, *The Rule of Law: Political Theory and the Legal System in Modern Society* (Leamington Spa: Berg, 1986), 175–86; and Guido de Ruggiero, *The History of European Liberalism*, trans. R.G. Collingwood (Oxford: Oxford University Press; London: Humphrey Milford, 1927), 251–64.

56 See Andrew E. Barshay, *State and Intellectual in Imperial Japan: The Public Man in Crisis* (Berkeley: University of California Press, 1988), 2–23; and Matsumoto Sannosuke, 'The Roots of Political Disillusionment: "Public" and "Private" in Japan,' in *Authority and the Individual in Japan: Citizen Protest in Historical Perspective*, ed. J. Victor Koschmann (Tokyo: University of Tokyo Press, 1978), 31–51.

57 Huang Ko-wu, *Ziyou de suoyiran: Yan Fu dui Yuehan Mier ziyou sixiang de renshi yu pipan* (Taibei: Yunchen wenhua, 1998), 193, 207, 217.

58 Hao Chang, *Chinese Intellectuals in Crisis: Search for Order and Meaning (1890–1911)* (Berkeley: University of California Press, 1987), 158–60; and

Charlotte Furth, 'Intellectual Change: From the Reform Movement to the May Fourth Movement, 1895–1920,' in *The Cambridge History of China*, vol. 12, *Republican China 1912–1949*, Part 1, ed. John K. Fairbank (Cambridge: Cambridge University Press, 1983), 382–8.

59 Liang, 'Shuo qun,' *Yinbingshi wenji* (Taibei: Zhonghua shuju, 1960), 2: 3–7; and *Xinmin shuo*, 12, 76–80. See also Hao Chang, *Liang Ch'i-ch'ao and Intellectual Transition in China* (Cambridge: Harvard University Press, 1971), 95–100; Brett McCormick, 'Liang Qichao's Liberal Statism and His Vision of a Modern Citizen,' *Asian Thought and Society* 25, no. 74 (2000): 123–36; James R. Pusey, *China and Charles Darwin* (Cambridge: Harvard University, Council on East Asian Studies, 1983), 107–12; and Peter Zarrow, 'The Reform Movement, the Monarchy, and Political Modernity,' in *Rethinking the 1898 Reform Period: Political and Cultural Change in Late Qing China*, ed. Rebecca E. Karl and Peter Zarrow (Cambridge: Harvard University Asia Center, 2002), 34–43.

60 See Charlotte Furth, 'Culture and Politics in Modern Chinese Conservatism,' in *The Limits of Change: Essays on Conservative Alternatives in Republican China*, ed. Charlotte Furth (Cambridge: Harvard University Press, 1976), 36; Chang, *Liang Ch'i-ch'ao and Intellectual Transition in China*, 104–5, 151–2; Hazama Naoki, 'On Liang Qichao's Conceptions of *Gong* and *Si*: "Civic Virtue" and "Personal Virtue" in the *Xinmin shuo*,' in *The Role of Japan in Liang Qichao's Introduction of Modern Western Civilization to China*, ed. Joshua A. Fogel (Berkeley: University of California, Institute of East Asian Studies, 2004), 205–21; Wang Fan-shen, 'Evolving Prescriptions for Social Life in the Late Qing and Early Republic: From *Qunxue* to Society,' in *Imagining the People: Chinese Intellectuals and the Concept of Citizenship, 1890–1920*, ed. Joshua A. Fogel and Peter Zarrow (Armonk, NY: M.E. Sharpe, 1997), 261–6; Mizoguchi Yūzō, 'Chūgoku ni okeru kō-shi gainen no tenkai,' *Shisō*, no. 669 (1980), 19–38; idem., 'Chūgoku no "kō-shi",' *Bungaku* 56 (9/ 1988): 88–102 and (10/1988): 73–84; Zarrow, 'The Reform Movement, the Monarchy, and Political Modernity,' 21–3, 34–5, 38–40; and Zhang Dainian, *Key Concepts in Chinese Philosophy*, trans. and ed. Edmund Ryden (New Haven: Yale University Press, 2002), 3, 11–21.

61 Liang, *Xinmin shuo*, 12–16, 50–4; Chang, *Liang Ch'i-ch'ao and Intellectual Transition in China*, 95–100, 105–8; and Pusey, *China and Charles Darwin*, 238–42. Yan Fu also expressed interest in the concept of 'renovating the people' (*xinmin*); see Onogawa Hidemi, *Shinmatsu seiji shisō kenkyū* (Tokyo: Misuzu shobō, 1969), 262–8.

62 Chang, *Liang Ch'i-ch'ao and Intellectual Transition in China*, 190–6; Philip C. Huang, *Liang Ch'i-ch'ao and Modern Chinese Liberalism* (Seattle: University of

Washington Press, 1972), 56–7, 80–5; Joseph R. Levenson, *Liang Ch'i-ch'ao and the Mind of Modern China*, 2d revised ed. (Berkeley: University of California Press, 1967), 115–20; and Xiaobing Tang, *Global Space and Nationalist Discourse of Modernity: The Historical Thinking of Liang Qichao* (Stanford: Stanford University Press, 1996), 19–27, 153–8. For a quite different interpretation of Liang, see Andrew J. Nathan, *Chinese Democracy* (Berkeley: University of California Press, 1985), 51–8, 62–5, 113, 133–4.

63 Jiwei Ci, *Dialectic of the Chinese Revolution: From Utopianism to Hedonism* (Stanford: Stanford University Press, 1994), 110–21; Huang, *Liang Ch'i-ch'ao and Modern Chinese Liberalism*, 72–3, 154; and Peter Zarrow, 'Late Qing Reformism and the Meiji Model: Kang Youwei, Liang Qichao, and the Japanese Emperor,' in *The Role of Japan in Liang Qichao's Introduction of Modern Western Civilization to China*, ed. Joshua A. Fogel (Berkeley: University of California, Institute of East Asian Studies, 2004), 40–67.

64 See especially Liang Qichao, 'Lun zhengfu yu renmin zhi quanxian,' *Yinbingshi wenji* 10: 1–6; Huang, *Liang Ch'i-ch'ao and Modern Chinese Liberalism*, 72–6; Levenson, *Liang Ch'i-ch'ao and the Mind of Modern China*, 71; and Wahkwan Cheng, 'Vox Populi: Language, Literature, and Ideology in Modern China' (Ph.D. diss., University of Chicago, 1989).

65 Chang, *Chinese Intellectuals in Crisis*, 173–4; and Peter Zarrow, *Anarchism and Chinese Political Culture* (New York: Columbia University Press, 1990), 83–96.

66 Mill, 'Utilitarianism,' 240–55; and John Gray, *Liberalisms: Essays in Political Philosophy* (London: Routledge, 1989), 150–3.

67 Arif Dirlik, *Anarchism in the Chinese Revolution* (Berkeley: University of California Press, 1991), 42.

68 Ibid., 91. Dirlik's reference here is Wu Zhihui, Liu's sometime rival in the 'Paris faction.' See also Mary Backus Rankin, *Early Chinese Revolutionaries: Radical Intellectuals in Shanghai and Chekiang, 1902–1911* (Cambridge: Harvard University Press, 1971), 35–9; Germaine A. Hoston, *The State, Identity, and the National Question in China and Japan* (Princeton: Princeton University Press, 1994), 155–69; Pusey, *China and Charles Darwin*, 427–32; and Zarrow, *Anarchism and Chinese Political Culture*, 120–5.

69 Chang, *Chinese Intellectuals in Crisis*, 177.

70 See Liang Qichao, *Yinbingshi ziyou shu* [1899] (Shanghai: Zhonghua shuju, 1936), 24–5, 30–1; idem., *Xinmin shuo*, 46–7; Stephen C. Angle, 'Should We All Be More English? Liang Qichao, Rudolf von Jhering, and Rights,' *Journal of the History of Ideas* 61, no. 2 (2000): 241–61; Chang, *Liang Ch'i-ch'ao and Intellectual Transition in China*, 102–8, 189–94, 201–5, 243–58; Huang, *Liang Ch'i-ch'ao and Modern Chinese Liberalism*, 78–9; Pusey, *China and Charles Dar-*

win, 260–78; Tang, *Gobal Space and Nationalist Discourse*, 130, 138–41, 178–83; Tsuchiya Hideo, 'Ryō Keichō no seiyō sesshu to kenri-jiyū ron,' in *Kyōdō kenkyū: Ryō Keichō, seiyō kindai shisō juyō to Meiji Nihon*, ed. Hazama Naoki, (Tokyo: Misuzu shobō, 1999), 132–67; and Zarrow, 'The Reform Movement, the Monarchy, and Political Modernity,' 45–6.

71 Dirlik, *Anarchism in the Chinese Revolution*, 59.

72 Liang, *Xinmin shuo*, 14, 54.

73 Ibid., 14–15, 52.

74 See Liang, *Ziyou shu*, 9–10, 33–4; Chang, *Chinese Intellectuals in Crisis*, 20, 54, 142–3, 165, 181; and Levenson, *Liang Ch'i-ch'ao and the Mind of Modern China*, 106, 120–1.

75 Gottfried-Karl Kindermann, 'An Overview of Sun Yat-sen's Doctrine,' in *Sun Yat-sen's Doctrine in the Modern World*, ed. Chu-yuan Cheng (Boulder, CO: Westview, 1989), 52–78; Thomas A. Metzger, 'Did Sun Yat-sen Understand the Idea of Democracy?' *American Asian Review* 10, no. 1 (Spring 1992): 9–22; and Sun Yat-sen, *The Three Principles of the People: San Min Chu I* (Taipei: China Publishing Co., [1963]).

76 Sun Yatsen, *Prescriptions for Saving China: Selected Writings of Sun Yat-sen*, trans. Julie Lee Wei, E-su Zen, and Linda Chao (Stanford: Hoover Institution Press, 1994), 45–8, 223, 229–35; Sun, *The Three Principles of the People*, 157–60; see also Pusey, *China and Charles Darwin*, 334–67.

77 Sun, *Prescriptions for Saving China*, 36–8, 86, 223, 228.

78 Ibid., 275–80; and Sun, *The Three Principles of the People*, 68–77. See also Yu-long Ling, 'The Doctrine of Democracy and Human Rights,' in *Sun Yat-sen's Doctrine in the Modern World*, ed. Chu-yuan Cheng, 179–90.

79 Sun, *The Three Principles of the People*, 32, 37–42.

Conclusion

1 John Gray, *Two Faces of Liberalism* (New York: New Press, 2000), 1–6, 29–30, 59–60.

2 See Uday Singh Mehta, *Liberalism and Empire: A Study in Nineteenth-Century British Liberal Thought* (Chicago: University of Chicago Press, 1999), 58; and C.B. Macpherson, *The Political Theory of Possessive Individualism: Hobbes to Locke* (London: Oxford University Press, 1962), 16–17, 53–62.

3 Michel Foucault, 'Governmentality,' in *The Foucault Effect: Studies in Governmentality*, ed. Graham Burchell et al. (Chicago: University of Chicago Press, 1991), 87–104.

4 Ernest Gellner, *Conditions of Liberty: Civil Society and Its Rivals* (London: Hamish Hamilton, 1994), 141–3.

5 Macpherson, *The Political Theory of Possessive Individualism*, 1–8, 263–77; and *Democratic Theory: Essays in Retrieval* (Oxford: Clarendon, 1973), 3–23.

6 Mehta, *Liberalism and Empire*, 26–37, 97–112 (quotation on p. 112).

7 See E.P. Thompson, *Customs in Common* (New York: Free Press, 1991), 97–184; and Elizabeth Fox-Genovese and Eugene D. Genovese, *Fruits of Merchant Capital: Slavery and Bourgeois Property in the Rise and Expansion of Capitalism* (New York: Oxford University Press, 1983), 337–87.

8 See Max Horkheimer, 'Materialism and Morality,' in *Between Philosophy and Social Science: Selected Early Writings*, trans. G. Frederick Hunter, et al. (Cambridge, MA: MIT Press, 1993), 16–21.

9 Theodor Adorno, *Problems of Moral Philosophy*, trans. Rodney Livingstone (Stanford: Stanford University Press, 2000), 13.

10 Bhikhu Parekh, 'Liberalism and Morality,' in *The Morality of Politics*, ed. Bhikhu Parekh and R.N. Berki (New York: Crane, Russak, & Co., 1972), 81–98; and Stuart Hampshire, 'Morality and Pessimism,' in *Public and Private Morality*, ed. Stuart Hampshire (Cambridge: Cambridge University Press, 1978), 1–22. See also Alasdair MacIntyre, *After Virtue: A Study in Moral Theory*, 2d ed. (Notre Dame: University of Notre Dame Press, 1985), 6–35; and the judicious comments of Michael Waltzer, 'The Communitarian Critique of Liberalism,' *Political Theory* 18, no. 1 (1990): 6–23.

11 John Roach, 'Liberalism and the Victorian Intelligentsia,' *Cambridge Historical Journal* 13, no. 1 (1957): 60.

12 Brian Harrison, 'State Intervention and Moral Reform in Nineteenth-Century England,' in *Pressure from Without in Early Victorian England*, ed. Patricia Hollis (London: Edward Arnold, 1974), 289–321; and Roach, 'Liberalism and the Victorian Intelligentsia,' 58–81.

13 Andrew Lawless, 'T.H. Green and the British Liberal Tradition,' *Canadian Journal of Political and Social Theory* 2, no. 2 (Spring–Summer 1978): 142–55; Anthony Skillen, *Ruling Illusions: Philosophy and the Social Order* (Atlantic Highlands, NJ: Humanities Press, 1978), 122–77 (esp. p. 166); and Andrew W. Vincent, 'The State and Social Purpose in Idealist Political Philosophy,' *History of European Ideas* 8, no. 3 (1987): 333–47.

14 Parekh, 'Liberalism and Morality.'

15 Stuart Hampshire, *Justice Is Conflict* (Princeton: Princeton University Press, 2000), 35–8, 41–6. C.L. Ten has called this our 'common political morality'; see 'Mill's Place in Liberalism,' *Political Science Reviewer* 24 (1995): 195–8. See also Harry M. Clor, 'Mill and Millians on Liberty and Moral Character,' *Review of Politics* 47, no. 1 (1985): 3–26; and William A. Galston, 'Liberal Virtues,' *American Political Science Review* 82, no. 4 (1988): 1277–90.

16 Rolf E. Sartorius, *Individual Conduct and Social Norms: A Utilitarian Account*

of Social Union and the Rule of Law (Encino, CA: Dickenson, 1975), 211–13; see also Ronald Dworkin, 'Foundations of Liberal Equality,' *The Tanner Lectures on Human Values*, vol. 11 (1990): 47–55; Gerald F. Gaus, *The Modern Liberal Theory of Man* (London: Croom Helm; NY: St Martin's Press, 1983); John Gray, *Liberalisms: Essays in Political Philosophy* (London: Routledge, 1989), 29–31; and John Kekes, *Against Liberalism* (Ithaca: Cornell University Press, 1997). For examples of the assumptions I note, see Joel Feinberg, *The Moral Limits of the Criminal Law*, vol. 1, *Harm to Others* (New York: Oxford University Press, 1984), 11; Robert P. George, *Making Men Moral: Civil Liberties and Public Morality* (Oxford: Clarendon Press, 1993), 189–229; J.P. Plamenatz, *Consent, Freedom, and Political Obligation* (London: Oxford University Press, 1938, 1968), 144–56; Nadia Urbinati, *Mill on Democracy: From Athenian Polis to Representative Government* (Chicago: University of Chicago Press, 2002), 93–104, 130, 185, 198–201; and Robert Paul Wolff, *The Poverty of Liberalism* (Boston: Beacon Press, 1968), 162–95.

17 Macpherson, *The Political Theory of Possessive Individualism*, 70–90.
18 See Gray, *Two Faces of Liberalism*, 99.
19 V.S. Naipaul, *The Middle Passage* (New York: Macmillan, 1963), 43, 128.
20 L.T. Hobhouse, *Democracy and Reaction* (London: T. Fisher Unwin, 1904), 125–9; also see his *Liberalism* (1911), repr. in *Liberalism and Other Writings*, ed. James Meadowcroft (Cambridge: Cambridge University Press, 1994).
21 Theodor Adorno, *Minima Moralia: Reflections from Damaged Life*, trans. E.F.N. Jephcott (London: NLB, 1974), 15–18, 63–4, 148–50.
22 See Andrew Hacker, 'The Underworld of Work,' *New York Review of Books* 51, no. 2 (12 February 2004): 38–40.
23 Horkheimer, 'Materialism and Morality,' 16, 43–5; Michael Lind, 'A Tragedy of Errors,' *The Nation* (23 February 2004): 23–32; and Macpherson, *Democratic Theory*, 32.
24 Jiwei Ci, *The Dialectic of the Chinese Revolution: From Utopianism to Hedonism* (Stanford: Stanford University Press, 1994), 1–23, 134–67. See also, for comparison, Baogang He, 'New Moral Foundations of Chinese Democratic Institutional Design,' and Dawn Einwalter, 'The Limits of the Chinese State: Public Morality and the Xu Honggang Campaign,' both in *China and Democracy: The Prospects for a Democratic China*, ed. Suisheng Zhao (New York: Routledge, 2000), 89–107 and 173–86 respectively.
25 See especially Wang Hui, *China's New Order: Society, Politics, and Economy in Transition*, ed. Theodore Huters (Cambridge: Harvard University Press, 2003); and Xudong Zhang, ed., *Whither China? Intellectual Politics in Post-Tiananmen China* (Durham: Duke University Press, 2001).

Bibliography

Adams, Willi Paul. 'The Historian as Translator: An Introduction.' *Journal of American History* 85, no. 4 (1999): 1283–98.

Adorno, Theodor. *Minima Moralia: Reflections from Damaged Life*, trans. E.F.N. Jephcott. London: NLB, 1974.

– *Problems of Moral Philosophy*, trans. Rodney Livingstone. Stanford: Stanford University Press, 2000.

Angle, Stephen C. 'Did Someone Say "Rights"? Liu Shipei's Concept of *Quanli*.' *Philosophy East and West* 48, no. 4 (1998): 623–51.

– 'Should We All Be More English? Liang Qichao, Rudolf von Jhering, and Rights.' *Journal of the History of Ideas* 61, no. 2 (2000): 241–61.

Antoni, Klaus. 'Inoue Tetsujirō (1855–1944) und die Entwicklung der Staatsideologie in der zweiten Hälfte der Meiji-Zeit.' *Oriens Extremus* 33, no. 1 (1990): 99–115.

Aruga, Tadashi. 'The Declaration of Independence in Japan: Translation and Transplantation, 1854–1997.' *Journal of American History* 85, no. 4 (1999): 1409–31.

Baker, Mona, ed., assisted by Kirsten Malmkjær. *The Routledge Encyclopedia of Translation Studies*. London: Routledge, 1995.

Barshay, Andrew E. *State and Intellectual in Imperial Japan: The Public Man in Crisis*. Berkeley: University of California Press, 1988.

Basileus, Harold. 'Neo-Humboldtian Ethnolinguistics.' *Word* 8, no. 2 (1952): 95–105.

Bassnett-McGuire, Susan. *Translation Studies*. London: Methuen, 1980.

Beasley, W.G. 'Political Groups in Tosa, 1858–68.' *Bulletin of the School of Oriental and African Studies* 30, no. 2 (1967): 382–90.

– 'Politics and the Samurai Class Structure in Satsuma, 1858–1868.' *Modern Asian Studies* 1, no. 1 (1967): 47–57.

Bell, Robert. 'Spiritual Freedom.' *Westminster Review*, no. 142 (1859); repr. in *Liberty: Contemporary Responses to John Stuart Mill*, ed. Andrew Pyle, 118–58. Bristol: Thoemmes, 1994.

Bellamy, Richard. 'T.H. Green and the Morality of Victorian Liberalism.' In *Victorian Liberalism: Nineteenth-Century Political Thought and Practice*, ed. Richard Bellamy, 131–51. London: Routledge, 1990.

– 'T.H. Green, J.S. Mill, and Isaiah Berlin on the Nature of Liberty and Liberalism.' In *Jurisprudence: Cambridge Essays*, ed. Hyman Gross and Ross Harrison, 257–85. Oxford: Clarendon, 1992.

Bennett, Tony. *Formalism and Marxism*. London: Methuen, 1979.

Benveniste, Emile. *Problems in General Linguistics*, trans. Mary Elizabeth Meek. Coral Gables: University of Miami Press, 1971.

Berkowitz, Peter. 'Mill: Liberty, Virtue, and the Discipline of Individuality.' In *Mill and the Moral Character of Liberalism*, ed. Eldon J. Eisenbach, 13–47. University Park: Pennsylvania State University Press, 1998.

Berlin, Isaiah. 'Two Concepts of Liberty.' In *Four Essays on Liberty*, 118–72. Oxford: Oxford University Press, 1969.

Bermeo, Nancy, and Philip Nord, eds. *Civil Society before Democracy: Lessons from Nineteenth-Century Europe*. Lanham, MD: Rowman and Littlefield, 2000.

Biagini, Eugenio F. *Liberty, Retrenchment, and Reform: Popular Liberalism in the Age of Gladstone, 1860–1880*. Cambridge: Cambridge University Press, 1992.

Bitō Masahide. 'Bushi and the Meiji Restoration.' *Acta Asiatica* 49 (1985): 78–96.

– 'Society and Social Thought in the Tokugawa Period.' *Japan Foundation Newsletter* 9, no. 2–3 (June–September 1981): 1–6.

Bloom, Irene. 'The Moral Autonomy of the Individual in Confucian Tradition.' In *Realms of Freedom in Modern China*, ed. William C. Kirby, 19–45. Stanford: Stanford University Press, 2004.

Böckenförde, Ernst-Wolfgang. *State, Society and Liberty: Studies in Political Theory and Constitutional Law*, trans. J.A. Underwood. Providence: Berg, 1991.

Bosanquet, Bernard. *Aspects of the Social Problem*. London: Macmillan, 1895.

– *The Philosophical Theory of the State*. 4th ed. London: Macmillan, 1923.

Bourdieu, Pierre. *Language and Symbolic Power*, ed. John B. Thompson, trans. Gino Raymond and Matthew Adamson. Cambridge: Harvard University Press, 1991.

Bowen, Roger W. *Rebellion and Democracy in Meiji Japan: A Study of Commoners in the Popular Rights Movement*. Berkeley: University of California Press, 1980.

Briggs, Asa. 'The Language of "Class" in Early Nineteenth-Century England.' In *Essays in Labour History*, ed. Asa Briggs and John Saville, 40–73. London: Macmillan, 1960.

Brook, Timothy, and B. Michael Frolic, eds. *Civil Society in China*. Armonk, NY: M.E. Sharpe, 1997.

Brower, Reuben A., ed. *On Translation*. Cambridge: Harvard University Press, 1959.

Buckle, Henry Thomas. 'Mill on Liberty,' *Fraser's Magazine* 59, no. 353 (May 1859); repr. in *Liberty: Contemporary Responses to John Stuart Mill*, ed. Andrew Pyle, 25–80. Bristol: Thoemmes, 1994.

Burns, J.H. 'J.S. Mill and Democracy, 1829–1861.' *Political Studies* 5 (1957); repr. in *Mill: A Collection of Critical Essays*, ed. J.B. Schneewind, 280–328. Notre Dame: University of Notre Dame Press, 1969.

Burrow, J.W. *The Crisis of Reason: European Thought, 1848–1914*. New Haven: Yale University Press, 2000.

– 'The "Village Community" and the Uses of History in Late Nineteenth-Century England.' In *Historical Perspectives: Studies in English Thought and Society in Honour of J.H. Plumb*, ed. Neil McKendrick, 255–84. London: Europa, 1974.

Bynon, Theodora. *Historical Linguistics*. Cambridge: Cambridge University Press, 1977, 1983.

Capaldi, Nicholas. *John Stuart Mill: A Biography*. Cambridge: University of Cambridge Press, 2004.

Chang, Hao. *Chinese Intellectuals in Crisis: Search for Order and Meaning (1890–1911)*. Berkeley: University of California Press, 1987.

– *Liang Ch'i-ch'ao and Intellectual Transition in China*. Cambridge, MA: Harvard University Press, 1971.

Cary, Otis. *A History of Christianity in Japan*. Rutland, VT: Tuttle, 1976.

Chen, Ping. *Modern Chinese: History and Sociolinguistics*. Cambridge: Cambridge University Press, 1999.

Chen Shude. '"Qunxue" yiming kaoxi.' *Shehuixue yanjiu*, no. 6 (1988): 74–8.

Cheng, Wah-kwan. 'Vox Populi: Language, Literature, and Ideology in Modern China.' Ph.D. diss., University of Chicago, 1989.

Chomsky, Noam. *Language and Responsibility*. New York: Pantheon, 1979.

Church, R.W. 'Mill on Liberty.' *Bentley's Quarterly Review* 2 (1860): 434–73; repr. in John Stuart Mill, *On Liberty*, ed. Edward Alexander, 220–38. Peterborough, Ont.: Broadview, 1999.

Ci, Jiwei. *Dialectic of the Chinese Revolution: From Utopianism to Hedonism*. Stanford: Stanford University Press, 1994.

Clark, E.W. *Life and Adventure in Japan*. New York: American Tract Society, 1878.

Clarke, Peter. *Liberals and Social Democrats*. Cambridge: Cambridge University Press, 1978.

Clor, Harry M. 'Mill and Millians on Liberty and Moral Character.' *Review of Politics* 47, no. 1 (1985): 3–26.

Cobbing, Andrew. *The Japanese Discovery of Victorian Britain: Early Travel Encounters in the Far West*. Richmond, Surrey: Japan Library, 1998.

Coetsem, Frans van. *Loan Phonology and the Two Transfer Types in Language Contact*. Dordrecht: Foris, 1988.

Collini, Stefan. 'From Sectarian Radical to National Possession: John Stuart Mill in English Culture, 1873–1945.' In *A Cultivated Mind: Essays on J.S. Mill Presented to John M. Robson*, ed. Michael Laine, 242–72. Toronto: University of Toronto Press, 1991.

– *Liberalism and Sociology: L.T. Hobhouse and Political Argument in England, 1880–1914*. Cambridge: Cambridge University Press, 1979.

– 'Liberalism and the Legacy of Mill.' *Historical Journal* 20, no. 1 (1977): 237–54.

– *Public Moralists: Political Thought and Intellectual Life in Britain, 1850–1930*. Oxford: Clarendon, 1991.

Confucius. *The Analects*, trans. D.C. Lau. Harmondsworth: Penguin, 1979.

Constant, Benjamin. 'The Liberty of the Ancients Compared with that of the Moderns.' In *Political Writings*, ed. Biancamaria Fontana, 307–28. Cambridge: Cambridge University Press, 1988.

Coulmas, Florian. 'Language Adaptation in Meiji Japan.' In *Language Policy and Political Development*, ed. Brian Weinstein, 69–86. Norwood: Ablex, 1990.

Cowell, Herbert. 'Liberty, Equality, Fraternity: Mr. John Stuart Mill.' *Blackwood's Edinburgh Magazine* 114 (1873); repr. in *Liberty: Contemporary Responses to John Stuart Mill*, ed. Andrew Pyle, 298–320. Bristol: Thoemmes, 1994.

Cowling, Maurice. *Mill and Liberalism*. Cambridge: Cambridge University Press, 1963.

Craig, Albert. *Chōshū in the Meiji Restoration*. Cambridge: Harvard University Press, 1961.

Dalby, Michael. 'Revenge and the Law in Traditional China.' *American Journal of Legal History* 25 (1981): 267–307.

Davis, Winston. 'The Civil Theology of Inoue Tetsujirō.' *Japanese Journal of Religious Studies* 3, no. 1 (1976): 5–40.

Dawson, Raymond. *Confucius*. Oxford: Oxford University Press, 1981.

De Bary, Wm. Theodore. *The Liberal Tradition in China*. Hong Kong: Chinese University Press; New York: Columbia University Press, 1983.

Den Otter, Sandra M. *British Idealism and Social Explanation: A Study in Late Victorian Thought*. Oxford: Clarendon Press, 1996.

Devigne, Robert. 'Mill on Liberty and Religion: An Unfinished Dialectic.' In *Mill and the Moral Character of Liberalism*, ed. Eldon J. Eisenach, 231–56. University Park: Pennsylvania State University Press, 1998.

Devlin, Lord. 'Mill on Liberty in Morals.' *The University of Chicago Law Review* 32, no. 2 (1965): 215–35.

Dewey, Clive. 'Images of the Village Community: A Study in Anglo-Indian Ideology.' *Modern Asian Studies* 6, no. 3 (1972): 291–328.

Dirlik, Arif. *Anarchism in the Chinese Revolution*. Berkeley: University of California Press, 1991.

Dopsch, Alfons. *The Economic and Social Foundations of European Civilization*. New York: Howard Fertig, 1969.

Dore, R.P. *Education in Tokugawa Japan*. Berkeley: University of California Press, 1965.

Ducrot, Oswald, and Tzvetan Todorov. *Encyclopedic Dictionary of the Sciences of Language*, trans. Catherine Porter. Oxford: Blackwell Reference, 1981.

Dumont, Louis. 'The "Village Community" from Munro to Maine.' *Contributions to Indian Sociology*, no. 9 (1966): 67–89.

Dworkin, Ronald. 'Foundations of Liberal Equality.' *The Tanner Lectures on Human Values*, vol. 11 (1990): 1–119.

Eastman, Lloyd E. *Family, Field, and Ancestors: Constancy and Change in China's Social and Economic History, 1550–1949*. New York: Oxford University Press, 1988.

Einwalter, Dawn. 'The Limits of the Chinese State: Public Morality and the Xu Honggang Campaign.' In *China and Democracy: The Prospects for a Democratic China*, ed. Suisheng Zhao, 173–86. New York: Routledge, 2000.

Eisenach, Eldon J. 'Mill and Liberal Christianity.' In *Mill and the Moral Character of Liberalism*, ed. Eldon J. Eisenach, 191–229. University Park: Pennsylvania State University Press, 1998.

Ellens, J.P. 'Which Freedom for Early Victorian Britain?' In *Freedom and Religion in the Nineteenth Century*, ed. Richard Helmstadter, 87–119. Stanford: Stanford University Press, 1997.

Elman, Benjamin A. *A Cultural History of Civil Examinations in Late Imperial China*. Berkeley: University of California Press, 2000.

Elshtain, Jean Bethke. 'Mill's Liberty and the Problem of Authority.' In John Stuart Mill, *On Liberty*, ed. David Bromwich and George Kateb, 203–23. New Haven: Yale University Press, 2003.

Feinberg, Joel. *The Moral Limits of the Criminal Law*, vol. 1, *Harm to Others*. New York: Oxford University Press, 1984.

Fénelon, François de. *Telemachus, Son of Ulysses*, ed. and trans. Patrick Riley. Cambridge: Cambridge University Press, 1994.

Ferguson, Adam. *An Essay on the History of Civil Society*, ed. Fania Oz-Salzberger. Cambridge: Cambridge University Press, 1995.

Fingarette, Herbert. *Confucius – The Secular as Sacred*. New York: Harper & Row, 1972.

Foucault, Michel. 'Governmentality.' In *The Foucault Effect: Studies in Govern-mentality*, ed. Graham Burchell, et al., 87–104. Chicago: University of Chicago Press, 1991.

Fox-Genovese, Elizabeth, and Eugene D. Genovese. *Fruits of Merchant Capital: Slavery and Bourgeois Property in the Rise and Expansion of Capitalism*. New York: Oxford University Press, 1983.

Freeden, Michael. *The New Liberalism: An Ideology of Social Reform*. Oxford: Clarendon, 1978.

Fridell, Wilbur M. 'Government Ethics Textbooks in Late Meiji Japan.' *Journal of Asian Studies* 29, no. 4 (1970): 823–33.

Fukuzawa Yukichi. *Zōtei kaei tsūgo*. In *Fukuzawa Yukichi zenshū*, vol 1: 67–274. Tokyo: Iwanami shoten, 1958.

Fung Yu-lan. *A History of Chinese Philosophy*, trans. Derk Bodde. 2 vols. Princeton: Princeton University Press, 1952–53.

Furth, Charlotte. 'Culture and Politics in Modern Chinese Conservatism.' In *The Limits of Change: Essays on Conservative Alternatives in Republican China*, ed. Charlotte Furth, 22–53. Cambridge: Harvard University Press, 1976.

– 'Intellectual Change: From the Reform Movement to the May Fourth Movement, 1895–1920.' In *The Cambridge History of China*. Vol. 12. *Republican China, 1912–1949*, Part 1, ed. John K. Fairbank, 322–405. Cambridge: Cambridge University Press, 1983.

Furukawa Tetsushi. *Nihon dōtoku kyōiku shi*. Tokyo: Kadokawa shoten, 1961.

Galston, William A. 'Liberal Virtues.' *American Political Science Review* 82, no. 4 (1988): 1277–90.

Gaus, Gerald F. *The Modern Liberal Theory of Man*. London: Croom Helm; New York: St Martin's Press, 1983.

Gavin, Masako. *Shiga Shigetaka, 1863–1927: The Forgotton Enlightener*. Richmond, Surrey: Curzon, 2001.

Gellner, Ernest. *Conditions of Liberty: Civil Society and Its Rivals*. London: Hamish Hamilton, 1994.

George, Robert P. *Making Men Moral: Civil Liberties and Public Morality*. Oxford: Clarendon Press, 1993.

Gosses, Frans. *The Management of British Foreign Policy before the First World War: Especially During the Period 1880–1914*, trans. E.C. Van der Gaaf. Leiden: Sijthoff, 1948.

Gray, John. *Liberalisms: Essays in Political Philosophy*. London: Routledge, 1989.

– 'The Light of Other Minds.' *Times Literary Supplement*, no. 5054 (11 February 2000): 12–13.

– *Mill on Liberty: A Defence*. London: RKP, 1983.

– *Two Faces of Liberalism*. New York: New Press, 2000.

Green, T.H. *Lectures on the Principles of Political Obligation and Other Writings*, ed. Paul Harris and John Morrow. Cambridge: Cambridge University Press, 1986.

Greengarten, I.M. *Thomas Hill Green and the Development of Liberal-Democratic Thought*. Toronto: University of Toronto Press, 1981.

Greenleaf, W.H. *The British Political Tradition*. Vol. 2. *The Ideological Heritage*. London: Methuen, 1983.

Guo Zhengzhao. *Yan Fu*. Taibei: Taiwan shangwu yinshuguan, 1978.

Habibi, Don A. *John Stuart Mill and the Ethics of Human Growth*. Dordrecht: Kluwer Academic, 2001.

Hacker, Andrew. 'The Underworld of Work.' *New York Review of Books* 51, no. 2 (12 February 2004): 38–40.

Hall, David L., and Roger T. Ames. *Thinking from the Han: Self, Truth, and Transcendence in Chinese and Western Culture*. Albany: SUNY Press, 1998.

– *Thinking through Confucius*. Albany: SUNY Press, 1987.

Hall, John W. 'Rule by Status in Tokugawa Japan.' *Journal of Japanese Studies* 1, no. 1 (Autumn 1974): 39–49.

Halliday, R.J. 'Some Recent Interpretations of John Stuart Mill.' In *Mill: A Collection of Critical Essays*, ed. J.B. Schneewind, 354–78. Notre Dame: University of Notre Dame Press, 1969.

Hamburger, Joseph. *John Stuart Mill on Liberty and Control*. Princeton: Princeton University Press, 1999.

Hampshire, Stuart. *Justice Is Conflict*. Princeton: Princeton University Press, 2000.

– 'Morality and Pessimism.' In *Public and Private Morality*, ed. Stuart Hampshire, 1–22. Cambridge: Cambridge University Press, 1978.

Hanks, William F. *Language and Communicative Practices*. Boulder: Westview, 1996.

Hansen, Phillip. 'T.H. Green and the Moralization of the Market.' *Canadian Journal of Political and Social Theory* 1, no. 1 (Winter 1977): 91–117.

Hara Heizō. 'Tokugawa bakufu no Eikoku ryūgakusei.' *Rekishi chiri* 79, no. 5 (1942): 21–50.

Harootunian, H.D. 'Jinsei, Jinzei, and Jitsugaku: Social Values and Leadership in Late Tokugawa Thought.' In *Modern Japanese Leadership: Transition and Change*, ed. Bernard Silberman and H.D. Harootunian, 83–119. Tucson: University of Arizona Press, 1966.

Harrison, Brian. 'State Intervention and Moral Reform in Nineteenth-Century England.' In *Pressure from Without in Early Victorian England*, ed. Patricia Hollis, 289–322. London: Edward Arnold: 1974.

Haskell, Thomas L. 'Persons as Uncaused Causes: John Stuart Mill, the Spirit of Capitalism, and the "Invention" of Formalism.' In *The Culture of the Market:*

Historical Essays, ed. Thomas L. Haskell and Richard F. Teichgraeber III, 441–502. Cambridge: Cambridge University Press, 1993.

Hazama Naoki. 'On Liang Qichao's Conceptions of *Gong* and *Si*: "Civic Virtue" and "Personal Virtue" in the *Xinmin shuo.*' In *The Role of Japan in Liang Qichao's Introduction of Modern Western Civilization to China,* ed. Joshua A. Fogel, 205–21. Berkeley: University of California, Institute of East Asian Studies, 2004.

He, Baogang. 'New Moral Foundations of Chinese Democratic Institutional Design.' In *China and Democracy: The Prospects for a Democratic China,* ed. Suisheng Zhao, 89–107. New York: Routledge, 2000.

Hegel, G.W.F. *Philosophy of Right,* trans. T.M. Knox. Oxford: Clarendon Press, 1957.

Henderson, Dan Fenno. 'Contracts in Tokugawa Villages.' *Journal of Japanese Studies* 1, no. 1 (1974): 51–81.

Hepburn, J.C. *A Japanese and English Dictionary.* Rutland, VT: Tuttle, 1983.

– A *Japanese-English and English-Japanese Dictionary.* 3d ed. Tokyo: Maruya, 1886.

Hida Yoshifumi, ed. *Eibei gairaigo no sekai.* Tokyo: Nan'undō, 1981.

Hilkey, Judy. *Character Is Capital: Success Manuals and Manhood in Gilded Age America.* Chapel Hill: University of North Carolina Press, 1997.

Himmelfarb, Gertrude. *On Liberty and Liberalism: The Case of John Stuart Mill.* San Francisco: Institute for Contemporary Studies, 1990.

Hirai Atsuko. 'Self-Realization and Common Good: T.H. Green in Meiji Ethical Thought.' *Journal of Japanese Studies* 5, no. 1 (1979): 107–36.

Hobhouse, L.T. *Democracy and Reaction.* London: T. Fisher Unwin, 1904.

– *Liberalism and Other Writings,* ed. James Meadowcroft. Cambridge: Cambridge University Press, 1994.

Holmes, Stephen. *Passions and Constraint: On the Theory of Liberal Democracy.* Chicago: University of Chicago Press, 1995.

Hori Tatsunosuke. *A Pocket Dictionary of the English and Japanese Language / Ei-Wa taiyaku shūchin jisho.* Edo: n.p., 1862.

Horkheimer, Max. 'Materialism and Morality.' In *Between Philosophy and Social Science: Selected Early Writings,* trans. G. Frederick Hunter, et al., 15–47. Cambridge, MA: MIT Press, 1993.

Hoston, Germaine A. *The State, Identity, and the National Question in China and Japan.* Princeton: Princeton University Press, 1994.

Howland, Douglas. *Borders of Chinese Civilization: Geography and History at Empire's End.* Durham: Duke University Press, 1996.

– 'Nishi Amane's Efforts to Translate Western Knowledge: Sound, Written Character, and Meaning.' *Semiotica* 83, no. 3/4 (1991): 283–310.

– 'The Predicament of Ideas in Culture: Translation and Historiography.' *History and Theory* 42, no. 1 (2003): 45–60.

– 'Samurai Status, Class, and Bureaucracy: A Historiographical Essay.' *Journal of Asian Studies* 60, no. 2 (2001): 353–80.

– 'Society Reified: Herbert Spencer and Political Theory in Early Meiji Japan.' *Comparative Studies in Society and History* 42, no. 1 (2000): 67–86.

– *Translating the West: Language and Political Reason in Nineteenth-Century Japan.* Honolulu: University of Hawai'i Press, 2002.

Huang Jiamo. 'Ma Junwu de zaoqi sixiang yu yanlun.' *Zhongyang yanjiuyuan jindaishi yanjiusuo jikan* 10 (1981): 303–49.

Huang Ko-wu. *Ziyou de suoyiran: Yan Fu dui Yuehan Mier ziyou sixiang de renshi yu pipan.* Taibei: Yunchen wenhua, 1998.

Huang, Philip C. *Liang Ch'i-ch'ao and Modern Chinese Liberalism.* Seattle: University of Washington Press, 1972.

Huber, Thomas M. *The Revolutionary Origins of Modern Japan.* Stanford: Stanford University Press, 1981.

Hudson, R.A. *Sociolinguistics.* Cambridge: Cambridge University Press, 1980.

Humboldt, Wilhelm von. *The Limits of State Action,* ed. J.W. Burrow. Indianapolis: Liberty Fund, 1993.

Hutton, R.H. 'Mill on Liberty.' *The National Review* 8 (1859); repr. in John Stuart Mill, *On Liberty: Annotated Text, Sources and Background, Criticism,* ed. David Spitz, 123–42. New York: Norton, 1975.

Imamura Yoshio. 'Jiyū no keifu.' In *Kōza Chūgoku,* vol. 3, *Kakumei no tenkai,* ed. Nohara Shirō, 155–99. Tokyo: Chikuma shobō, 1967.

Inden, Ronald. *Imagining India.* London: Routledge, 1990.

Inoue, Kyoko. *Individual Dignity in Modern Japanese Thought: The Evolution of the Concept of Jinkaku in Moral and Educational Discourse.* Ann Arbor: Center for Japanese Studies, 2001.

Inoue Tetsujirō. *Chokugo engi.* In *Meiji shisō shū,* ed. Matsumoto Sannosuke, vol. 2: 85–116. Tokyo: Chikuma shobō, 1977.

– *Inoue Tetsujirō jiden.* Tokyo: Fuzanbō, 1973.

– *Kyōiku to shūkyō no shōtotsu.* In *Meiji tetsugaku shisō shū,* ed. Senuma Shigeki, 124–60. Tokyo: Chikuma shobō, 1974.

– 'Kyōikusha to shite no Nakamura Masanao.' *Kyōiku* 1, no. 5 (8/1933): 71–81.

– 'Miru no Jiyū no ri o hakusu.' *Tōyō gakugei zasshi* 9 (1883): 13–17.

– *Rinri shinsetsu.* In *Meiji bunka zenshū,* vol. 23, *Shisō hen,* 411–30. Tokyo: Nihon hyōronsha, 1968.

Ion, A. Hamish. 'Edward Warren Clark and Early Meiji Japan: A Case Study of Cultural Contact.' *Modern Asian Studies* 11, no. 4 (1977): 557–72.

– 'Edward Warren Clark and the Formation of the Shizuoka and Koishikawa

Christian Bands (1871–1879).' In *Foreign Employees in Nineteenth-Century Japan*, ed. Edward R. Beauchamp and Akira Iriye, 171–89. Boulder, CO: Westview, 1993.

Ishida Takeshi. 'J.S. Miru *Jiyū ron* to Nakamura Keiu oyobi Gen Fuku.' In his *Nihon kindai shisōshi ni okeru hō to seiji*, 1–46. Tokyo: Iwanami shoten, 1976.

Ishizuki Minoru. *Kindai Nihon no kaigai ryūgaku shi*. [Rev. ed.] Tokyo: Chūōkōron sha, 1992.

Jacobsen, Eric. *Translation: A Traditional Craft*. Copenhagen: Gyldendalske Boghandel; Nordisk Forlag, 1958.

Jakobson, Roman. 'On Linguistic Aspects of Translation.' In *On Translation*, ed. Reuben A. Brower, 232–9. Cambridge: Harvard University Press, 1959.

Jones, Raymond A. *The British Diplomatic Service, 1815–1914*. Waterloo, Ont.: Wilfrid Laurier University Press, 1983.

Kahan, Alan S. *Aristocratic Liberalism: The Social and Political Thought of Jacob Burckhardt, John Stuart Mill, and Alexis de Tocqueville*. New York: Oxford University Press, 1992.

Kaigo Tokiomi. *Nihon kyōkasho taikei – kindai hen*. Vol. 1 [*Shūshin*, part 1]. Tokyo: Kōdansha, 1961.

Kamei Hideo. *Transformations of Sensibility: The Phenomenology of Meiji Literature*, trans. ed. Michael Bourdaghs. Ann Arbor: Center for Japanese Studies, The University of Michigan, 2002.

Karasawa Tomitarō. *Kyōkasho no rekishi*. Tokyo: Sōbunsha, 1956.

Karatani Kōjin. *Origins of Modern Japanese Literature*, trans. ed. Brett de Bary. Durham: Duke University Press, 1993.

Karl, Rebecca E. *Staging the World: Chinese Nationalism at the Turn of the Twentieth Century*. Durham: Duke University Press, 2001.

Kekes, John. *Against Liberalism*. Ithaca: Cornell University Press, 1997.

Kindermann, Gottfried-Karl. 'An Overview of Sun Yat-sen's Doctrine.' In *Sun Yat-sen's Doctrine in the Modern World*, ed. Chu-yuan Cheng, 52–78. Boulder, CO: Westview, 1989.

Kinmonth, Earl H. 'Nakamura Keiu and Samuel Smiles: A Victorian Confucian and a Confucian Victorian.' *American Historical Review* 85 (1980): 535–56.

Kobayashi Toshihiro. *Meiji zenki shisō*. Tokyo: Sanwa shobō, 1988.

Krieger, Leonard. *The German Idea of Freedom: History of a Political Tradition*. Chicago: University of Chicago Press, 1957.

Lackner, Michael, Iwo Ameling, and Joachim Kurtz, eds. *New Terms for New Ideas: Western Knowledge and Lexical Change in Late Imperial China*. Leiden: Brill, 2001.

Lawless, Andrew. 'T.H. Green and the British Liberal Tradition.' *Canadian Journal of Political and Social Theory* 2, no. 2 (Spring–Summer 1978): 142–55.

Lehrer, Adrienne. *Semantic Fields and Lexical Structures.* Amsterdam: North–Holland, 1974.

Levenson, Joseph R. *Liang Ch'i-ch'ao and the Mind of Modern China.* 2d rev. ed. Berkeley: University of California Press, 1967.

Levi, Albert William. 'The Value of Freedom: Mill's Liberty (1859–1959).' *Ethics* 12 (1959): 37–46.

Lewis, Mark Edward. *Sanctioned Violence in Early China.* Albany: SUNY Press, 1990.

Li, Frank. 'East Is East and West Is West: Did the Twain Ever Meet? The Declaration of Independence in China.' *Journal of American History* 85, no. 4 (1999): 1432–48.

Liang Qichao. 'Lun zhengfu yu renmin zhi quanxian.' In *Yinbingshi wenji.* Vol. 10: 1–6. Taibei: Zhonghua shuju, 1960.

– 'Shuo qun.' In *Yinbingshi wenji,* vol. 2: 3–7. Taibei: Zhonghua shuju, 1960.

– *Xinmin shuo.* Shanghai: Zhonghua shuju, 1936.

– *Yinbingshi ziyou shu.* Shanghai: Zhonghua shuju, 1936.

Lin Anwu. 'Gexing ziyou yu shehui quanxian.' *Si yu yan* 27, no. 1 (1989): 1–18.

Lin Caijue. 'Yan Fu dui ziyou de lijie.' *Donghai Daxue lishi xuebao,* no. 5 (1982): 85–159.

Lind, Michael. 'A Tragedy of Errors.' *The Nation* (23 February 2004): 23–32.

Ling, Yu-long. 'The Doctrine of Democracy and Human Rights.' In *Sun Yat-sen's Doctrine in the Modern World,* ed. Chu-yuan Cheng, 175–200. Boulder, CO: Westview, 1989.

Liu, Lydia H. *Translingual Practice: Literature, National Culture, and Translated Modernity: China, 1900–1937.* Stanford: Stanford University Press, 1995.

– 'Translingual Practice: The Discourse of Individualism Between China and the West.' *positions: east asia cultures critique* 1, no. 1 (1993): 160–93.

Liu Zhengtan, et al. *Hanyu wailaici cidian / A Dictionary of Loan Words and Hybrid Words in Chinese.* Shanghai: Shanghai cishu chubanshe, 1984.

Lyons, John. *Semantics.* 2 vols. Cambridge: Cambridge University Press, 1977.

Ma Junwu. *Ma Junwu ji,* ed. Mo Shixiang. Wuhan: Huazhong shifan daxue chubanshe, 1991.

Ma Xiaoquan. 'Local Self-Government: Citizenship Consciousness and the Political Participation of the New Gentry-Merchants in the Late Qing.' In *Imagining the People: Chinese Intellectuals and the Concept of Citizenship, 1890–1920,* ed. Joshua A. Fogel and Peter Zarrow, 183–211. Armonk, NY: M.E. Sharpe, 1997.

MacIntyre, Alasdair. *After Virtue: A Study in Moral Theory.* 2nd ed. Notre Dame: University of Notre Dame Press, 1985.

Mackay, Thomas, ed. *A Plea for Liberty: An Argument against Socialism and Social-istic Legislation*. New York: Appleton, 1891.

Macpherson, C.B. *Democratic Theory: Essays in Retrieval*. Oxford: Clarendon, 1973.

– *The Political Theory of Possessive Individualism: Hobbes to Locke*. London: Oxford University Press, 1962.

Maeda Ai. *Bakumatsu – Ishinki no bungaku*. Tokyo: Hōsei daigaku shuppan-kyoku, 1972.

Maine, Henry. *Lectures on the Early Histories of Institutions*. 7th ed. Port Washington, NY: Kennikat Press, 1966.

– *Village Communities in the East and West*. 3d ed. New York: Henry Holt, 1889.

Maruyama Masao. *Chūsei to hangyaku: tenkeiki Nihon no seishinshiteki isō*. Tokyo: Chikuma, 1992.

– *Studies in the Intellectual History of Tokugawa Japan*, trans. Mikiso Hane. Princeton: Princeton University Press; Tokyo: University of Tokyo Press, 1974.

Marx, Karl. *Critique of Hegel's Doctrine of the State*. In *Early Writings*, trans. R. Livingstone and G. Benton, 57–198. New York: Vintage, 1975.

Masini, Federico. *The Formation of the Modern Chinese Lexicon and Its Evolution toward a National Language*. Published as *Journal of Chinese Linguistics, Monograph Series*, no. 6 (1993).

Masuda Wataru. *Chūgoku bungakushi kenkyū: bungaku kakumei to zen'ya no hitobito*. Tokyo: Iwanami, 1967.

Matsumoto Sannosuke. 'The Roots of Political Disillusionment: "Public" and "Private" in Japan.' In *Authority and the Individual in Japan: Citizen Protest in Historical Perspective*, ed. J. Victor Koschmann, 31–51. Tokyo: University of Tokyo Press, 1978.

Matsuo Shōichi. *Jiyūminken shisō no kenkyū*. Rev. and expanded ed. Tokyo: Nihon keizai hyōronsha, 1990.

Matsuzawa Hiroaki. '*Saikoku risshi hen* to *Jiyū no ri* no sekai: bakumatsu jugaku – bikutoria-chō kyūshinshugi – bunmeikaika.' *Nihon seijigakkai nenpō* (1975): 9–53.

Mayer, Arno J. *The Persistence of the Old Regime: Europe to the Great War*. New York: Pantheon, 1981.

McCloskey H.J. 'A Critique of the Ideals of Liberty.' *Mind* 74 (1965): 483–508.

– *John Stuart Mill: A Critical Study*. London: Macmillan, 1971.

– 'Liberty of Expression: Its Ground and Limits.' *Inquiry* 13, no. 3 (1970): 219–37.

– 'Mill's Liberalism.' *Philosophical Quarterly* 13, no. 52 (April 1963): 143–56.

McCormick, Brett. 'Liang Qichao's Liberal Statism and His Vision of a Modern Citizen.' *Asian Thought and Society* 25, no. 74 (2000): 123–36.

Mehta, Uday Singh. *Liberalism and Empire: A Study in Nineteenth-Century British Liberal Thought*. Chicago: University of Chicago Press, 1999.

Meiroku Zasshi: Journal of the Japanese Enlightenment, trans. William Braisted. Cambridge: Harvard University Press, 1976.

Mencius. *Mencius*, trans. D.C. Lau. London: Penguin, 1970.

Metzger, Thomas A. 'Did Sun Yat-sen Understand the Idea of Democracy?' *American Asian Review* 10, no. 1 (Spring 1992): 1–41.

Metzger-Court, Sarah. 'Economic Progress and Social Cohesion: Self-Help and the Achieving of a Delicate Balance in Meiji Japan.' *Japan Forum* 3, no. 1 (1991): 11–21.

Mill, James. *Essay on Government*. In *Political Writings*, ed. Terence Ball, 1–42. Cambridge: Cambridge University Press, 1992.

Mill, John Stuart. *Autobiography*. In *Collected Works of John Stuart Mill*. Vol. 1. *Autobiography and Literary Essays*, 1–290. Toronto: University of Toronto Press, 1981.

– 'Coleridge.' In *Collected Works of John Stuart Mill*. Vol. 10. *Essays on Ethics, Religion, and Society*, 117–63. Toronto: University of Toronto Press, 1969.

– *Considerations on Representative Government*. In *Collected Works of John Stuart Mill*. Vol. 19. *Essays on Politics and Society*, Part 2, 371–577. Toronto: University of Toronto Press, 1977.

– *On Liberty*. In *The Collected Works of John Stuart Mill*. Vol. 18. *Essays on Politics and Society*, Part 1, 213–310. Toronto: University of Toronto Press, 1977.

– *On Liberty*, ed. Edward Alexander. Peterborough, Ont.: Broadview, 1999.

– *On Liberty: Annotated Text, Sources and Background Criticism*, ed. David Spitz. New York: Norton, 1975.

– *Principles of Political Economy*. In *The Collected Works of John Stuart Mill*. Vols. 2–3. Toronto: University of Toronto Press, 1965.

– 'Utilitarianism.' In *Collected Works of John Stuart Mill*. Vol. 10. *Essays on Ethics, Religion, and Society*, 203–59. Toronto: University of Toronto Press, 1969.

Miller, Roy Andrew. *The Japanese Language*. Chicago: University of Chicago Press, 1967.

Min, Tu-ki. *National Polity and Local Power: The Transformation of Late Imperial China*, ed. Timothy Brook and Philip Kuhn. Cambridge: Harvard University Council on East Asian Studies, 1989.

Mitsukuri Rinshō. '*Riberuchii* no setsu.' *Meiroku zasshi*, no. 9 (1874): 2b–4b.

Miyanaga Takashi. *Keiō ninen bakufu Igirisu ryūgakusei*. Tokyo: Shinjinbutsu ōraisha, 1994.

Mizoguchi Yūzō. 'Chūgoku ni okeru kō-shi gainen no tenkai.' *Shisō*, no. 669 (1980): 19–38.

– 'Chūgoku no kō-shi.' *Bungaku* 56 (9/1988): 88–102 and (10/1988): 73–84.
– 'Zhongguo minquan sixiang de tese.' In *Zhongguo xiandaihua lunwenji*, ed. Zhongyang yanjiuyuan jindaishi yanjiusuo, 343–62. Taibei: Zhongyang yanjiuyuan jindaishi yanjiusuo, 1991.
Monro, D.H. 'Liberty of Expression: Its Ground and Limits.' *Inquiry* 13, no. 3 (1970): 238–53.
Morioka Kenji. *Kaitei kindaigo no seiritsu: goi hen*. Tokyo: Meiji shoin, 1991.
Morrow, John. 'Liberalism and British Idealist Political Philosophy: A Reassessment.' *History of Political Thought* 5, no. 1 (1984): 91–108.
Motoda Eifu. 'Lectures Delivered in the Presence of His Imperial Majesty the Emperor of Japan,' trans. N. Asaji and J.C. Pringle. *Transactions of the Asiatic Society of Japan* 40 (1912): 45–113.
Naipaul, V.S. *The Middle Passage*. New York: Macmillan, 1963.
Nakamura Keiu. 'Gi taiseijin jōsho.' In *Meiji keimō shisō shū*, ed. Ōkubo Toshiaki, 281–3. Tokyo: Chikuma, 1967.
Nakamura Keiu, trans. [John Stuart Mill.] *Jiyū no ri*. Suruga: Kihira Keiichirō, 1871. Repr. in *Meiji bunka zenshū*, vol. 5, *Jiyū minken hen*, 1–84. Tokyo: Nihon hyōronsha, 1927.
Nathan, Andrew J. *Chinese Democracy*. Berkeley: University of California Press, 1985.
Neumann, Franz. 'The Concept of Political Freedom.' In *The Democratic and the Authoritarian State: Essays in Political and Legal Theory*, ed. Herbert Marcuse, 160–200. Glencoe: The Free Press, 1957.
– *The Rule of Law: Political Theory and the Legal System in Modern Society*. Leamington Spa: Berg, 1986.
Newmeyer, Frederick J. *The Politics of Linguistics*. Chicago: University of Chicago Press, 1986.
Nicholson, Peter P. *The Political Philosophy of the British Idealists: Selected Studies*. Cambridge: Cambridge University Press, 1990.
– 'T.H. Green and State Action: Liquor Legislation.' In *The Philosophy of T.H. Green*, ed. Andrew Vincent, 76–103. Aldershot: Gower, 1986.
Nida, Eugene. *Towards a Science of Translating*. Leiden: Brill, 1964.
Nida, Eugene, and Charles R. Taber. *The Theory and Practice of Translation*. Leiden: Brill, 1969.
Nishimura Shigeki. 'Nihon dōtokugaku no shurui.' Repr. in *Meiji keimō shisō shū*, ed. Ōkubo Toshiaki, 359–60. Tokyo: Chikuma shobō, 1967.
– *Nihon dōtoku ron*. Tokyo: Iwanami shoten, 1936.
– 'On Free Trade.' In *Meiroku Zasshi: Journal of the Japanese Enlightenment*, trans. William Braisted, 356–8. Cambridge: Harvard University Press, 1976.
– *Shōgaku shūshin kun*. Repr. in *Nihon kyōkasho taikei – kindai hen*, vol. 2 [*Shūshin*, part 2], ed. Kaigo Tokiomi, 6–37. Tokyo: Kōdansha, 1962.

- 'Shūshin chikoku futamichi arazu ron.' *Meiroku zasshi*, no. 31 (1875): 3b-6.
- 'Shūshin kyōkasho no setsu.' In *Hakuō sōsho*, vol. 2: 536–43. Tokyo: Nihon kōdōkai, [1912].

Norman, Jerry. *Chinese*. Cambridge: Cambridge University Press, 1988.

Notehelfer, F.G. *American Samurai: Captain L.L. Janes and Japan*. Princeton: Princeton University Press, 1985.

Ogihara Takashi. *Nakamura Keiu kenkyū: Meiji keimō shisō to risōshugi*. Tokyo: Waseda Daigaku shuppanbu, 1990.

Ōkubo Toshiaki. *Meiji no shisō to bunka*. Tokyo: Yoshikawa kōbunkan, 1988.
- 'Meiji shoki bunka shijō ni okeru Shizuoka: Shizuoka no bunmeikaika.' *Rangaku shiryō kenkyūkai kenkyū hōkoku*, no. 217 (1969): 4–24.

Onogawa Hidemi. *Shinmatsu seiji shisō kenkyū*. Tokyo: Misuzu shobō, 1969.

Ōta Aito. *Meiji Kirisutokyō no ryūiki: Shizuoka bando to bakushintachi*. Tokyo: Tsukiji shokan, 1979.

Ozawa Saburō. *Nihon purotesutanto shi kenkyū*. Tokyo: Tōkai daigaku, 1964.

Parekh, Bhikhu. 'Liberalism and Morality.' In *The Morality of Politics*, ed. Bhikhu Parekh and R.N. Berki, 81–98. New York: Crane, Russak, & Co., 1972.

Parent, William A. 'Some Recent Work on the Concept of Liberty.' *American Philosophical Quarterly* 11, no. 3 (1974): 149–67.

Pedlar, Neil. *The Imported Pioneers: Westerners Who Helped Build Modern Japan*. New York: St Martin's Press, 1990.

Peires, J.B. *The Dead Will Arise: Nongqawuse and the Great Xhosa Cattle-Killing Movement of 1856–7*. Bloomington: Indiana University Press, 1989.

Perkin, Harold. *The Origin of Modern English Society, 1780–1880*. London: Routledge & Kegan Paul, 1969.

Pittau, Joseph. *Political Thought in Early Meiji Japan, 1868–1889*. Cambridge: Harvard University Press, 1967.

Plamenatz, J.P. *Consent, Freedom, and Political Obligation*. London: Oxford University Press, 1938, 1968.

Plant, Raymond. *Hegel: An Introduction*. 2d ed. Oxford: Basil Blackwell, 1983.

Pocock, J.G.A. 'Virtues, Rights, and Manners: A Model for Historians of Political Thought.' *Political Theory* 9, no. 3 (1981): 353–68.

Porter, Brian A. 'The Social Nation and Its Futures: English Liberalism and Polish Nationalism in Late Nineteenth-Century Warsaw.' *American Historical Review*, 101, no. 5 (1996): 1470–92.

Pusey, James R. *China and Charles Darwin*. Cambridge: Harvard University, Council on East Asian Studies, 1983.

Pyle, Andrew, ed. *Liberty: Contemporary Responses to John Stuart Mill*. Bristol: Thoemmes, 1994.

Pyle, Kenneth B. *The New Generation in Meiji Japan: Problems of Cultural Identity, 1885–1889*. Stanford: Stanford University Press, 1969.

Rankin, Mary Backus. *Early Chinese Revolutionaries: Radical Intellectuals in Shanghai and Chekiang, 1902–1911.* Cambridge: Harvard University Press, 1971.
– *Elite Activism and Political Transformation in China: Zhejiang Province, 1865–1911.* Stanford: Stanford University Press, 1986.
Rees, J.C. *Mill and His Early Critics.* Leicester: University College, 1956.
– 'A Re-Reading of Mill *On Liberty.' Political Studies* 8, no. 2 (1960): 113–29.
Reitan, Richard M. '*Rinrigaku*: The Emergence of Ethics in Meiji Japan.' Ph.D. diss., University of Chicago, 2002.
Richter, Melvin. *The Politics of Conscience: T.H. Green and His Age.* Cambridge: Harvard University Press, 1964.
Riley, Jonathan. 'Individuality, Custom, and Progress.' *Utilitas* 3, no. 2 (1991): 217–44.
Ritchie, David G. *The Moral Function of the State.* London: Women's Printing Society, 1887.
– *Natural Rights: A Criticism of Some Political and Ethical Concepts.* London: Allen & Unwin, 1894.
– *The Principles of State Interference: Four Essays on the Political Philosophy of Mr. Herbert Spencer, J.S. Mill, and T.H. Green.* London: Swan Sonnenschein, 1902.
– *Studies in Political and Social Ethics.* London: Swan Sonnenschein, 1902.
Roach, John. 'Liberalism and the Victorian Intelligentsia.' *Cambridge Historical Journal* 13, no. 1 (1957): 58–81.
Roberts, John. 'T.H. Green.' In *Conceptions of Liberty in Political Philosophy,* ed. Zbigniew Pelzynski and John Gray, 243–62. New York: St Martin's Press, 1984.
Robson, John M. *The Improvement of Mankind: The Social and Political Thought of John Stuart Mill.* Toronto: University of Toronto Press; London: RKP, 1968.
Roper, Jon. *Democracy and Its Critics: Anglo-American Democratic Thought in the Nineteenth Century.* London: Unwin Hyman, 1989.
Rowe, William T. 'The Public Sphere in Modern China.' *Modern China* 16, no. 3 (1990): 309–29.
Ruggiero, Guido de. *The History of European Liberalism,* trans. R.G. Collingwood. Oxford: Oxford University Press; London: Humphrey Milford, 1927.
Saitō Tsuyoshi. *Meiji no kotoba: higashi kara nishi e no kakehashi.* Tokyo: Kōdansha, 1977.
Sakai, Naoki. *Translation and Subjectivity: On "Japan" and Cultural Nationalism.* Minneapolis: University of Minnesota Press, 1997.
– *Voices of the Past: The Status of Language in Eighteenth-Century Japanese Discourse.* Ithaca: Cornell University Press, 1991.
Sakakura Atsuyoshi et al. *Kōza kokugoshi,* vol. 3, *Goi shi.* Tokyo: Taishūkan, 1971.

Sakata Yoshio. 'Meiji ishin to kaikyū shikan.' *Jimbun gakuhō*, no. 1 (1950): 43–60.

Sartorius, Rolf E. *Individual Conduct and Social Norms: A Utilitarian Account of Social Union and the Rule of Law*. Encino, CA: Dickenson, 1975.

Sasaki Akira. *Dōtoku kyōiku no kenkyū to jissen*. Tokyo: Kyōiku kaihatsu kenkyūjo, 1996.

Saussure, Ferdinand de. *Course in General Linguistics*, trans. Roy Harris. La Salle: Open Court, 1986.

Scheiner, Irwin. *Christian Converts and Social Protest in Meiji Japan*. Berkeley: University of California Press, 1970.

Schmitt, Carl. *The Crisis of Parliamentary Democracy*, trans. Ellen Kennedy. Cambridge, MA: MIT Press, 1985.

Schogt, Henry. 'Semantic Theory and Translation Theory.' In *Theories of Translation: An Anthology of Essays from Dryden to Derrida*, ed. Rainer Schulte and John Biguenet, 192–203. Chicago: University of Chicago Press, 1992.

Schwartz, Benjamin. *In Search of Wealth and Power: Yen Fu and the West*. Cambridge: Harvard University Press, 1964.

Semmel, Bernard. *John Stuart Mill and the Pursuit of Virtue*. New Haven: Yale University Press, 1984.

– 'John Stuart Mill's Coleridgean Neoradicalism.' In *Mill and the Moral Character of Liberalism*, ed. Eldon J. Eisenbach, 49–76. University Park: Pennsylvania State University Press, 1998.

Shibatani, Masayoshi. *The Languages of Japan*. Cambridge: Cambridge University Press, 1990.

Shih, Shu-mei. *The Lure of the Modern: Writing Modernism in Semicolonial China, 1917–1937*. Berkeley: University of California Press, 2001.

Shimoide Junkichi. '*Jiyū no ri* kaidai.' In *Meiji bunka zenshū*, vol. 5, *Jiyū minken hen*, 2–5. Tokyo: Nihon hyōronsha, 1927.

Shively, Donald H. 'Motoda Eifu: Confucian Lecturer to the Meiji Emperor.' In *Confucianism in Action*, ed. David S. Nivison and Arthur F. Wright, 302–33. Stanford: Stanford University Press, 1959.

– 'Nishimura Shigeki: A Confucian View of Modernization.' In *Changing Japanese Attitudes toward Modernization*, ed. Marius B. Jansen, 193–241. Princeton: Princeton University Press, 1965.

'Shōgaku ni kōyō aru shūshin kyōiku.' *Kyōiku zasshi*, no. 22 (23 December 1876): 1–16.

Shōwa Joshi Daigaku Kindai Bungaku Kenkyūshitsu, ed. *Kindai bungaku kenkyū sōsho*. Tokyo: Kōyōkai, 1956.

Silberman, Bernard S. *Cages of Reason: The Rise of the Rational State in France, Japan, the United States, and Great Britain*. Chicago: University of Chicago Press, 1993.

Sinn, Elizabeth. 'Yan Fu.' In *An Encyclopedia of Translation: Chinese-English, English-Chinese*, ed. Chan Sin-wai and David E. Pollard, 429–47. Hong Kong: Chinese University Press, 1995.

Skillen, Anthony. *Ruling Illusions: Philosophy and the Social Order*. Atlantic Highlands, NJ: Humanities Press, 1978.

Skinner, Quentin. 'The Idea of Negative Liberty: Philosophical and Historical Perspectives.' In *Philosophy in History: Essays on the Historiography of Philosophy*, ed. Richard Rorty, et al., 193–221. Cambridge: Cambridge University Press, 1984.

Skorupski, John, ed. *The Cambridge Companion to Mill*. Cambridge: Cambridge University Press, 1998.

Smith, Craig A. 'The Individual and Society in T.H. Green's Theory of Virtue.' *History of Political Thought* 2, no. 1 (1981): 187–201.

Smith, G.W. 'J.S. Mill on Freedom.' In *Conceptions of Liberty in Political Philosophy*, ed. Zbigniew Pelczynski and John Gray, 182–216. New York: St Martin's Press, 1984.

Smith, Steven B. *Hegel's Critique of Liberalism: Rights in Context*. Chicago: University of Chicago Press, 1989.

Smith, Thomas C. *Native Sources of Japanese Industrialization, 1750–1920*. Berkeley: University of California Press, 1988.

Smith Jr., Warren W. *Confucianism in Modern Japan: A Study of Conservatism in Japanese Intellectual History*. Tokyo: Hokuseido Press, 1959.

Snell-Hornby, Mary. *Translation Studies: An Integrated Approach*. Amsterdam: John Benjamins, 1988.

Spencer, Herbert. *Social Statics*. New York: Schalkenbach Foundation, 1995.

Steiner, George. *After Babel: Aspects of Language and Translation*. London: Oxford University Press, 1975.

Stephen, James Fitzjames. *Liberty, Equality, Fraternity*, ed. Stuart D. Warner. Indianapolis: Liberty Fund, 1993.

Sullivan, Eileen P. 'A Note on the Importance of Class in the Political Theory of John Stuart Mill.' *Political Theory* 9, no. 2 (1981): 248–56.

Sun Yatsen. *Prescriptions for Saving China: Selected Writings of Sun Yat-sen*, trans. Julie Lee Wei, E-su Zen, and Linda Chao. Stanford: Hoover Institution Press, 1994.

– *The Three Principles of the People: San Min Chu I*. Taipei: China Publishing Co., [1963].

Suzuki Shūji. *Bunmei no kotoba*. Hiroshima: Bunka hyōron, 1981.

'Symposium: "Public Sphere" / "Civil Society" in China?' *Modern China* 19, no. 2 (1993).

Takahashi Kamekichi. *Nihon kindai keizai keiseishi*. Tokyo: Tōyō keizai shin-pōsha, 1968.

Takahashi Masajirō, trans. [John Stuart Mill.] *Jiyū no kenri*. Tokyo: Miyamoto insatsujo, 1895.

Takahashi Masao. *Nakamura Keiu*. Tokyo: Yoshikawa kōbunkan, 1966.

– *Nishimura Shigeki*. Tokyo: Yoshikawa kōbunkan, 1987.

Takata Atsushi. 'Gen Fuku no *Ten'en ron* no shisō.' *Tōkyō Jōshidaigaku fuzoku hikakubunka kenkyūjo kiyō* 20 (1965): 1–61.

Takeda Kiyoko. 'Japanese Christianity: Between Orthodoxy and Heterodoxy.' In *Authority and the Individual in Japan: Citizen Protest in Historical Perspective*, ed. J. Victor Koschmann, 82–107. Tokyo: University of Tokyo Press, 1978.

Tang, Xiaobing. *Global Space and Nationalist Discourse of Modernity: The Historical Thinking of Liang Qichao*. Stanford: Stanford University Press, 1996.

Taylor, Charles. 'What's Wrong with Negative Liberty.' In *Philosophical Papers*, vol. 2, *Philosophy and the Human Sciences*, 211–29. Cambridge: Cambridge University Press, 1985.

Taylor, M.W. *Men Versus the State: Herbert Spencer and Late Victorian Individualism*. Oxford: Clarendon Press, 1992.

Ten, C.L. *Mill on Liberty*. Oxford: Oxford University Press, 1980.

– 'Mill's Place in Liberalism.' *Political Science Reviewer* 24 (1995): 179–204.

Thelle, Notto R. *Buddhism and Christianity in Japan: From Conflict to Dialogue, 1854–1899*. Honolulu: University of Hawai'i Press, 1987.

Thomas, Geoffrey. *The Moral Philosophy of T.H. Green*. Oxford: Clarendon, 1987.

Thomas, William. *Mill*. Oxford: Oxford University Press, 1985.

Thompson, Dennis F. *John Stuart Mill and Representative Government*. Princeton: Princeton University Press, 1976.

Thompson, E.P. *Customs in Common*. New York: Free Press, 1991.

Thompson, Roger R. *China's Local Councils in the Age of Constitutional Reform, 1898–1911*. Cambridge, MA: Council on East Asian Studies, Harvard University, 1995.

Tillman, Hoyt Cleveland. 'Yan Fu's Utilitarianism in Chinese Perspective.' In *Ideas across Cultures: Essays on Chinese Thought in Honor of Benjamin I. Schwartz*, ed. Paul A. Cohen and Merle Goldman, 63–84. Cambridge: Harvard University Press, 1990.

Tocqueville, Alexis de. *Democracy in America*. Ed. J.P. Mayer and Max Lerner, trans. George Lawrence. New York: Harper & Row, 1966.

Tonomura, Hitomi. *Community and Commerce in Late Medieval Japan: The Corporate Villages of Tokuchin-ho*. Stanford: Stanford University Press, 1992.

Toury, Gideon. *Descriptive Translation Studies and Beyond*. Amsterdam: John Benjamins, 1995.

– *In Search of a Theory of Translation*. Tel Aviv: Tel Aviv University, The Porter Institute for Poetics and Semiotics, 1980.

Tōyama Shigeki. 'Reforms of the Meiji Restoration and the Birth of Modern Intellectuals.' *Acta Asiatica* 13 (1967): 55–99.

Tsuchiya Hideo. 'Ryō Keichō no seiyō sesshu to kenri-jiyū ron.' In *Kyōdō kenkyū: Ryō Keichō, seiyō kindai shisō juyō to Meiji Nihon*, ed. Hazama Naoki, 132–167. Tokyo: Misuzu shobō, 1999.

Tsurumi, E. Patricia. 'Meiji Primary School Language and Ethics Textbooks: Old Values for a New Society.' *Modern Asian Studies* 8, no. 2 (1974): 247–61.

Ullmann, Stephen. *The Principles of Semantics*. Oxford: Blackwell; Glasgow: Jackson, Son & Co., 1951, 1957.

Urbinati, Nadia. *Mill on Democracy: From the Athenian Polis to Representative Government*. Chicago: University of Chicago Press, 2002.

Urmson, J.O. 'The Interpretation of the Moral Philosophy of J.S. Mill.' *Philosophical Quarterly* 3 (1953); repr. in *Mill: A Collection of Critical Essays*, ed. J.B. Schneewind, 179–89. Notre Dame: University of Notre Dame Press, 1969.

Venuti, Lawrence. *The Translator's Invisibility: A History of Translation*. London: Routledge, 1995.

Vincent, Andrew. 'The State and Social Purpose in Idealist Political Philosophy.' *History of European Ideas* 8, no. 3 (1987): 333–47.

Vincent, Andrew, and Raymond Plant. *Philosophy, Politics, and Citizenship: The Life and Thought of the British Idealists*. Oxford: Basil Blackwell, 1984.

Vološinov, V.N. *Marxism and the Philosophy of Language*, trans. Ladislav Matejka and I.R. Titunik. New York: Seminar Press, 1973.

Waldron, Jeremy. 'Mill as a Critic of Culture and Society.' In *John Stuart Mill, On Liberty*, ed. David Bromwich and George Kateb, 224–45. New Haven: Yale University Press, 2003.

Waltzer, Michael. 'The Communitarian Critique of Liberalism.' *Political Theory* 18, no. 1 (1990): 6–23.

Wang Fan-shen. 'Evolving Prescriptions for Social Life in the Late Qing and Early Republic: From *Qunxue* to Society.' In *Imagining the People: Chinese Intellectuals and the Concept of Citizenship, 1890–1920*, ed. Joshua A. Fogel and Peter Zarrow, 258–78. Armonk, NY: M.E. Sharpe, 1997.

Wang Hui. *China's New Order: Society, Politics, and Economy in Transition*, ed. Theodore Huters. Cambridge: Harvard University Press, 2003.

Wang Kefei. *Zhong-Ri jindai dui xifang zhengzhi zhexue sixiang de shequ: Yan Fu yu Riben qimeng xuezhe*. Beijing: Zhongguo shehuikexue chubanshe, 1996.

Wang Quchang. *Yan Jidao nianpu*. Shanghai: Shangwu yinshuguan, 1936.

Wang Shi. *Yan Fu zhuan*. Shanghai: Renmin chubanshe, 1975.

Wang Shi, and Yu Zheng. *Yan Fu*. Shanghai: Jiangsu guji chubanshe, 1984.

Watson, George. *The English Ideology: Studies in the Language of Victorian Politics*. London: Allen Lane, 1973.

Weber, Max. 'Bureaucracy.' In *From Max Weber: Essays in Sociology*, trans. H.H. Gerth and C. Wright Mills, 196–244. New York: Oxford University Press, 1946.

Weiler, Peter. *The New Liberalism: Liberal Social Theory in Great Britain, 1889–1914*. New York: Garland, 1982.

Weinstein, W.L. 'The Concept of Liberty in Nineteenth-Century English Political Thought.' *Political Studies* 13, no. 2 (1965): 145–62.

Wempe, Ben. *Beyond Equality: A Study of T.H. Green's Theory of Positive Freedom*. Delft: Eburon, 1986.

West, E.G. 'Liberty and Education: John Stuart Mill's Dilemma.' *Philosophy* 40 (1965): 129–42.

West, Rebecca. *Black Lamb and Grey Falcon: A Journey through Yugoslavia*. New York: Viking, 1941.

Williams, Raymond. *Marxism and Literature*. Oxford: Oxford University Press, 1977.

Wolff, Robert Paul. *The Poverty of Liberalism*. Boston: Beacon Press, 1968.

'The Wood and the Trees.' *Times Literary Supplement*, 10 March 1961: 153.

Wright, Terence R. *The Religion of Humanity: The Impact of Comtean Positivism on Victorian Britain*. Cambridge: Cambridge University Press, 1986.

Xiong Yuezhi. *Xixue dongjian yu wanqing shehui*. Shanghai: Renmin chubanshe, 1994.

Xu Gaoruan. 'Yan Fu xing de quanwei zhuyi ji qi tongshidai ren dui cixing sixiang zhi piping.' In *Jindai Zhongguo sixiang renwu lun*, vol. 3, *Ziyou zhuyi*, ed. Zhou Yangshan and Yang Xiaoxian, 137–64. Taibei: Shibao wenhua chuban, 1980.

Xun Kuang. *Xunzi: A Translation and Study of the Complete Works*, [by] John Knoblock. 3 vols. Stanford: Stanford University Press, 1988–1994.

Yamaji Aizan. *Essays on the Modern Japanese Church: Christianity in Meiji Japan*, trans. Graham Squires. Ann Arbor: Center for Japanese Studies, The University of Michigan: 1999.

Yamashita Shigekazu. 'Nakamura Keiu yaku *Jiyū no ri* ni tsuite.' *Kokugakuin daigaku Tochigi tanki daigaku kiyō*, no. 6 (1972): 61–75.

Yan Fu, trans. [John Stuart Mill.] *Qun ji quan jie lun*. [Shanghai]: Shangwu yinshuguan, n.d.

Yanabu Akira. 'Fukuzawa Yukichi ni okeru "individual" no hon'yaku.' In *Hon'yaku*, ed. Zasshi *Bungaku* henshūbu, 276–93. Tokyo: Iwanami shoten, 1982.

– *Hon'yaku bunka o kangaeru*. Tokyo: Hōsei daigaku shuppankyoku, 1978.

Yanazaki, Masakazu, and Tōru Miyakawa. 'Inoue Tetsujirō: The Man and His Works.' *Philosophical Studies of Japan* (Japan Society for the Promotion of Science), vol. 7 (1966): 111–26.

Yang Yiyin, and Tang Xinglin. 'Yan Fu bing fei tianfu ziyouzhe bian.' *Chongqing shiyuan xuebao (zhe she ban)*, no. 56 (1994): 106–11.

Yoshino Sakuzō. 'Shizuoka gakkō no kyōshi Kurāku sensei.' *Shinkyū jidai*, 3, no. 2 (1927): 18–25.

Zarrow, Peter. *Anarchism and Chinese Political Culture*. New York: Columbia University Press, 1990.

– 'Introduction: Citizenship in China and the West.' In *Imagining the People: Chinese Intellectuals and the Concept of Citizenship, 1890–1920*, ed. Joshua A. Fogel and Peter Zarrow, 3–38. Armonk, NY: M.E. Sharpe, 1997.

– 'Late Qing Reformism and the Meiji Model: Kang Youwei, Liang Qichao, and the Japanese Emperor.' In *The Role of Japan in Liang Qichao's Introduction of Modern Western Civilization to China*, ed. Joshua A. Fogel, 40–67. Berkeley: University of California, Institute of East Asian Studies, 2004.

– 'The Reform Movement, the Monarchy, and Political Modernity.' In *Rethinking the 1898 Reform Period: Political and Cultural Change in Late Qing China*, ed. Rebecca E. Karl and Peter Zarrow, 34–43. Cambridge: Harvard University Asia Center, 2002.

Zastoupil, Lynn. *John Stuart Mill and India*. Stanford: Stanford University Press, 1994.

Zhang Dainian. *Key Concepts in Chinese Philosophy*, trans. and ed. Edmund Ryden. New Haven: Yale University Press, 2002.

Zhang Foquan. *Ziyou yu renquan*. Hong Kong: Yazhou chubanshe, 1955.

Zhang, Xudong, ed. *Whither China?: Intellectual Politics in Post-Tiananmen China*. Durham: Duke University Press, 2001.

Zhang Zhijian. *Yan Fu sixiang yanjiu*. Guilin: Guangxi shifan daxue chubanshe, 1989.

Zhou Zhenfu. *Yan Fu sixiang shuping*. Taibei: Taiwan Zhonghua shuju, 1964.

Zhu Xi, ann. *Sishu jizhu*. Taibei: Xuehai chubanshe, 1979.

Zhuangzi. *Chuang-tzu: The Seven Inner Chapters*, trans. A.C. Graham. London: Allen & Unwin, 1981.

– *Complete Works of Chuang Tzu*, trans. Burton Watson. New York: Columbia University Press, 1968.

– *Zhuangzi jinzhu jinyi*, ann. Chen Guying. Taibei: Taiwan shangwu yinshuguan, 1975.

Index

Adorno, Theodor, 140
Ames, Roger T., 94–5
Andō Shōeki, 69
atheism, 42
anarchism, 7, 12, 51, 130, 131
authoritarianism, 14, 15, 30, 45, 95, 96, 111, 112, 134

Bacon, Francis, 72, 73
Bell, Robert, 41
Bentham, Jeremy, 49, 109, 110
Berlin, Isaiah, 9, 47
Bodin, Jean, 138
Bosanquet, Bernard, 11, 14, 48, 166n72; on evolution, 58; on the general will, 55–6; on improvement of local government, 57; on individual improvement, 60; on reformist goals of the state, 56–7; on social recognition of 'ideal facts,' 55; as social reformer, 54, 57, 166n68; on self-government, 54; on the state as an organization, 56; *The Philosophical Theory of the State*, 56
bourgeoisie, domination of libertarian state, 10, 15, 51, 68, 130, 131, 134–5, 137, 140

British Idealism, 48, 164n45
Buddhism, 107, 115
bureaucracy, 158n42; in China, 35; in England, 32; in Japan, 33–4, 37–8
bushidō, 115

Carlyle, Thomas, 43
character, 5, 6, 9, 77. *See also* Yan Fu, on character
China: bureaucratic government of, 32, 35; Chinese Communist Party, 147; civil service examinations in, 31–2, 35; desire for new socio-moral system, 12, 13, 107, 114, 116; failure of Qing dynasty, 9, 11, 35–6, 62, 126; models of private and public from antiquity, 93–6; public morality for, 126, 128–34, 146, 147; reform plans for, 7, 9, 36–7; revolutionary movements against Qing government, 7, 8, 9, 11, 12, 14, 36, 51, 105, 126, 129, 131, 132, 133; sale of opium to, 80; Westernization in, 29, 146
Chomsky, Noam, 21
Charity Organization Society, 57, 59
Christianity, 42, 63, 71–5, 77–8, 114,